PRIVATE LAW AND THE VALUE OF CHOICE

Some say that private law ought to correct wrongs or to protect rights. Others say that private law ought to maximise social welfare or to minimise social cost. In this book, Emmanuel Voyiakis claims that private law ought to make our responsibilities to others depend on the opportunities we have to affect how things will go for us. Drawing on the work of HLA Hart and TM Scanlon, he argues that private law principles that require us to bear certain practical burdens in our relations with others are justified as long as those principles provide us with certain opportunities to choose what will happen to us, and having those opportunities is something we have reason to value. The book contrasts this 'value-of-choice' account with its wrong- and social cost-based rivals, and applies it to familiar problems of contract and tort law, including whether liability should be negligence-based or stricter; whether insurance should matter in the allocation of the burden of repair; how far private law should make allowance for persons of limited capacities; when a contract term counts as 'unconscionable' or 'unfair'; and when tort law should hold a person vicariously liable for another's mistakes.

Volume 8 in the series Law and Practical Reason

Law and Practical Reason

The intention of this series is that it should encompass monographs and collections of essays that address the fundamental issues in legal philosophy. The foci are conceptual and normative in character, not empirical. Studies addressing the idea of law as a species of practical reason are especially welcome. Recognising that there is no occasion sharply to distinguish analytic and systematic work in the field from historico-critical research, the editors also welcome studies in the history of legal philosophy. Contributions to the series, inevitably crossing disciplinary lines, will be of interest to students and professionals in moral, political, and legal philosophy.

General Editor

Prof George Pavlakos (Antwerp and Glasgow)

Advisory Board

Prof Robert Alexy (Kiel)
Prof Samantha Besson (Fribourg, CH)
Prof Emilios Christodoulidis (Glasgow)
Prof Sean Coyle (Birmingham)
Prof Mattias Kumm (New York and Berlin)
Prof Stanley Paulson (St Louis and Kiel)
Prof Joseph Raz (Columbia Law School)
Prof Arthur Ripstein (Toronto)
Prof Scott Shapiro (Yale Law School)
Prof Victor Tadros (Warwick)

Editorial Assistant
Triantafyllos Gouvas (Antwerp)

Recent titles in the series

Private Law and the Value of Choice

Emmanuel Voyiakis

·HART·
PUBLISHING
OXFORD AND PORTLAND, OREGON
2017

Hart Publishing

An imprint of Bloomsbury Publishing Plc

Hart Publishing Ltd
Kemp House
Chawley Park
Cumnor Hill
Oxford OX2 9PH
UK

Bloomsbury Publishing Plc
50 Bedford Square
London
WC1B 3DP
UK

www.hartpub.co.uk
www.bloomsbury.com

Published in North America (US and Canada) by
Hart Publishing
c/o International Specialized Book Services
920 NE 58th Avenue, Suite 300
Portland, OR 97213-3786
USA

www.isbs.com

**HART PUBLISHING, the Hart/Stag logo, BLOOMSBURY and the
Diana logo are trademarks of Bloomsbury Publishing Plc**

First published 2017

© Emmanuel Voyiakis 2017

British Library Cataloguing-in-Publication Data

A catalogue record for this book is available from the British Library.

ISBN: HB: 978-1-84113-886-2
       ePDF: 978-1-50990-283-5
       ePub: 978-1-50990-284-2

Library of Congress Cataloging-in-Publication Data

Names: Voyiakis, Emmanuel, author.

Title: Private law and the value of choice / Emmanuel Voyiakis.

Description: Oxford [UK] ; Portland, Oregon : Hart Publishing, 2016. | Series: Law and practical reason ;
volume 8 | Includes bibliographical references and index.

Identifiers: LCCN 2016037917 (print) | LCCN 2016038124 (ebook) |
ISBN 9781841138862 (hardback : alk. paper) | ISBN 9781509902842 (Epub)

Subjects: LCSH: Private law. | Civil law.

Classification: LCC K600 .V69 2016 (print) | LCC K600 (ebook) | DDC 346—dc23

LC record available at https://lccn.loc.gov/2016037917

Typeset by Compuscript Ltd, Shannon
Printed and bound in Great Britain by TJ International, Padstow, Cornwall

To find out more about our authors and books visit www.hartpublishing.co.uk. Here you will find extracts, author
information, details of forthcoming events and the option to sign up for our newsletters.

To my beloved parents
Για τους αγαπημένους μου γονείς

Acknowledgements

I am very grateful to Aditi Bagchi, Hugh Beale, Jacco Bomhoff, Neil Duxbury, Andromachi Georgosouli, Peter Jaffey, David Kershaw, Stuart Lakin, George Letsas, Katie Nixon, Dan Priel, Helen Reece, Prince Saprai, Nick Sage, Sandy Steel, Andy Summers, Victor Tadros, Leah Trueblood and Charlie Webb for their comments on earlier work on which this book is based. I am also grateful to the audiences and the convenors of the Contracts Section of the 2012 Association of American Law Schools Annual Conference, the 2014 Private Law and Moral Values Conference at King's College London, the 2014 UCL Private Law Theory Group, the 2015 Legal and Political Theory Workshop at NUI Galway, the 2015 Oxford Jurisprudence Discussion Group, and staff seminars at Brunel Law School, LSE Law Department and Warwick Law School.

I owe a debt of gratitude to Richard Hart who agreed to take on an 'iffy' project, to George Pavlakos who proposed its inclusion in the Law & Practical Reason series and offered most valuable guidance during its development, and to everyone in the Hart Publishing editorial team for all their wonderful work.

Table of Contents

Introduction

SOME THEORIES SAY that private law ought to correct wrongs, or to protect rights. Others say that it ought to minimise social cost, or to maximise social welfare. This book says that private law ought to make our responsibilities to others depend on the opportunities we have to affect how things will go for us. One might perhaps call this the 'opportunity' theory of private law, but I have opted to name it after the 'value-of-choice' account of moral responsibility on which I have based most of my argument. That account has been developed by TM Scanlon, who credits HLA Hart as his own inspiration. The purpose of the book is to explain how we can deploy that account to measure the moral merits of private law (which for my present purposes means contract and tort law).

The main idea is simple. We have reason to want what happens to us to be sensitive to our choices. Most obviously, life is more likely to go well for us—we will enjoy our meal, our profession, our evening's entertainment, a nice and safe drive—if what happens depends on how we choose. Hart saw that this does not matter just for our own decisions about what to do. It also matters for our responsibilities to others, and the role of the law in holding us to those responsibilities. Hart was making a point about criminal punishment, but he found it easier to state his idea by drawing what he called, drily, a 'mercantile analogy' with private law contexts. He asked us to look at legal rules that create certain familiar institutions, such as those of a will or a contract or a marriage, as setting up a '*choosing* system', in which individuals can find out, in general terms at least, the benefits they may expect to receive and the costs they may expect to pay if they act in certain ways.[1] Such institutions, Hart argued,

> provide individuals with two inestimable advantages in relation to the areas of conduct they cover. These are (1) the advantage to the individual of determining by his choice what the future shall be and (2) the advantage of being able to predict what the future will be. For these institutions enable the individual (1) to bring into operation the coercive forces of the law so that those legal arrangements he has chosen shall be carried into effect and (2) to plan the rest of his life with certainty or at least the confidence (in a legal system that is working normally) that the arrangements

---

[1] HLA Hart, 'Legal Responsibility and Excuses' in *Punishment and Responsibility: Essays in the Philosophy of Law*, 2nd edn (Oxford, Oxford University Press, 2008) 44 (emphasis in original). Hart's essay first appeared in S Hook (ed), *Determinism and Freedom in the Age of Modern Science* (New York, Collier Books, 1958) 95.

he has made will in fact be carried out. By these devices the individual's choice is brought into the legal system and allowed to determine its future operations in various areas thereby giving him a type of indirect coercive control over, and a power to foresee the development of, official life.[2]

Scanlon argues that the value for a person of having a choice does not matter only in the justification of the institutions that Hart wrote about. It matters in the justification of any principle that requires a person to bear a substantive burden (duty, liability, obligation) in their relations with others. In this view, which Scanlon has put forward as the 'value-of-choice' account of responsibility, to justify the imposition of a substantive burden on people in a given situation, we must attend to the reasons people have to value the opportunity to affect, through their choices and other responses, how things will go for them in that situation. As he puts it:

> Once we understand the positive reasons that people have for wanting opportunities to make choices that will affect what happens to them, what they owe to others, and what others owe to them, we can see also how their having had such opportunities can play a crucial role in determining what [principles] they can reasonably object to.[3]

I propose to take this general idea back to the private law settings that Hart first applied it to. In particular, I suggest that we should see principles of contract and tort law as making up a 'choosing system', which does its job well when it makes a person's responsibilities in a situation depend on the value for that person of the opportunities they have to affect how things will go for them. In this view, it is OK for the law to force a person to make repair for breaching their bargain, as long as that person has reason to value the opportunity to make and receive legally enforceable voluntary commitments. It is OK to impose the burden of repair on a careless driver, as long as this person has reason to value the opportunity to decide where, when, and how to drive, and so on. We can generalise: it is OK for a principle of private law to impose some burden on a person in the context of an activity, as long as that person has reason to value the opportunities that the principle affords them to affect how things will go in relation to that activity. Applying that idea in specific settings will involve asking questions like the following. What sort of opportunities does a given principle of private law allow a person in a certain situation or in the context of some activity? Under which conditions is that person called upon to act on those opportunities? Does giving that person a choice in that situation make it generally more likely that things will go well

---

[2] Ibid at 45.

[3] TM Scanlon, *What We Owe To Each Other* (Cambridge, Mass, Belknap Press of Harvard University Press, 1998) 251.

for them? Our answers to these questions may lead us down several different paths. Sometimes they will match our view about the responsibilities of the contract-breaker or the careless driver. Those persons have a valuable opportunity to choose how they go about their respective activities, so they must bear the responsibility in case their choices—to breach the contract; to drive carelessly—cause harm to others. Sometimes we will conclude that the burden of repair may not be imposed on a person precisely because they do not have reason to value the opportunity that they were presented with, eg because the other party deceived them about the cost of certain options, or because they lacked the capacity to avoid causing certain outcomes. Sometimes we will reach more complex conclusions, eg that we may require a person to bear the burden of repair only as long as we have given that person a measure of protection against the consequences of their poor choices, say, by giving them access to affordable insurance coverage. Maybe *that* is the proper conclusion in the careless driver's case.

This way of thinking is strikingly dissimilar to that of a corrective justice or of a consequentialist account of private law. It does not ask who wronged whom, or who violated whose rights. It does not ask which principle is likely to be socially optimific. Rights and costs matter under the value-of-choice account too, but their significance is 'filtered' though the idea of the value for people of having certain opportunities in certain contexts. Consider rights first. Promising, driving, hunting, operating and working in a factory are activities that come with bundles of rights and corresponding duties. Promisors may serve their interests by giving certain commitments, but they also incur the duty not to mislead promisees; drivers may drive where and when they please, but they also incur the duty to exercise a level of skill and advertence; hunters may go about their activity, but they also incur a duty to comply with the applicable regulations; entrepreneurs are entitled to a managerial prerogative, but may be required to bear the burden of repair for a worker's mistakes, and so on. Change the design of those bundles (eg give promisees a right to force promisors to perform rather than compensate; abolish car insurance; ban certain types of hunting weapons; make workers personally liable for workplace negligence) and you change the value for each of those persons of the opportunity to engage in the relevant activities. The value-of-choice account says that the justification of any particular design for those bundles of rights and duties turns precisely on whether those persons have reason to value the opportunities that the bundle comes with, eg on whether having those opportunities is more likely to make things go well for those persons. In turn, the application of this 'filter' suggests a particular explanation of the significance of rights in the justification: rights matter *because* they provide people with certain opportunities to affect how things will go for them. Similar filtering applies to costs. The cost of the options available to a person affects the value for that person of the opportunity to act on those options. Driving would be too risky and expensive if people were prohibited from insuring themselves. People would not start enterprises unless they could pass on the cost of insurance for industrial accidents to their consumer base, and so on. Again, the value-of-choice account filters the idea that costs matter into the particular claim that considerations of cost are an element in the assessment of the value for a person of the opportunities that they have in the context of an activity. But the same token suggests that certain other aspects of the idea that rights and costs matter should be filtered out. This goes for the claim that one ought to make repair because one has committed a *wrong*, except when this is shorthand for the idea that one had reason to value the opportunities one had under the bundle of rights and duties that now requires one to make repair. The same goes for the claim that one ought to bear the burden of repair because a principle to that effect maximises *aggregate* (or social) welfare or minimises social cost. Under the value-of-choice account, costs matter only as grounds on which particular *individuals* may object to a principle that imposes a burden on them, not as social aggregates.

That is the value-of-choice account in a nutshell. I claim two broad advantages for it. One is that it allows us to explain in a reasonably straightforward way why both rights and costs matter in private law. We do not have to say that considerations of cost matter only in the context of determining what rights people have or that rights matter only insofar as protecting them is socially optimific. We can say that considerations of cost and rights matter because they concern the opportunities people have, and the value for them of having those opportunities. Furthermore, focusing on the opportunities people have can help us decide when the law ought to prohibit some activities altogether, and when it ought to give people the choice to engage in them; when the standard of liability in the context of those activities ought to be negligence-based and when it ought to be stricter, and so on. And it does this without being committed to a consequentialist view of reasons.[4]

Another advantage of the value-of-choice account is that it shows why certain ideas that have been often thought to lie outside the domain of private law are, in fact, an integral part of its moral justification. Take the availability of *insurance*. Those who think about private law in terms of rights and wrongs have tended to say that problems of insurance and insurability are 'downstream' matters, ie problems about managing liabilities one already has. The value-of-choice account disagrees. The availability of insurance in relation to some activity will sometimes be part of the reason why a person has reason to value

---

[4] In that sense, the value-of-choice account picks up the gauntlet that Barbara Fried has thrown to non-consequentialist accounts of tort law, see B Fried, 'The Limits of a Nonconsequentialist Approach to Torts' (2012) 18 *Legal Theory* 231, 259–61.

the opportunity to engage in that activity, and to bear the practical burdens that the activity involves. People value the opportunity to decide where, when, and how to drive in part because our compulsory car insurance laws make it easier for them to obtain affordable insurance against the possibility that they will make a driving mistake and cause a traffic accident. If Parliament, in a fit of libertarianism, abolished car insurance in order to encourage people to 'take responsibility' for their driving, it would not just make driving less valuable for everyone. It would also undermine the justification of private law principles that make drivers pay for the harms caused by their driving mistakes. Something similar goes for our growing understanding of the impact of certain *rational biases* that make us choose poorly in some situations. The value-of-choice account can explain how far such biases affect people's responsibilities in private law without appealing to the idea that decisions made under their influence are not really 'free' or 'voluntary', or that a principle that took those decisions as a basis for enforcement would be socially suboptimal. It simply asks whether, despite the fact that a person's choice is affected by such a bias in a given situation, things are more likely to go well for that person if what happens in that situation depends on that person's choice. That is why product advertising that trades on such biases does not excuse adults from the responsibility to pay for what they have purchased, but distance selling that denies consumers a reasonable 'change of mind' period may well do so. If you find all this trivially true, try generating similar explanations through a corrective justice account. It will be a challenge.

The book has seven chapters. Chapter 1 discusses the most characteristic burden that private law principles place on people, the burden of repair, and aims to destabilise the intuition that the reason one ought to bear that burden is that, in failing, say, to perform one's side of a bargain or to drive safely, one has done something *wrongful*. This intuition, I argue, invites the following challenge: wrongful conduct is not a condition for imposing on one the *original* burdens of performing one's bargains or driving safely. One bears those original burdens because a range of substantive considerations about the reasonable interests of the persons involved, the demandingness of the burden, the ease of discharging or of avoiding it etc, say so. If wrongfulness is not a condition for imposing those original burdens, why should it be a condition for imposing on one the *further* burden of making repair whenever one has failed to discharge the original ones? To give the challenge bite, I contrast wrongfulness-based accounts of the burden of repair with a 'direct' alternative. The 'direct' account treats the burden of repair just like any other original burden and justifies its imposition accordingly. It asks whether a principle that imposes that burden on a person is sufficiently sensitive to the applicable substantive considerations, such as the reasonable interests of the parties concerned, how easy it might be for someone to discharge the relevant burden or to avoid it by choosing appropriately, and so on. That account does not take the fact that a person's failure to discharge some original burden is wrongful as determining either on whom the burden of repair ought to fall, or what form such repair ought to take. I then claim that the 'direct' account is consistent with many moral ideas that underlie wrongfulness-based accounts. However, the overlap is partial, not total. So we have a fight.

Chapters 2 and 3 try to settle that fight by appealing to our ideas about moral responsibility. Chapter 2 distinguishes two kinds of judgements of moral responsibility. One involves expressions of moral praise or criticism of a person and their conduct. Scanlon calls these judgements of *attributive* responsibility. The other involves allocations of practical burdens (duties, obligations, liabilities etc) to people. These are judgements of *substantive* responsibility. I claim that private law is concerned only with the latter kind of judgement: the job of private law is to decide whose problem it is to make repair or to bear certain other practical burdens (eg to desist from certain conduct), not to express moral criticism or praise. I hope that this claim will sound banal. The less banal aspect of it is that the two senses of responsibility are so different that it does not help to think that they even have a common root, say, in certain ideas about capacity for reason-responsiveness or our acting, rational agency. Many important theorists think otherwise, and I try to show why they are mistaken.

Chapter 3 lays out Scanlon's value-of-choice account of substantive responsibility. It considers the different reasons for which people may value having the opportunity to choose in a situation, and how those reasons help explain why people may not object to principles that make their substantive responsibilities contingent on them having that opportunity (I discuss and deflect certain objections to Scanlon's argument along the way). The account's punchline, anticipated by Hart, is that one's responsibilities turn on the choices one *has*, not on the choices one *makes*. You are not responsible to make repair for injuring me because you were careless. You are responsible because you had the opportunity to take care, and that opportunity was something you had reason to value in the context of the activity you were undertaking. This idea has a less apparent, but equally important aspect. Whether you have reason to value that opportunity will sometimes depend on what others have done to ensure that you will choose well, or to protect you against the consequences of your poor choices. That is, sometimes you value having a choice because there is a safety net in place to catch you if you fall. If all this is right, the case against accounts that emphasise wrongdoing, wrongfulness, corrective justice etc is reasonably obvious. Those accounts place the moment of responsibility too late: they miss that who is responsible for the harm is settled before any wrong has actually occurred. The value-of-choice account cuts against consequentialist theories of private law in a different way. While it shares their interest in the costs of the opportunities people have, it treats costs as grounds of individual complaints against principles rather than as social aggregates.

Chapters 4 and 5 begin the task of applying the value-of-choice account to some familiar questions of private law theory. They go about it in a slightly unusual order. Chapter 4 takes up the idea that sometimes the opportunity to engage in an activity will be valuable for a person on the condition that others have done enough to give that person a measure of protection against the risk of choosing poorly. Chapter 5 then looks at the significance of the fact that this person could have avoided some harmful outcome by choosing appropriately. The intuitive way of doing things is the reverse: to begin by asking why avoidability matters for responsibility, and then to discuss whether a person might nevertheless be entitled to some protection against the consequences of their avoidable mistakes (eg to require others to give them access to certain insurance structures). I do not object to this order, but in Chapter 4 I argue that it carries the risk of portraying the provision of protection as a 'bail out', ie to make us think that the responsibility belongs originally to that person, but that we then have good reason to 'lift' or 'shift' it onto someone else. That is true in some situations, but not in others. Sometimes giving a person some protection against the consequences of their mistakes in some activity is part of what makes the opportunity to engage in that activity valuable for that person. That is, sometimes others may require that person to take on certain duties or to observe certain standards of conduct in part *because* they have that person covered in case that person makes a harmful mistake (ie that person's complaint against not having such protection would be 'it is not OK for you to be putting me in this situation!'). When that is the case, no protection means no responsibility, even if that person could have avoided the mistake in question by choosing appropriately. I then fashion a 'protection principle' out of the value-of-choice account in order to describe the situations in which protection has that function. I also claim that this principle identifies a moral thread running through familiar common law principles, including those of contributory negligence and mitigation, principles of vicarious liability for workplace accidents and various activity- or hazard-specific compulsory insurance schemes.

Chapter 5 turns to the significance for a person's responsibilities of the fact that this person could have avoided a certain outcome. I claim that this significance is best explained by treating avoidability as an opportunity, and reflecting on the value for that person of having that opportunity. In turn, this idea can account for two important features of private law. One is the distinction between contexts in which a person's liability is negligence-based, and contexts in which the conditions of such liability are stricter. The other is the allowance that private law sometimes makes for persons whose capacities fall below the normal standard. I conclude by discussing how the value-of-choice account would approach a very recent English statute which purports to be driven by considerations of responsibility, the Social Action, Responsibility and Heroism (SARAH) Act 2015.

Chapter 6 applies the value-of-choice account in the context of contracting, and takes issue with a set of principles proposed by Scanlon regarding the enforceability of voluntary undertakings. I argue that the main principle Scanlon puts forward requires amendment because it is insufficiently sensitive to the fact that the value for a person of the main opportunities that contracting offers—not to seek a deal in the first place, to negotiate, to weigh one's options, to say yes or no to the deal on the table—depends on that person's *structural position*, ie on the position from which the social structure causes that person to enter into transactions with others. More specifically, Scanlon's principle fails to justify what is often the most plausible institutional response to the fact that the value of those opportunities is compromised for persons in a weaker structural position, namely to keep the transaction alive and enforce it under modified terms (eg enforce the minimum wage in the place of any lower agreed rate). I propose a modified version of that principle, and claim two things. First, that the modified principle is not exposed to certain objections levelled against accounts that see the aim of contract law as the pursuit of social justice. Secondly, that it can justify not only familiar common law doctrines like unconscionability, but also modern statutory regimes for the protection of consumers, especially legislation on fair terms.

Chapter 7 considers vicarious liability in tort. It notes two ideas that have tended to underlie accounts of vicarious liability. One is that vicariously liable persons *participated* in the conduct that is being attributed to them. The other is that those persons are well *placed* either to deter that conduct, or to deal with its consequences. While many justifications of vicarious liability have tended to hedge their bets between the two ideas, existing accounts have not been able to account properly for their respective significance. I claim that we can do this by treating vicarious liability as an instance of the 'protection principle' proposed in Chapter 4. In this view, the aim of principles of vicarious liability is not to hold entrepreneurs liable for the costs of their activities, or to give victims a more secure route to compensation, but to protect employees against the consequences of their workplace mistakes.

1

Private Law and the Burden of Repair

WHEN YOU CARELESSLY injure another person, or fail to keep your bargain with them, that person may require you to bear the burden of repairing the harm that results from your failure to do as you ought to have done. For example, that person may require you to pay them some form of compensation, to cease the conduct that caused the injury, to live up to your part of the deal as soon as possible, and so on. It is natural to think that the reason why the other person is justified in requiring you to do those things is that, in failing to discharge the burden that you owed originally, you have *wronged* them.[1] If you ask 'why ought I to compensate you?', the other person could reply 'because your failure to take due care, or to perform your end of the deal, wronged me'. The answer retains its natural feel when we bring legal institutions into the picture. If you ask 'why are courts justified in imposing on me the burden of compensating you, on pain of further legal sanction?', the other person could still reply 'because you wronged me'. That answer would rely both on the wrongful character of your conduct and on the further implicit claim that our institutions may justifiably coerce wrongdoers into making repair, but it is the first of those points that gives the answer its intuitive force.

The case for this looks ever stronger when we contrast wrongdoing to harming, which for present purposes I will understand as the causing of a setback to another person's interests. 'You ought to compensate me because you harmed me' is not a good general basis for explaining why one may owe someone the duty to make repair. Much of what one does in life causes setbacks to the interests of others, and yet this does not entitle others to require one to make repair. Your refusal to renew your tenancy agreement may cause a setback to your landlord's interest in making a certain rate of return from their property,

---

[1] Jules Coleman distinguishes two senses in which conduct might be wrongful. It might be wrongful in that it violates someone's rights (Coleman calls this a 'wrong'), or in that it causes unjustified harm to a person's legitimate interests (he calls this 'wrongdoing'): J Coleman, *Risks and Wrongs*, Reprint (New York, Oxford University Press, 2002) 331-2. For present purposes, I will be using 'wrong', 'wrongdoing' and 'wrongfulness' in a looser sense, which covers both that Coleman has in mind. Section III(C) considers the special force of rights with regard to the burden of repair.

but it does not entitle that person to require you to renew, or to make up for the income they will be losing in case you decide to move out. Asking you to undertake either of those burdens, we could say, would demand too much of you, and too little of your landlord. Moreover, sometimes others may be entitled to require a person to make repair, even if that person has not caused and is not likely to cause others any harm at all. You may be a far better gardener than I ever will be, and your touch is guaranteed to make my garden look wonderful, but the mere fact that I do not want you in my property is sufficient ground for me to be entitled to require you to get out of there, if you have made your way in uninvited. Making your responsibility to keep out of my garden contingent on your presence there causing me harm would demand too little of you, and too much of me.

Compared to harming, wrongdoing provides a better measure of our respective responsibilities, precisely because it gives us a more accurate account of what burdens we may require each other to bear in such cases. Your landlord may not require you to take on the burden involved in renewing your tenancy because they have no right to that effect, and you would commit no wrong in failing to renew. I may require you to stay out of my garden no matter what benefits your skill would bring to it because I have a right to do so and your entering my garden without permission would wrong me. We could, of course, try to arrive at similar explanations through the notion of harming. For example, we might say that your entering my garden without permission is harm *enough*, in that it causes a setback to my interest in having exclusive control over my garden, even if the further consequences of your conduct are actually beneficial to me. However, that manoeuvre fails to explain why harm to my interest in exclusive control over my garden allows me to require you to bear the burden of staying out, while harm to your landlord's interest in making a return from the property does not allow them to require you to renew the tenancy. Focusing on wrongfulness allows us to draw that important distinction in a clear and intuitive way.

In Chapter 3 I will argue that, its intuitive force notwithstanding, wrongfulness is not relevant to the justification of the burden of repair. My aim here is to set the scene for that argument, by getting a better grip on the role that the appeal to wrongfulness is supposed to play in that justification, and on the moral stakes of ascribing that role to it. Wrongfulness-based accounts (of which corrective justice and civil recourse accounts are the prime representatives) claim that you ought to bear that burden when your failure to discharge an original burden you owed to another person is wrongful. In section I, I lay out a simple challenge to centrality of the idea of wrongfulness in such accounts. As a general matter, we do not need to appeal to that idea to explain why you have to bear an *original* burden, eg to keep your promises or to drive safely. You have to keep your promises and drive safely because certain substantive considerations—from the rights and interests of parties to the situation, the nature and demandingness of the burden involved, the ease of avoiding that burden and so on—say that you do. Your failure to respond to those considerations may indeed be wrongful, but this would add nothing to the justification of why you have to bear the relevant original burdens. If this story works for original burdens, why would it not *also* work for any further burdens you have to bear (eg pay compensation, perform, stop doing something) to make up for your failure to discharge the original ones?

Section II sharpens this question by asking what we gain by making wrongfulness a requirement for imposing the burden of repair, and what we lose by going without it. To that end, it puts on the table an alternative account of the burden of repair, which I will call 'direct'. The direct account does exactly what it says, ie it thinks about the justification for imposing the burden of repair in the same way we would think about the justification for imposing any original burden. It holds that the reason why you ought to bear the burden of repair, when you do, is not that you have committed a wrong, but that the rights and interests of the persons involved in the situation point to that conclusion; it would not be too demanding on you to require you to bear that burden; you had the opportunity to avoid it by choosing appropriately, and so on. Put in the negative, the direct account says that, just as we need not see you as a wrongdoer to decide that you ought to bear the burden of driving safely, we need not see you as a wrongdoer to decide that you ought to bear the burden of repair for the driving accident that your carelessness caused.

Section III asks whether wrongfulness-based accounts give us anything that the direct account does not, and makes two claims. The first is that the direct account allows us to say many of the things that wrongfulness-based accounts say, eg that there is a continuity between the case for imposing an original burden on a person and the case for imposing on them the burden of repair; that repair will typically involve doing the 'next best thing'; that rights matter; that the burden of repair is agent-relative; that the justification for imposing it will not normally turn on distributive considerations, and so on. But the direct account does not give us everything wrongfulness-based accounts do. In some respects, it gives us less. In particular, it has no place for the idea that wrongdoers may be made to suffer because they did wrong (or that the aim of private law is to allow victims to 'get even'). In other respects, it gives us more, in the sense that it allows into the moral calculus considerations that wrongfulness-based accounts tend to block or exclude. For example, it allows that sometimes a person may not be required to do the 'next best thing' in repair; that the parties who stand in the relationship of repair need not be the same as the parties that stand in the original relationship; that considerations of distribution and punishment may sometimes affect what repair ought to consist in, and so on.

Section IV draws two conclusions from this, the first more important that the second. One is that the direct account gives us a whole lot of what we get from wrongfulness-based accounts. If tomorrow we decided to drop all talk of wrongs, wrongdoing and corrective justice in private law, and followed the direct account instead, the only claim we would be dropping completely is that it is OK to make a wrongdoer suffer on account of their wrong. Beyond that, we would interpret some otherwise very strong claims of wrongfulness-based accounts in a more relaxed way, eg we would no longer feel compelled to say that repair must *always* be the 'next best thing', or that repair must come *only* from the wrongdoer, or that distributive considerations are *never* relevant in justifying the imposition of the burden of repair, and so on. My second conclusion is that at least some advocates of wrongfulness-based accounts appreciate all this. They proclaim their allegiance to the significance of wrongfulness and corrective justice, but their heart is not really in it.

Whether or not this second conclusion is right, it is clearly less important because many other theorists remain committed to the strong claims that the direct account asks us to drop or relax. Do we have reason to think that those theorists are making a mistake? I think we do. These strong claims are not consistent with our considered ideas about moral responsibility, though it will take me a couple of chapters to make the case for this.

I. ORIGINAL BURDENS AND BURDENS OF REPAIR

Many of the burdens and responsibilities that others may require you to bear are not conditional in any way on you having committed a wrong. Once you become a parent, your children may require you to bear the burden of raising them and caring for them. When you agree to a sale, the other party may require you to bear the burden of keeping your end of the deal. When you join a club, other members may require you to shoulder the burdens of membership. When you drive your car, other road users may require you to bear the burden of observing certain traffic norms and driving standards. Your failure to discharge those burdens may sometimes be wrongful, but the justification of why you may be required to bear them in the first place is not grounded on wrongdoing of any sort.[2] It is grounded, respectively, on

---

[2] Ernest Weinrib has been interpreted as suggesting that those failures would be in themselves corrective injustices, insofar as they would allow a person to make a normative gain (ie to claim more freedom) at another's expense, see E Weinrib, *The Idea of Private Law*, Revised edn (Oxford, Oxford University Press, 2012) 76: 'corrective justice serves a normative function: a transaction is required, on pain of rectification, to conform to its contours'. While the passage does not seem to me clear evidence that Weinrib regards both the failure and its correction to be governed by norms of corrective justice, I agree with John Gardner and Scott Hershovitz that this view (which they attribute to Weinrib) would be a non-starter, see J Gardner, 'What Is Tort Law For? Part 1—The Place of Corrective Justice' (2011) 30 *Law & Philosophy* 1, 23; S Hershovitz, 'Corrective Justice for Civil Recourse Theorists' (2011) 39 *Florida State University LR* 107, 114.

the substantive morality of family relationships and parenting, of promise-keeping, of sharing projects with others, of taking care not to injure others in daily life and so on. There are many plausible ways of thinking about those substantive matters. For present purposes, I will assume that the determination of the precise burden that the applicable moral principles impose on you ought to be sensitive to considerations like the reasonable interests that you and others have in the situation, the cost for each of you of promoting or protecting those interests in certain ways, your relative ability to discharge the burdens in question or to avoid them by choosing appropriately and so on. It is to the sum of those substantive considerations that we will look to determine what form this burden ought to take (eg whether it should amount to the imposition of mere liability, a duty owed to the holder of a claim-right etc), and whether asking you to bear it would demand too much of you (as a parent, promisor, club member, driver) and too little of others.

It would be odd if we needed a very different story to explain why you have to bear certain *further* burdens, including burdens of repair, in case you have failed to discharge the burdens you had to bear originally. After all, what is good for the goose should be good for the gander. If we have a story that justifies the imposition of original burdens, why can't we use the same story to justify the imposition of the burden of repair too? The fact that your failure to discharge the original burdens may have been wrongful does not give us reason to think otherwise. Say that your failure to discharge certain burdens and responsibilities towards others is, indeed, wrongful. Let it also be true that your failure to discharge the original burdens matters when we discuss whether others may require you to bear some burden of repair. It does not follow that your failure to discharge those original burdens matters *because* it is wrongful. Perhaps it matters because an assessment of the substantive considerations that apply in the situation as it stands after your failure says so. More simply, maybe the burden of repair is just another burden, and its imposition falls to be justified in much the same way as the imposition of any original burden.

A strong tradition in private law theory nonetheless holds that, in one or another guise, the burden of repair is special and that the appeal to wrongfulness is a central part of the case for its imposition. Private law models of wrongs—models of corrective justice and civil recourse in particular—are explicitly premised on the idea that the justification of the burden of repair in the context of an accident or a breached voluntary undertaking turns on whether the failure to discharge the relevant original burden was wrongful. The wide appeal of those models makes it important to consider in more detail the job or jobs that the ideas of wrongfulness and corrective justice might be doing in that regard.

II. A 'DIRECT' ACCOUNT OF THE BURDEN OF REPAIR

Jules Coleman writes:

> Corrective justice imposes a duty to repair wrongful losses on the agents responsible
> for them. In this way corrective justice *mediates* the relationship between agents and
> a subset of losses that individuals absorb. Its central feature is that it brings agents
> together with these losses by *creating* agent-relative reasons for acting. The particular
> duty it imposes is to repair the loss. There may be other agent-relative reasons for
> acting that arise as a consequence of wrongfully injuring another, for example, the
> duty to apologize or to forbear from future harming, but these are not derived from
> corrective justice.[3]

Say that you have failed to take due care not to injure me and that we are now
wondering how that failure might matter for the appropriate allocation of
the cost of repairing the injury I have suffered. Coleman says that answering
this question requires us to appeal to some idea that 'mediates' between your
failure to discharge your original burden and the burden of making repair for
that injury. That mediating idea then creates a reason to the effect that the
burden of making such repair ought to fall on you, or on someone else, as the
case may be.

The question I want to ask is this. When we think about an original burden (eg to keep one's promises, or to drive safely), we do not appeal to some
mediating idea to account for the relationship between that burden and the
substantive considerations that support its imposition. Rather, we take those
considerations to count *directly* in favour of or against imposing that burden on
a certain person. When you ask why you have a duty to drive safely, we can say
that you have it because other people can reasonably require anyone who uses
the roads to observe certain driving standards, which—properly followed—
reduce the risk of driving accidents, those standards are not too demanding
in terms of skill and advertence, and so on. Why should we expect the relationship between those considerations and the justification for imposing the
burden of repair to be any less direct?

To sharpen this question, I will outline an alternative account, which justifies
the imposition of the burden of repair just as we would justify the imposition
of an original burden, ie by appealing directly to the substantive considerations that apply in each situation (ie to the considerations that apply before the
failure to discharge the original burden, and to the considerations that apply
after that failure, respectively). To keep on the table many options about how
that justification might proceed, I will frame it in terms of what the parties
'could reasonably require of each other', making only light assumptions about
the grounds on which they might do so.

---

[3] Coleman, above n 1, at 329 (emphasis added).

Say that you and I are discussing the substantive considerations that determine what promisees may generally require of promisors. We conclude that promisees may require promisors to bear the burden of doing as they promised, and we justify our conclusion on the basis that both parties have an interest in being able to give and receive voluntary undertakings, and that once the promisor has led the promisee to entertain certain expectations by giving such an undertaking, the promisee may reasonably require the promisor not to disappoint them (one may substitute one's preferred explanation of the binding character of promises here).[4] Looking at things from the promisor's point of view, we also conclude that the promisor could not object to being required to bear the burden of living up to those expectations, say because the promisor could have easily avoided that burden by not leading the promisee to entertain them. The story would not change if we made the further claim that the promisee may require the promisor to bear that burden as a matter of moral *right*. The fact that the promisee acquires a right would just be a further specification of the nature and demandingness of the burden to be imposed on the promisor. To settle debates about whether the promisee indeed has a moral right, rather than, say, a mere moral interest, we would appeal directly to the relevant substantive considerations, and show that they justify the imposition of that more demanding burden. We would not need to invoke any mediating idea to do this.

Our discussion then goes further and we start to think about the considerations that determine what a promisee may require of a promisor in case the latter fails to live up to the original burden. We conclude that the promisee may require the promisor to perform as soon as possible, or to pay compensation. We justify our conclusion on the basis that, as long as the promisee still has an interest in performance, the promisee may require the promisor to serve that interest even after the initial breach, and to make up any loss that the breach has led the promisee to suffer. We also conclude that the promisor cannot reasonably object to being required to bear either of those burdens, as long as the promisor had sufficient and easily available opportunity to avoid them, either by not undertaking to perform, or by performing as agreed. Again, we have reached those conclusions by appealing directly to what we take to be the applicable considerations in the situation as it stands after the default. We did this *ex ante*, just as we did with the original burden. In either case, no mediation was necessary.

---

[4] For an account of promises that explains their force as an exercise of a normative power, see J Raz, 'Promises in Morality and Law' (1982) 95 *Harvard LR* 916; D Owens, *Shaping the Normative Landscape* (Oxford, Oxford University Press, 2012).

Consider this in a little more detail. Our way of justifying the burden of repair attaches significance to the promisor's failure to live up to the original burden. However, it traces that significance not in the fact that the failure in question has been wrongful, but in the fact that the promisee has an interest in being able to obtain repair in the event of the promisor defaulting, and in the fact that the promisor had the ability to avoid the burden of repair by choosing appropriately. In effect, this way of thinking justifies the burden of repair in the same way it justifies the original burden. In both cases, that justification is *direct*, in that it relies on the range of substantive considerations that determine what the parties could reasonably require of each other in the situation (in the present example, and for the purpose of discussion, I have taken these considerations to include the promisee's interest in performance, the fact that the promisor has led the promisee to expect such performance, the promisor's ability to avoid the burden of performing and the burden of repair by choosing appropriately and so on). The only difference is that justifying the imposition of the burden of repair in this way requires us to pay *ex ante* attention to the considerations that would apply in the situation as would stand after the promisor's default.[5] This does not deny that the promisor's failure to perform as agreed may, in fact, be wrongful. It only suggests that the wrongfulness of the default does not do any useful work in justifying the burden of repair. That work is done directly by whichever considerations apply in the post-default situation, considered *ex ante*.

III. THE SIGNIFICANCE OF WRONGFULNESS

The direct account gives us a no-frills story about the burden of repair. It asks us to think about the justification for imposing that burden in more or less the same way we think about any original burden. In both cases, we look at the applicable substantive considerations (most notably, the reasonable interests of the parties, how demanding the burden is for them, how easily they may discharge or avoid it etc) and decide whether they count in favour of imposing a certain burden on a certain person. We do not appeal to any sort of mediating idea to explain why or how those considerations bear on the justification of the relevant burden. If the story works for original burdens, why would it not work for the burden of repair too?

---

[5] *cf* C Schroeder, 'Causation, Compensation and Moral Responsibility' in D Owen, *Philosophical Foundations of Tort Law* (New York, Oxford University Press, 1995) 360: 'the question of what is to be done next is simply another question of responsible moral action, and thus raises issues fully on par with those raised in giving content to the obligation to prevent harm in the first place'.

Maybe the reason is that the fact that someone is a wrongdoer ought to make a difference in how we treat that person. Perhaps a wrongdoer's actions 'lock' a wrongdoer into a special normative relationship to the victim of the wrong, so that none other than the wrongdoer must make repair, and such repair must go to none other than the victim. Or perhaps the reason why wrongdoing matters is that a victim ought to be allowed to make the wrongdoer suffer, and imposing the burden of repair on the wrongdoer is a good way to facilitate this. Or perhaps wrongdoing matters because it allows us to say that some considerations, eg where wrongdoer and victim stand in the society-wide distribution of resources, should *not* matter when we think about the burden of repair. Some of these explanations may be better than others, but they all agree that a morally plausible account of the burden of repair ought to register the significance of what a wrongdoer has done, how this affects the wrongdoer's relationships with others, and how all these things impact on what others (and the state) may now require the wrongdoer to do in response. My aim in this section is to look more closely at those explanations, and ask how far they could be accommodated under the direct account.

I will report mixed results. Some of the ideas favoured by advocates of wrongfulness-based accounts are straightforwardly compatible with the direct account too. One idea is flatly incompatible with it. And one or two others are compatible with the direct account, but only as long as we understand them in a more relaxed way.

A. Derivativeness and Priority

It seems intuitively clear that the burden of repair is normatively *derivative* from the original burden, and that discharging the original burden has normative *priority* over making repair. The appeal to wrongfulness is perfectly suited to express both intuitions. Calling the failure to discharge an original burden 'wrongful' is a neat and natural way of saying that one ought to avoid that failure rather than simply make repair for it. And taking the wrongfulness of that failure as a reason for imposing the burden of repair on the wrongdoer is an equally natural way of pointing out that the latter bears the burden of repair because they failed to discharge the original burden.

The direct account is actually no less consistent with both intuitions. For a start, it is consistent with the thought that the case for requiring one to make repair is normatively derivative from the case for requiring one to discharge the original burden of performing as promised. The derivation obtains because the considerations that justify the imposition of an original burden will generally be an important part of the case for justifying the imposition of the burden of repair too. For example, the promisee's interest in receiving performance is part of the case of why that person also has an interest in a measure of protection in case the promisor defaults. What the direct account resists is the more particular claim that the justification of the burden of repair is derived from the *wrongfulness* of the promisor's failure to discharge the original burden. Something similar goes with regard to the priority of discharging the original burden over making repair. If we have made a deal that you are to perform some undertaking towards me, and you turn your mind to how you ought to conduct yourself in the situation, you ought to not allow yourself to consider compensating me as being morally equivalent to performing. Under the direct account, the reason for this is not provided by the fact that your failure to perform would be wrongful. It is provided by the very considerations that justified imposing on you the original burden of performing. If you happen to think that, morally speaking, compensating me for your failure to perform is as good as doing as you promised, you have misunderstood what promising is about, and the moral reasons that making a promise brings into play. Saying that not performing would be wrongful is a handy way of expressing that point, but it is not a necessary part of the case for it.

Finally, it seems to me an advantage of the direct account that it can accommodate the possibility that a person may be required to make repair for some harm even *without* having failed to discharge some original burden, eg because that person is under what Peter Jaffey calls a 'primary liability' to bear the costs of certain activities, like the liability to pay tax or the liability to pay for the use of other people's resources in emergencies.[6] Primary liabilities pose a challenge for wrongfulness-based accounts precisely because those accounts claim that the justification of the burden of repair is always derivative from a failure to discharge some original burden. The direct account does not face this challenge. If we do not need to 'switch gears' depending on whether a burden is an original or a further one, it does not matter whether we describe the burden of repair as a further burden owed because a person has failed to discharge an original one, or as an original burden owed because a person is under a primary liability.

---

[6] P Jaffey, 'Duties and Liabilities in Private Law' (2006) 12 *Legal Theory* 137. Jaffey argues that cases of mistaken payment and cases like *Vincent v Lake Erie*, 109 Minn 456, 124 NW 221 (1910), in which a ship's master was held liable for the damage to a dock as a result of the master having prudently used the dock to protect the ship from a severe storm, are examples of primary liabilities. For the view that the master had committed a wrong against the owner of the dock in *Vincent*, see J Gardner, 'Wrongs and Faults' in AP Simester (ed), *Appraising Strict Liability* (Oxford, Oxford University Press, 2005) 55–7.

B. Continuity and Doing the 'Next Best Thing'

Suppose that a promisor has breached a promise, and that now we are wondering whether the promisor ought to make repair, and what form such repair ought to take. We can expect that our response to those questions will be heavily informed by the considerations that explained why the promisor incurred the duty to perform in the first place (or 'originally'). To use John Gardner's apt term, when we turn our mind to the normative consequences of the fact that the promisor has failed to do as promised, we are 'continuing' our reflections on the moral implications of the original promise, treating that failure as an occasion to flesh out the duties of the promisor and the entitlements of the promisee now that their relationship has taken a certain practical turn.[7] Gardner goes on to suggest that this continuity has one distinctive normative consequence: it entails that, once one has failed to discharge the original burden, one ought to do the 'next best thing'.[8] In his view, it is this idea of having to do the 'next best thing' that identifies the place of corrective justice in the justification of private law.

The direct account agrees that the normative force of the considerations that justify the imposition of an original burden on a person is not exhausted or extinguished when that person has failed to discharge that burden. Those considerations will be part of the case for imposing on that person the further burden (or obligation) to make repair. However, the direct account does not assume either that such 'continuity' will always obtain, or that its normative consequence will always be that one ought to do the 'next best thing' in repair. Since it treats the burden of repair just like any other burden, it remains open to the possibility that sometimes considerations that did not bear on the justification of the original burden may bear on the justification of the burden of repair, and vice versa.

To see why this difference matters in practice, consider *Ruxley Electronics v Forsyth*.[9] Forsyth hired the defendant contractor to build a pool that would be 7 ft 6 in deep. The contractor built a pool that was only 6 ft 9 in deep at its furthest end, and 6 ft deep at the point one would naturally dive in. Forsyth had made clear to the contractors that he requested a deeper pool because he was anxious about suffering injury when diving. After consulting the applicable professional standards, the trial judge found that the pool was good and safe

---

[7] Gardner, above n 2, at 33; E Weinrib, *Corrective Justice* (Oxford, Oxford University Press, 2012) at 84: 'Because what is rightfully the plaintiff's remains constant throughout, the remedy is the continuation of the right; together they make up a single unbroken juridical sequence'.

[8] Ibid at 33–4.

[9] *Ruxley Electronics and Construction Ltd v Forsyth* [1996] AC 344.

to use for all purposes, and that the difference in the market value of the shallower pool compared to the one requested was negligible. Forsyth nevertheless argued that he felt less safe than he would have felt if the pool had had the agreed depth. He did not settle his account with the contractors, who sued for their fee. Forsyth counter-claimed damages to the amount of £21,560, which would have covered the cost of demolishing the pool and building it again to the agreed specifications. The trial judge rejected the contractor's claim and allowed Forsyth's counter-claim, but awarded him only £2,500 in damages for loss of amenity, and £750 in further damages for inconvenience. The Court of Appeal allowed Forsyth's appeal and made an award for the full cost of reinstating the pool to the agreed specifications. A unanimous House of Lords allowed the contractor's appeal and affirmed the judge's decision. Citing the judgment of Cardozo J in *Jacob & Youngs Inc v Kent*,[10] Lord Lloyd held that 'the cost of reinstatement is not the appropriate measure of damages if the expenditure would be out of all proportion to the good to be obtained'.[11] Lord Bridge said: 'to hold in a case such as this that the measure of the building owner's loss is the cost of reinstatement, however unreasonable it would be to incur that cost, seems to me to fly in the face of common sense'.[12]

A principle to the effect that the contractor ought to do the 'next best thing' would require the contractor to bear the burden of paying for reinstatement.[13] The contractor was required to build a pool of certain depth and failed to do that. The '*next* best thing' to doing the job right the first time is to do it right the second time, or to pay Forsyth the amount of money that would be required for someone else to do the job.[14] Unless it is qualified in some way, the principle of doing the 'next best thing' has no room for the idea that the content of the burden that the contractor ought to bear must stand in some

[10] *Jacob & Youngs Inc v Kent* (1921) 230 NY 239, 244–5.

[11] *Ruxley* at 367. See also the opinions of Lord Jauncey at 359: 'the trial judge found that it would be unreasonable to incur the cost of demolishing the existing pool and building a new and deeper one. In so doing he implicitly recognised that the respondent's loss did not extend to the cost of reinstatement. He was, in my view, entirely justified in reaching that conclusion'; and Lord Mustill at 361: 'the test of reasonableness plays a central part in determining the basis of recovery, and will indeed be decisive in a case such as the present when the cost of reinstatement would be wholly disproportionate to the non-monetary loss suffered by the employer'.

[12] Ibid, 354.

[13] Gardner, above n 2, at 35 discusses *Ruxley* in a footnote (fn 57), but his discussion has a different aim, namely to show that breach of a contract plus payment of damages is not the moral equivalent of performance, even when the measure of damages includes an award meant to compensate for the disappointment of the promisee's 'performance interest'.

[14] *cf Robinson v Harman* (1848) 1 Ex Rep 850, 855 *per* Parke B: 'The rule of the common law is, that where a party sustains a loss by reason of a breach of contract, he is, so far as money can do it, to be placed in the same situation, with respect to damages, as if the contract had been performed'.

reasonable proportion to the loss suffered by Forsyth, where such loss is not calculated *solely* by reference to what Forsyth was entitled to receive under the agreement. The reason is that the principle of doing the 'next best thing' ties the content of the burden of repair to Forsyth's original entitlement. It does not allow considerations that arise after the contractor's failure to honour that entitlement to influence what the contractor ought to do in repair.

The direct account takes a different view. It asks us to approach questions about the burden of repair just as we approach questions about the original burden. Suppose, then, that the case concerned questions not about what the contractor ought to do in repair, but about what he ought to do originally under the agreement. We would obviously determine that question by looking at the terms of that agreement. However, sometimes the parties will not have considered a particular question, or the solution they provided will have been based on some mistaken assumption. So suppose that the cost of building the pool has turned out to be far in excess of what the parties anticipated at the time of agreement, and that the agreement contains no clause on whether the contractor has undertaken to build the pool at the agreed price, irrespective of the actual cost that performing might involve, or whether the contractor may request some additional payment. To determine whether that party must indeed perform 'no matter the cost', we will consider both the interests of the party who expects performance and the interests of the party who undertakes to perform. We will consider, in particular, the value of performance for the party who requests it, the likely cost of performance, the parties' relative ability to assess that cost in advance, the value for the parties (typically, the contractors) that proposed a fixed fee of having the opportunity to do so, the ability of each party to deal with unexpected rises in that cost, any relevant assurances given between the parties and so on. The contribution of each of those considerations to the content of original burden will depend on the contribution of the others. For instance, we will not take the fact that performance has value for the promisee as settling *by itself* what level of sacrifice the promisor ought to undertake in order to provide such performance. That level of sacrifice must also be sensitive to the cost of performance for the other party. It is possible that, in some cases, we will conclude that, unless the agreement features an explicit clause to the contrary, the contractor did not actually undertake to perform 'no matter the cost', but only as long as the cost of doing so stood in some reasonable proportion to what the parties expected it to be. The general idea is not really controversial in the context of contract interpretation. For example, in *L Schuler AG v Wickman Machine Tool Sales Ltd*, it was held that the fact that the parties had used the label 'condition' to describe a term that set out a rather minor duty on the part of the defendants did not necessarily allow the claimants to treat any breach of the relevant term, however small, as sufficient ground for rescinding the contract. That result would be unreasonable because it would place a much too demanding burden on the defendants for the sake of something rather trivial. As Lord Reid put it:

> The fact that a particular construction leads to a very unreasonable result must be a relevant consideration [in interpreting the agreement]. The more unreasonable the result the more unlikely it is that the parties can have intended it, and if they do intend it the more necessary it is that they should make that intention abundantly clear.[15]

The appeal to reasonableness as a standard of contract interpretation is a well-settled principle of English law.[16]

The direct account asks us to engage in similar reasoning when we consider the content of the burden of repair. Sometimes the parties will have specified that, if performance is not up to what was agreed, the defaulting party ought to undertake reinstatement 'no matter the cost'. Sometimes the answer will not be given in the agreement, chiefly because the parties may not have considered what repair would amount to in every case that performance fell short of the original specification. In such cases, to determine whether a party must provide repair in the form of reinstatement 'no matter the cost', we would need to attend to the value of the repair for the party that requests it, the likely cost of repair, the relative ability of the parties to estimate that cost in advance, the value for them of leaving the particular method of repair unspecified, any relevant assurances given between the parties and so on. As with the original burden, we will not take the fact that repair has value for one party as settling by itself what level of sacrifice the other party ought to accept in providing that value. And just as a party could sometimes reasonably object to being required to *perform* 'no matter the cost', maybe sometimes that party could object to being required to *make repair* 'no matter the cost'. In Chapter 3, I discuss whether *Ruxley* is indeed correctly decided.[17] My present point is that the direct account fits the now settled view of English law expressed in *Ruxley* in a way that the idea of doing the 'next best thing' does not.

C. Rights

Perhaps the most obvious challenge to the direct account is that it does not seem to give due weight to the fact that, very often, one's failure to discharge an original burden owed to another person will constitute a violation of that person's rights. The challenge is obvious because the appeal to the significance

---

[15] *L Schuler AG v Wickman Machine Tool Sales Ltd* [1974] AC 235, 251.

[16] *cf* C Staughton, 'How do the Courts Interpret Commercial Contracts?' (1999) 58 CLJ 303, 308–11, where the former Lord Justice of Appeal said: 'When speaking to students I tell them that what Lord Reid said is something which they should learn by heart'.

[17] See ch 3(IV)(B).

of rights can offer a very plausible explanation of what is special about the burden of repair. Unlike original burdens, the burden of repair seems to be a burden that one owes to a person precisely *because* one has violated that person's rights. Compare two situations. In one, the front door of my flat is old and needs repair. In the other, you have carelessly broken my front door. It is intuitively clear that the burden of repair should lie with me in the first situation, and with you in the second. The only difference between the two situations is that, in the second, you have violated my property rights. Wrongfulness-based accounts seem well-placed to capture that difference.

It seems to me that the direct account is consistent with the idea that rights have special significance in the justification of the burden of repair. The fact that a person has a right and that another has a correlative duty is a matter that concerns the stringency (or the demandingness) of one's entitlement and the other's corresponding burden. It does not speak to whether the wrongfulness of the failure to discharge that burden is a necessary part of justifying the imposition of the burden of repair. Indeed, there is no obvious reason why we would ever need to appeal to wrongfulness, or to corrective justice, or to some other mediating idea in order to explain why the fact that one has violated another person's rights matters when we consider who ought to bear the burden of repair. We could say directly that the considerations that justify the right *also* justify imposing on one the burden of repair for its violation. This is clearest if we suppose, for the purposes of illustration, that rights are the *only* kind of consideration that matters in the justification of the burden of repair. Those who buy into this 'strict' view have all the grounds they need to explain why a person who violates rights ought to bear the burden of repair. Once those rights are violated, as Coleman notes, 'that is enough for the strict liability theorist to justify both liability and recovery; the wrongfulness of the invasion is, in effect, otiose'.[18] This is not to deny that there is some distance between saying that a person has a right to require one to bear some original burden, and saying that this person has a right that one bear the burden of repair for one's failure to discharge that original burden. The two rights, and the corresponding obligations, are not analytically identical, so we will need some explanation of how we go from one to the other. Coleman's point is that we can travel that distance without needing to appeal to the idea that one's failure to live up to the original right was wrongful. For advocates of the strict view he has in mind, the fact that someone had an original right and that one's failure has violated it suffices for that purpose. In the broken door example, we could say that my right that others do not damage my property entitles me to require them not just to refrain from causing such damage, but also to make

---

[18] Coleman, above n 1, at 344.

repair in case they do cause it. Your conduct has caused some such damage, so I am entitled to require you to make repair for it. If the further fact that the violation constitutes a wrong is supposed to connect the considerations that justify the property right with the justification of what ought to happen when you violate that right, it builds a bridge where there is no river.

Of course, the 'strict' view which says that only rights matter may be mistaken. Maybe rights are not the only kind of consideration that goes into determining who ought to make repair and what such repair ought to consist of.[19] However, highlighting that view serves to show that those who take rights very seriously have no reason to subscribe to a wrongfulness-based account of the burden of repair. If anything, the direct account seems a much more natural ally, because it allows them to say exactly what they want: that the justification of the burden of repair turns on the very considerations that justified the imposition of the original burden.

D. Agent-relativity

Another idea central to wrongfulness-based justifications of the burden of repair says that, when you have failed to discharge the original burden that you owed to the other person, it is you, rather than anyone else, who ought to make repair, and it is to that person, rather than to anyone else, that you ought to make such repair. In fact, one could say that repair made by a third party would not be 'repair' properly so called at all. If you owed me a bicycle and failed to deliver it, but someone else stepped in and gave me that very same bicycle, that person would be benefiting me, but they would not be making repair for anything. The idea of repair seems to require a failure to discharge an original burden, and the benefactor is not guilty of any such failure. One way to put the point is to say that the very notion of repair, and the duty to make it, is agent-relative.[20] Ernest Weinrib advocates a strong version of this position:

---

[19] Weinrib, above n 7, at 112–3 seems to me to come close to endorsing this view in respect of damages *in lieu* of an injunction, arguing that the right to an injunction is not derived solely by reference to the claimant's violated right, but by reference to the 'system' of rights from which the claimant's particular right draws its normative force. Presumably, Weinrib thinks that the same system gives the wrongdoer-defendant a right not to be subjected to onerous burdens that produce only minimal benefits for the victim-claimant, whose harm can be easily monetised etc.

[20] The force of this idea convinced Jules Coleman to abandon his 'annulment' conception of corrective justice, under which the aim of corrective justice is to annul the claimant's wrongfully-inflicted loss. Coleman's critics pointed out that the annulment conception did not account for the fact that it is the defendant, rather than anyone else, who ought to make repair. See J Coleman, 'The Mixed Conception of Corrective Justice' (1992) 77 *Iowa LR* 427, 433–6.

If the law took money from the defendant without giving it to the plaintiff, the injustice suffered by the plaintiff would remain uncorrected. Similarly, if the law gave money to the plaintiff without taking it from the defendant, the injustice done by the defendant would remain uncorrected. And even if the law took money from the defendant and gave an equivalent amount of money to the plaintiff in separate operations (say, by requiring payment into one government fund and out of another), the injustice as something done by the defendant to the plaintiff—and therefore as being of relational significance between them—would still remain uncorrected.[21]

As Weinrib makes clear, wrongfulness-based accounts justify the burden of repair by focusing on the burdens generated under the original relationship between two agents. They then treat the failure of one agent to discharge the original burden owed to the other as causing that relationship to enter a new stage. This stage involves a different burden for that agent, namely the burden of repair required under corrective justice,[22] but that burden is as special between the parties, or as 'agent-relative', as the original one.

The direct account is sensitive to the idea that some of the burdens you owe to others may be agent-relative, but it is not committed to the claim that the relation in question must be the same for both the original burden and the burden of repair. Consider original burdens. To determine who stands in the appropriate relation to whom, or who owes agent-relative duties to another, we need to look into the applicable substantive considerations, eg who made a voluntary undertaking, to whom they made it, who owed a duty of care to others and so on. The direct account recommends that we proceed in the same fashion when we think about the burden of repair. That is, to figure out who owes a duty of repair to whom, we should attend to the substantive considerations applicable in that situation as it stands after a person's failure to discharge the original burden. If those considerations happen to be different from those that applied in the original situation, it is possible that they will ground different agent-relative duties between the same or even between different persons. Consider the example of contributory negligence. Suppose that I carelessly injured you, but that you could have avoided the injury by taking some easy steps of self-protection. When we consider the original burdens each of us bears in the situation, the only burden that 'connects' us is my duty of care towards you. Your original burden of self-protecting does not connect us, as it does not take the form of a duty that you owe to me (it is not, as Weinrib might say, a 'bilateral' consideration). Still, your failure to discharge that burden now entitles me to require you to bear part of the burden of making repair for the

---

[21] Weinrib, above n 7, at 88.

[22] Ibid at 93: 'The continuity of right and remedy means that the same relationship of right and duty continues through a sequence of stages that, on the duty side, require different specific actions'.

harm you have suffered. You did not owe it to me to self-protect, but, now that you failed to do so, I may require you to pick up part of the bill for the injury you have suffered (I return to this example in Chapter 4).

All this is consistent with the agent-relativity of the burden of repair, as it settles not only what repair is due but also who ought to provide it and to whom.[23] The difference is that, under the direct account, the relationship that binds the person who ought to make repair and the person who ought to receive it need not be the same as the relationship that binds the person who owed the original burden and the person that burden was owed to (in the contributory negligence example, my ability to self-protect does not connect us in the context of the original burden, but it does connect us in the context of the burden of repair). In that sense, the characteristic feature of Weinrib's position is not so much that it sees the burden of repair as agent-relative, but that it blocks any considerations that do not bear on the justification of the original burden from determining who stands in the appropriate relationship for the purpose of justifying the burden of repair.

That difference matters for the justification of familiar community insurance schemes, such as those requiring everyone to take out third-party insurance in respect of accidents commonly associated with some important everyday activity, eg driving. Suppose that our community would save a lot in transaction costs by having an institutional arrangement that prohibits victims of driving accidents from trying to recover compensation from careless drivers, and allows them instead to recover full compensation straight from the careless drivers' insurers. Under that arrangement, the person who failed to discharge the original burden of driving safely and the person who bears the burden of repair are not the same, and the victim has no option of demanding that repair be made by the former. Weinrib's understanding of agent-relativity as pertaining to the relationship between the wrongdoer and the victim would treat such an arrangement as unjust, inasmuch as it bars the latter from bringing action against the former. Under the direct account, the arrangement would be justified to the extent that careless drivers could object to having to bear the burden of repair for their carelessness; that insurers would not have an objection to bearing that burden; and that victims could not object to receiving repair from someone other than careless drivers. Whether these conditionals are satisfied will depend on the substantive considerations in play (in Chapters 4 and 5, I will argue that it

---

[23] Coleman, above n 20, at 436: 'If one person has wronged another, then corrective justice imposes a duty on the wrongdoer to rectify his wrong. In the annulment thesis, in contrast, the fact that one person wrongs another creates a state of the world that is the concern of justice, but perhaps not of anyone in particular, including the wrongdoer. In the relational view, the fact that one person wrongs another affects the system of rights and responsibilities *between them*'.

depends on the value of those persons of having the opportunities that this arrangement offers them), but the arrangement in question would not count as unjust simply because it allows the burden of repair to fall on a person other than the wrongdoer.

Note that the contrast between the direct account and its rivals remains under even more relaxed conceptions of agent-relativity. For instance, Coleman has argued for a conception of agent-relativity that connects the pool of wrongdoers with the pool of their victims, rather than individual wrongdoers with their individual victims.[24] Stephen Perry has suggested that the question of who should bear the burden of repair in corrective justice may be determined, at least in part, by considerations that are not agent-relative in character.[25] While these positions may have some affinity to the direct account in some respects, they both remain committed to a view that the direct account rejects: that the *only* eligible candidates for bearing the burden of repair are the agents who stand in the relationship constituted by the substantive considerations that justified the original burden.

E. 'Getting Even'

Most theorists who think that private law is there to correct wrongs agree with Aristotle that the purpose of this is to *undo* or at least to *repair* the victim's wrongful harm. Scott Hershovitz thinks that the 'Aristotelian' view gets it badly wrong.[26] He argues that the real purpose of corrective justice as a response to wrongdoing is to give the victim a good substitute for revenge against the wrongdoer, or to allow the victim to 'get even'. Under Aristotelian accounts of corrective justice, the proper normative response to a wrong is necessarily *exhausted* in the repair of the harm suffered by one's victim. As Hershovitz notes, this commitment puts Aristotelian accounts in an awkward position. Many familiar harms, from the harm of losing a limb or a life, to the harm of having one's cherished possessions destroyed, cannot actually be repaired. Classical accounts therefore have to try to explain why a wrongdoer may nevertheless be required to pay damages in such situations by describing

---

[24] J Coleman, 'Moral Theories of Torts—Their Scope and Limits: Part I' (1982) 1 *Law & Philosophy* 371, 375–6. Coleman develops this suggestion with discrete activities (like driving) in mind, but the argument could plausibly be extended to link the group of all wrongdoers and the group of all their victims.

[25] S Perry, 'Loss, Agency, and Responsibility for Outcomes: Three Conceptions of Corrective Justice' in K Cooper-Stephenson, E Gibson (eds) *Tort Theory* (Ontario, Captus Press, 1993) 24, 47.

[26] Hershovitz, above n 2. See also S Hershovitz, 'Tort as a Substitute for Revenge' in J Oberdiek (ed), *Philosophical Foundations of the Law of Torts* (Oxford, Oxford University Press, 2014) 86.

such remedies as approximations of actual repair. This, Hershovitz says, is skirting around the hard truth that, in those cases, the proper and often only possible normative response to a person's wrong is to allow the victim to subject the wrongdoer to a harm that bears some appropriate relation to the gravity of the harm that the victim suffered. Corrective justice is simply a way of doing this in a more civil and controlled fashion than allowing the victim to take revenge. On this 'talionic' account, the reason one is required to pay damages (and why this requirement is agent-relative on one's part, and the right to act on it is agent-relative on the victim's) is not that this makes things the way they were, but that it gives victims a way of dealing with the non-repairable harm they have suffered, by enlisting the help of our institutions to 'get even' with the wrongdoer. This fulfils two aims. First, it satisfies the victim's moral sentiments and obviates the need for that person to take revenge or fashion some other violent response to the wrong. Secondly, it communicates to wrongdoers that they cannot treat others in certain ways and avoid being held to account for it.

I have no stakes in discussing whether Hershovitz's intuition that tort law is about 'getting even' captures the true point of corrective justice as a concept and a practice. The question I want to consider is whether the direct account can accommodate his suggestion that victims should be allowed to make wrongdoers suffer on account of their wrongs. In the course of the argument, I will try to disassociate the idea of allowing victims to 'get even' from two neighbouring but different ideas. One is that the manner in which a person failed to discharge an original burden owed to another may aggravate the magnitude of the victim's injury. The other is that a person who engages in certain forms of conduct may be legitimately subject to punishment at the request, and to the practical benefit, of the victim of such conduct. I will argue that while the direct account has no place for the idea of allowing victims to 'get even', it is hospitable to both of those other ideas.

In line with the overall thrust of the direct account, consider original burdens first. Say that we are dealing with a really complex moral problem, and we are not sure who should bear which practical burden. Maybe we are trying to decide how much, if anything, persons ought to do to check the truth or other justification for statements made by someone else before repeating those statements to others, say, by retweeting them (I gladly confess to finding this a really tough nut to crack). We think about the question as best as we can, decide on an answer, and pass a law that lays out the duties that people have in that regard, and the conditions of their liability for retweeting defamatory statements. Sometime later, it occurs to us that our answer was wrong. We now believe that the law we passed is asking too much of retweeters by way of advertence, or that it imposes too serious a constraint on their freedom of expression. We proceed to amend the law to match our considered convictions about the matter.

Consider the position of retweeters who were held liable under the original law. Those persons bore burdens that should never have been imposed on them. In a very plausible sense, we might say that, in demanding too much of them, we wronged them. Now suppose that our revised law not only absolves those persons of liability under the old law, but also refunds them on application, and from the public coffers, for any damages and legal costs they have had to pay (let us say that we are happy to let the claimants keep the damages as a windfall). This would not return things to the way they were. People's reputations will still have suffered, other persons' freedoms will have been temporarily curtailed, and some persons will have spent time and money on lawyers and courts. Yet it seems to me that we would not regard allowing those persons to claim those refunds as allowing them to 'get even' with anyone. Instead, we would treat the occasion as a morally more complex version of what happens when, say, someone is charged too much tax in one year, and gets a refund in the next. In both cases, we would recognise that we made a mistake in designing or implementing a policy, and we are now focusing on allowing those that the policy saddled with excess burdens to protect themselves from its adverse effects and, as much as possible, to reverse those effects. Maybe we can even achieve a communicative aim by admitting publicly that we got it wrong, and that next time we should take more care when making policy.

Why not think the same way about the burden of repair in standard tort and contract settings? If the thought of allowing one to 'get even', or allowing one to make a wrongdoer suffer, does not carry much moral weight when we think about failures to discharge the burden of allocating original burdens in the right way (eg the burden of deciding how much to ask of people who retweet statements by others), why should that thought carry more weight when we think about the failure to discharge one of those original burdens? Maybe a wrongdoer is, in that respect, like the careless legislator: each failed to get it right the first time, and must now make repair for the consequences of that failure. Of course, their respective victims may experience the moral sentiment of having been wronged and of wanting to make the wrongdoer suffer, and that requires some accounting for. But it does not follow that those sentiments are part of the explanation of why our community ought to repeal its latest defamation laws, or why wrongdoers ought to make repair to their victims.

Note that while the direct account has no taste for the idea of 'getting even', it does not exclude two other possibilities. One is that the repair that a person has to make may depend on the manner in which that person has behaved. The direct account allows that particularly egregious or callous failures to discharge an original burden, eg 'oppressive' and 'unconstitutional' actions by public officials, may aggravate the magnitude of the victim's injury, and therefore justify awarding the victim higher than normal damages.[27] But the justification for this has nothing to do with allowing the victim to make a wrongdoer suffer. It simply accepts that the character of what a person has done (the injury that requires repair) may sometimes be affected by who that person is (say, a public official) and how that person went about doing it (say, by abusing public powers to oppress the victim).

Moreover, the direct account is perfectly consistent with the possibility that some forms of conduct may be subject to punishment, that the power to request such punishment may be placed in the hands of the victim of that conduct, and that the punishment may take the form of a benefit conferred by the punished person to the victim. These are, to be sure, exceptional possibilities. Much of the time, the reasons that justify imposing certain burdens on certain persons will also explain why those persons are *not* taking on the additional burden of risking punishment in case they fail to discharge them. Suppose that someone proposed that, as a general matter, defaulting promisors should be jailed until they make good their promises. We might plausibly say that such a measure would be too burdensome on promisors, because the breach of a promise is not, at least in the general instance, the kind of failure against which we may use the threat of jail or other punishment as a disincentive.

By the same token, however, in other situations we may well be justified in using that threat in order to ensure that people have a clear and powerful incentive not to ignore the original burdens that they owe to others. That may be the case especially when the interests protected by the discharge of those burdens are important; the failure to discharge them is tempting; the detection and prevention of such failures is not easy; such failures have a considerable adverse effect on social peace and people's sense of security; the appropriate institutions have announced the threatened sanctions in advance, and so on. That is the stuff criminal law is typically concerned with, but we have no reason to think that the protection they provide people with cannot be useful in civil law contexts too. For a start, we could justify giving the power to request and pursue the application of those sanctions to the person to whom the original burden was owed, insofar as this makes it more likely that this person's interests will be better protected. We could appeal to the same idea to justify giving the victim the benefit of any monetary penalty that the person who failed to discharge the original burden has to pay.

This is not the only way to think about the justification of punishment, but it is certainly plausible (HLA Hart, for one, held it),[28] and it does not appeal

---

[27] *Rookes v Barnard* [1964] AC 1129 per Lord Devlin at 1226–7; *Kuddus v Chief Constable of Leicestershire Constabulary* [2002] 2 AC 122 per Lord Slynn at 133–4.
[28] See introduction.

to the idea that the person on whom those stronger sanctions are imposed is a wrongdoer, or that the reason why this person must be punished is that the victim is entitled to make them suffer. Its claim, rather, is that sometimes it is necessary to protect other people's interests by creating an extra (ie not repair-based) disincentive for persons who might otherwise be tempted to fail in their original duties to others. This justification seems to me to achieve the communicative and accountability-enhancing purposes that Hershovitz has in mind. It tells people that they *really* ought to not do certain things, on pain of being held accountable and suffering punishment. Sometimes it also allows victims to pull the strings in holding those persons to account and requesting their punishment, and to get the benefit of any monetary penalty imposed in the course of that process. But it does not accept that the reason why victims have that power is that they are entitled to 'get even' with those persons.

This view also accounts for the example that animates Hershovitz's own discussion, the case of *Alcorn v Mitchell* before the Supreme Court of Illinois.[29] At the end of litigation between the two parties on a trespass suit, Alcorn, who lost the case, spat at Mitchell's face. Mitchell sued him for battery. The Supreme Court of Illinois awarded Mitchell $1,000, which, at the time, was a rather substantial sum.[30] Hershovitz notes that, while Mitchell certainly suffered an indignity, the facts of the case give us no reason to think that he suffered any injury beyond that, or even that the injury he suffered was one that money might repair. The Court justified the severity of the award as follows:

> The act in question was one of the greatest indignity, highly provocative of retaliation by force, and the law, as far as it may, should afford substantial protection against such outrages, in the way of liberal damages, that the public tranquility may be preserved by saving the necessity of resort to personal violence as the only means of redress.[31]

Hershovitz reads this passage as suggesting that 'Alcorn had to pay so that Mitchell would not have to strike back. The tort suit was to substitute for the revenge the Court worried Mitchell might take absent a civil means of redress'.[32] I think we should read the court's decision differently. Alcorn had to pay because the nature of the indignity that he committed was such that the law should, in the court's own words, protect people from suffering it, by putting in place a substantial disincentive for anyone who might be tempted

---

[29] *Alcorn v Mitchell* 65 Ill. 553 (1872); Hershovitz, above n 26, at 85–8.

[30] Hershovitz, ibid at 86, reports that in today's money that would be somewhere between $20,000 and $250,000 depending on one's assumptions about change in the value of money over time.

[31] Above n 29, at 554.

[32] Hershovitz, above n 26, at 87.

to inflict it on others. This reading focuses on how the imposition of a strong sanction would prevent people in Alcorn's position from inflicting injury. Hershovitz's reading focuses on what the imposition of such a sanction would prevent people in Mitchell's position from doing in response. Both actions are clearly worth preventing in the way the court tried to prevent them. My point is that preventing the incidence of the original injury in the future gives us enough reason to justify the court's award. In fact, it seems to me that the court drew attention to the likely consequences for social peace of allowing such injuries to go unpunished by the state precisely in order to justify why it is important to for the state to give a strong disincentive to those tempted to inflict such injuries. The court was saying 'look at what injuries people will be tempted to inflict on others if we don't send a strong message'. It was not claiming that this message would be 'substituting' a natural entitlement of persons in Mitchell's position to send a similar message themselves.[33]

F. Distribution

Consider, finally, how the direct account might approach another idea that wrongfulness-based accounts take to heart: that the justification of the burden of repair should not depend on considerations of *distribution*.

Suppose that unjustly Poor carelessly drives into unjustly Rich. It seems intuitively clear that Poor may not disclaim responsibility for repairing the injury on the mere ground that Poor is the victim of an unjust distribution of resources. Similarly, Rich does not lay down an entitlement to repair just because Rich has been the beneficiary of that unjust distribution. It follows that Poor may not complain against the fact that being required to bear the burden of repair would have the effect of sustaining this distributive injustice. Poor's complaint about the injustice of the distribution may be valid, but it will not undermine the justification for imposing on Poor the burden of repair.

---

[33] Stephen Darwall suggests that conceptions of corrective justice that see its function as allowing a victim to be 'vindictive' or to act 'in revenge' are not consistent with the general conditions of moral accountability between equals; S Darwall, 'Justice and Retaliation' (2010) 39 *Philosophical Papers* 315, 335–7. In a community of such persons, Darwall writes, 'individuals never have the moral standing to retaliate or take vengeance. As private individuals we do give up a right of *punishment*, which we would otherwise have had as representative persons, to the state. And we give up also rights to seek compensation through extra-judicial means. But we never had the right to vengeance, or to retaliate except to the extent necessary for self-defense, so the state need provide citizens no legal forum to act against other private individuals in return for giving up these "private rights"' (original emphasis).

Jules Coleman thinks that examples like that illustrate the special value and identify the special domain of corrective justice. He writes:

> If sustaining or protecting a less than fully just distribution of wealth or resources can sometimes be a matter of justice, it cannot be a matter of distributive justice. Then what sort of justice is it that permits, if it does not explicitly endorse, distributive injustice? The answer is, corrective justice.[34]

I suspect that Coleman's conception of distributive justice may be a little too limiting.[35] Any plausible theory of distributive justice cares not only about how much you have, but also about how you get to acquire it (I am not familiar with any theory of distribution that allows people to adjust their relative shares by stealing or by inflicting personal harm on others). However, it seems to me that the essence of Coleman's point is not that corrective justice does the explanatory job that distributive justice cannot, but that corrective justice sets a principled limitation to how a theory of distributive justice might go about the job of distribution. The real claim is that the demands of corrective justice, or the wrongfulness of the injury, give us reason not to allow people to respond to distributive injustice by refusing to bear the burden of repair for injuries caused by their carelessness.

That said, I think that Coleman is missing a third possible answer to the question he asks. The reason why distributive considerations do not excuse Poor from the burden of repair is actually provided by the considerations that required Poor to bear the relevant original burden. Poor's duties to Rich and to other road users were not contingent on the justice of their respective distributive shares. That is, the standard of conduct Poor ought to observe is 'drive safely', not 'drive safely as long as this achieves a certain distributive pattern'.[36] Equally clearly, it is part of the justification for imposing that burden on Poor that Poor's position in the society-wide distribution of resources does not, as a general matter, make it more difficult for Poor to observe the relevant driving standards. We could appeal to a similar thought when we consider whether Poor may object to having to bear the burden of repair. For example, we could say that the fact that Poor has an unjustly small share of resources may make it harder for Poor to *discharge* the burden of repair, but it does not make it harder for Poor to *avoid* that burden. All Poor needs to do for that purpose is

---

[34] Coleman, above n 1, at 305.

[35] *cf* E Voyiakis, 'Rights, Social Justice, and Responsibility in the Law of Tort' (2012) 35 *University of New South Wales Law Journal* 449.

[36] I am not aware of any theorist who suggests that, as a general matter, our promissory duties or our duties of care are contingent on the justice of the society-wide distribution of resources. This makes it hard to see who advocates of wrongfulness-based accounts take themselves to be arguing against when they urge that private law is not there to do distributive justice.

to observe the applicable driving standards. The upshot is that we do not need to appeal to some special normative idea (be that wrongdoing, wrongfulness or corrective justice) to block considerations of distributive justice from affecting whether Poor may be required to bear the burden of repair. The blocking device may be built into the substantive considerations that justify imposing on Poor the original burden of driving safely.[37]

At the same time, there may be cases where the applicable substantive considerations will actually *require* us to take the justice of the society-wide resource distribution into account when we justify the original burden that one person owes to another. Consider the example of pay agreements between employers' unions and labour unions.[38] Suppose that a society features one of each sort of union, and that each of them represents 100 per cent of their potential constituents. The two unions conclude a five-year pay agreement. One year into the implementation of the pay agreement, and other things being equal, the government increases the tax rates for labour income by 25 per cent, to fund the equivalent of a tax break for capital income. It seems to me plausible that this shift in the distribution of tax burdens would entitle labour unions to object not only to the tax laws in question, but also to the continued implementation of the pay agreement and to employers' attempts to enforce it. In particular, labour unions could argue that their failure to continue to abide by the pay agreement does not entitle employers to require them to bear any further burdens, precisely because the justification of the original burdens that each party undertook *was* contingent on a certain pattern of distribution of resources between owners of capital and labourers. Their complaint would be that, applied to the pay agreement, the moral principles of promise-keeping *themselves* require that the parties' respective burdens be sensitive to the society-wide pattern of resource distribution.

IV. REPAIR WITHOUT WRONGFULNESS OR CORRECTIVE JUSTICE

I have argued that it would be odd if the justification of the burden of repair were very different in character, or were built out of very different moral materials, from the justification of any original burden. When we ask whether a person should bear the burden of performing an agreed task, of taking care not to injure others, or of paying a certain rate of tax, we look at the reasonable interests of that person and of others involved in the situation. We look at

---

[37] I discuss this point, and the significance of insurance for driving accidents, in more detail in ch 4(IV).

[38] I am ignoring trivial examples, such as those in which the parties make a bet on the tax policy of a newly elected government.

their ability to discharge that burden, and their ability to avoid it by choosing appropriately. In assessing those abilities, we look at the demandingness of the particular burden for each of those persons, the range of options available to them, the stakes for others of those persons not discharging the relevant burden and so on. Sometimes our assessment is sensitive to issues that arise after one has acquired the original burden, or to where those persons stand in the distribution of resources across society, or to the possibility of adding the threat of punitive sanctions to induce those persons to live up to the burden in question. In doing all this, we do not think that the relationship between those considerations and some putative original burden must be somehow 'mediated'. Those considerations do or do not justify the imposition of that burden on a person, but in either case their impact is direct. If this story works for original burdens, why would it not work for the burden of repair?

A well-known and vibrant tradition in private law theory answers that the burden of repair is special because its imposition is justified only when a person has committed a wrong in failing to discharge some original burden owed to another. To get a better grip on the role that the appeal to wrongfulness, or to the related idea of corrective justice, is supposed to play in these accounts, I contrasted them with a 'direct' account. The direct account says that the burden of repair is, in fact, nothing special: it is a burden that falls to be justified just like any other, by direct appeal to all considerations applicable in the situation as it stands after the failure to discharge the burden one owed originally (eg to do as promised, or to drive safely). Accordingly, under the direct account, the reason why you ought to bear the burden of repair, when you do, is not that you have committed a wrong. It is, rather, that the relevant substantive considerations point to that conclusion, eg that the other party could reasonably want some protection against your failure to discharge the original burden, it would not be too demanding on you to require you to bear the burden of making repair, you had the opportunity to avoid that burden by choosing appropriately, and so on.

I have argued that the direct account conflicts with one idea that might be thought to support a wrongfulness-based view of the burden of repair: that repair is a way of making wrongdoers suffer on account of their wrong. But it is consistent with very many other ideas that underpin its wrongfulness-based rivals, even if it does not always understand those ideas in the same way, or develop them in the same direction. It can explain why discharging the original burden has normative priority; why the burden of repair is normatively derivative from the original one; why rights may have special significance in the justification of the burden of repair; why that burden is agent-relative; why it may often take the form of requiring one to do the next best thing; and why considerations of distribution and punishment may sometimes be inapplicable to its justification. The main difference is that the direct account understands some of those claims in a more relaxed way. It allows that (and explains why) repair need not always involve doing the next best thing; that such repair need not always come from the wrongdoer; and that the justification for imposing the burden of repair may sometimes be sensitive to the parties' distributive shares and to punitive considerations.

Maybe the differences between the direct account and its wrongfulness-based rivals are big and important. If you think this, the rest of this book will try to convince you that the direct account has the better of the debate, ie that the ideas that we would have to drop if we stopped talking about wrongs, wrongdoing, wrongfulness and corrective justice were not really worth keeping in the first place.

But maybe you will think that the distance between the two accounts is quite small. Take the idea that the direct account flatly rejects, namely that repair in tort law is a way of allowing the victim to make the wrongdoer suffer. To my knowledge, only Scott Hershovitz has defended it in print. I suspect that even theorists who appreciate the force of his anti-Aristotelian cry 'we cannot go back to the way things were!' may hesitate to buy his talionic alternative.[39] Whether or not it stands up to scrutiny, the claim that we may legitimately make wrong-doers suffer is basically an outlier within its own tradition. And if my enemy's enemy is my friend, the fact that both the direct account and its (mainstream) wrongfulness-based counterparts reject that claim might be the beginning of a beautiful friendship. If you find this happier picture appealing, the rest of the book will try to convince you that we should interpret the ideas that the two accounts share in the more relaxed way that the direct account recommends.

Either way, though, if something like the direct account is right, this is terrible news for those who think that we cannot do the job of justifying the burden of repair without appealing to wrongdoing, wrongfulness, corrective justice and similar ideas. It is terrible news because it shows that those ideas either commit us to claims we should not endorse, or tell us nothing that we cannot get by treating the burden of repair just like any other burden, and justifying

---

[39] *cf* B Zipursky, 'Substantive Standing, Civil Recourse and Corrective Justice' (2011) 39 *Florida State University LR* 299, 314–5 gives some reasons why he is not likely to revise his and John Goldberg's civil recourse theory in that direction: 'The first [problem] is that many unanswered empirical questions jump out: How pervasive is th[e] desire [for retaliation]? How valuable is it actually to act upon it? How successful is an avenue of civil recourse as a substitute for a privilege of violent retaliation? A second is that there is a characteristic function or operation of a right of civil recourse, and it is in huge part to require the defendant to compensate the plaintiff and to repair the injury he or she inflicted. Retaliation is typically not constructive but destructive, and appears to have little to do with repair. A third is that—even apart from legal systems—a huge part of morality is learning to deal with having been wronged without acting upon vengeful desires. It is implausible to think of tort law as existing for those who lack the moral development to do that without civil litigation.'

its imposition accordingly. I have not made the substantive case for all this yet. I have simply thrown around some intuitions that seem to me to support that view (eg that the direct account fits cases like *Ruxley* better). But it seems to me that some advocates of wrongfulness-based accounts have seen the trouble ahead, and have qualified their support for the idea that wrongfulness matters in the justification of the burden of repair to such a degree that they might not mind if we put that idea out of commission.

I think that is true of John Gardner. As we have seen, Gardner believes that there is continuity between the reasons that justify the imposition of an original burden (to keep one's promises, to drive safely etc) and the reasons that justify the imposition of the burden of repair when one has failed to discharge an original one. The distinctive role of corrective justice, in his view, is to explain how we move from one burden (Gardner puts this in terms of an 'obligation') to the other (eg to explain why if I don't turn up at the time we agreed, I ought to turn up, or give you a call, as quickly as possible). Corrective justice, in Gardner's view, fulfils that role by telling us that the relevant reasons require the wrongdoer to do the next best thing.[40] I hope it is clear that the direct account likes the continuity thesis almost as much as Gardner does. It certainly agrees that there is a normative distance to travel between the failure to discharge an original burden and the justification for imposing the burden of repair. It accepts that making repair will very often require one to do the next best thing. And, though I have not argued this yet, it is perfectly consistent with a non-consequentialist approach to reasons.[41] Of course, Gardner may not be OK with every aspect of the direct account (eg the two may still disagree about *Ruxley*). However, if the direct account holds water, none of the normative claims Gardner wants us to accept is distinctive of corrective justice as he understands it. In fact, the continuity thesis is not a thesis about corrective justice at all; it is a thesis about the content and force of reasons that apply in the situation originally, and completely independently of any notion of wrong-correction. Instead of defending the place of that idea in the justification of the burden of repair, Gardner's account has—in my view, rightly—shown it the door.

Gardner is not alone in this. Stephen Perry is generally counted as a corrective justice theorist. But look at the case he makes for that idea. Taking simple situations where one person has harmed another as his examples, Perry asks

which of these two should most appropriately suffer the interference with well-being that *either* the original loss *or* the payment of compensation necessarily entails?

---

[40] Gardner, above n 2 at 33–35 and 50. Gregory Keating's position is substantively similar, see G Keating, 'The Priority of Respect over Repair' (2012) 18 *Legal Theory* 293.

[41] I discuss how some insights of consequentialist theories (eg economic models of private law) could be incorporated into a non-consequentialist account of responsibility in ch 3(IV)(D).

> In general, determining whether there is 'sufficient reason' to hold someone to be under an obligation requires us to look at the nature and importance of the interest at stake, on the one hand, and the nature and importance of the conduct from which it would be protected if a right were recognized or imposed, on the other…[42] [This enquiry is an] open-ended one: it is possible to take many different factors into consideration, and there is no pre-established list of what these are… This suggests in turn that corrective justice is less a matter of fixed substantive principles than it is a framework for certain kinds of moral argument.[43]

I will let you decide whether Perry's version of corrective justice makes any claims, or requires any normative commitments, that he could not generate through the direct account. Perhaps I am misreading Gardner and Perry because I am in the grip of my own account and simply much too keen get rid of talk of wrongdoing, wrongfulness and corrective justice in private law theory. Even so, I cannot help being struck by the fact that many prominent defences of the idea of corrective justice and cognate notions end up either defending certain particularly strong claims (Weinrib, Hershovitz) or qualifying their support for that idea in terms that deny its distinctiveness (Gardner, Perry). Both strategies suggest to me that maybe something is not quite right about the idea itself.

The rest of the book argues that this is indeed the case. We should reject the claim that a person ought to bear the burden of repair when that person is a wrongdoer, because that claim is not consistent with our considered ideas about moral responsibility.

---

[42] Perry, above n 25, at 44 (original emphasis).
[43] Ibid at 47.

2

Responsibility, but the Right Kind

MANY THEORISTS CLAIM that one ought to bear the burden of repair when one's failure to discharge an original burden owed to another person has been wrongful. I have raised a challenge to that claim. One need not be a wrongdoer for others to require one to bear many familiar burdens, from the burden of performing one's promises to that of driving safely. One ought to bear those burdens because the applicable considerations in the situation—particularly considerations about the parties' reasonable interests, the demandingness of the particular burden, the ease of avoiding it and so on—say that one ought to. Why should we think any differently about the burden of repair? To give the challenge bite, I put on the table a 'direct' alternative. The 'direct' account gets its name from the fact that it asks us to approach the justification for imposing the burden of repair on a person in very much the same way we would approach the imposition of an original burden. And it is consistent with many moral ideas that underlie wrongfulness-based alternatives, though it is not consistent with all of them, and understands some of them in a rather different way.

So which account is right? As advertised, I think we can make progress by comparing the two accounts against some general ideas about moral responsibility. Broadly stated, the idea I have in mind is that people's responsibilities ought to depend on the opportunities that they have to affect how things will go for them. Of course, neither the claim that we can think about questions of private law by appealing to the ideas about responsibility, nor the more specific claim that responsibility is related to the opportunities one has in a situation are new to private law theorists. However, I believe that existing accounts of those claims and their significance for private law are unsatisfactory, so I need to undertake the ground-clearing exercise of explaining where those accounts go wrong, before I offer my own alternative in the next chapter.

The need for some ground-clearing arises partly because we can use the language of responsibility to express a whole array of different judgements. Some of them are judgements about who caused what. Others are judgements of moral praise or blameworthiness. Others are judgements about whose job it is to do something. The distinction between those kinds of judgements matters a lot for my argument because I will insist that each kind turns on different considerations, and that private law is concerned with one kind only. In particular, I will argue that the business of private law is to tell us whose job it is to do certain things, or to undertake certain practical burdens (duties, liabilities, obligations etc). That is, private law is concerned with what I will call—following T.M. Scanlon's term—ascriptions of *substantive* responsibility. It is not concerned with praising or blaming people, with what Scanlon calls judgements of *attributive* responsibility. It is also not concerned with questions of who caused what, except to the extent required to settle substantive questions about whose job it is to do certain things.

Consider a beautifully simple example by Stephen Perry:

> I am playing snooker, and announce that I am going to sink the black ball in the far corner pocket … [T]he shot goes badly awry. The black ball caroms around the table a number of times, bouncing off the cushion and other balls along the way. Amazingly, however, it eventually rolls into the far corner pocket.[1]

The example means to illustrate that even though I may claim *credit* for the shot, I am not to be *praised* for having made it. Both assessments attach significance to the fact that I held the cue, declared a pocket, struck the ball and the ball went where I said it would. But each assessment is interested in different aspects of that fact, or frames it against a different background. The first frames it against the background of the rules of snooker. The second frames it against the background of the skills of a good snooker player. Moreover, one assessment does not preoccupy the other. The rules of snooker are the same for me whether or not my shots are skilful, and playing by the rules is only one, and fairly pedestrian, consideration in the assessment of whether I am a good player. Like Perry, I think that nothing much changes if we substitute 'burden and blame' for 'credit and praise'. Blaming people and imposing practical burdens on them are different matters, for similar reasons.

I hope this claim will sound completely obvious, even banal. I am certainly not aware of any private law theorist who rejects it. But I will try to show that this claim has a sharper end too. More specifically, I will claim that many private law theorists have not realised just *how* different questions of attributive and substantive responsibility are. They are, in fact, so different that it is unhelpful even to think that they have a common root. This is a more controversial claim. Stephen Perry, Tony Honoré, John Gardner, and Joseph Raz deny it. In their respective ways, they argue that both kinds of judgements of responsibility share certain basic features, eg that they both assume that one is able to respond to reasons, or that they both follow from some deeper ideas about our acting, rational agency. I will argue that those theorists are

---

[1] S Perry, 'Responsibility for Outcomes, Risk and the Law of Torts' in G Postema (ed), *Philosophy and the Law of Torts* (Cambridge, Cambridge University Press, 2001) 72, 82–3.

mistaken in this. Generally stated, my argument will be that judgements of substantive responsibility are *divisions of labour* between persons, while judgements of attributive responsibility are *expressions of moral criticism*, and the two projects are so different that it does not help to focus on their areas of overlap. While both projects are interested in facts about a person, their actions and attitudes, and the resulting outcomes, each project frames those facts against a different background and ascribes significance to different aspects of them. My case for insisting on the significance of that distinction will only be fully made in the next chapter, once I have developed an account that is specific to questions of substantive responsibility. For the moment, I will be content to throw stones at those who think that attributive and substantive responsibility have a common root in a more 'basic' sense of responsibility, or in some ideas about our acting, rational agency. Those stones will be mainly examples where others may require a person to bear some substantive burden, including the burden of repair, even though those 'basic' or agency-related conditions are not satisfied. If that is so, we cannot hope to build an account of the kind of responsibility that private law is concerned with, substantive responsibility, upon those conditions, and should look for an alternative that is specific to substantive concerns.

I. SUBSTANTIVE AND ATTRIBUTIVE RESPONSIBILITY

The phrase 'this person is responsible for X' could mean many different things. We could use it to say that it was this person, rather than anyone else, who *caused* X, as in 'the livestock sector is responsible for a great part of the increase in greenhouse gas emissions'. We could use it to say that that this person is to *blame* for X, as in 'you are responsible for your crimes'.[2] We could also use it to say that this person ought to *bear the practical burden* of dealing with X, as in 'you are responsible for the well-being of your children'. These claims may be related in a number of ways, but they are distinct. 'Who caused this?', 'Who is to blame for this?', and 'Whose problem is this to deal with?' sometimes will and sometimes will not receive the same response. In the greenhouse gas example, the increase is caused by the animals' natural functions, but we might consider that the blame should lie with their owners (eg, they have failed to put in place affordable greener farming methods) or with the competent national and international authorities (eg because they have failed to come up with and enforce viable policies on emissions). We come across a similar variety of options when we consider whether the burden of limiting greenhouse gas

---

[2] This sense is also reflected in familiar uses of responsible/irresponsible, as in 'she is a responsible driver' or 'drink responsibly'.

emissions should be borne by individual livestock owners, or be spread over a national or the global community as part of an overall environmental policy. To take a more typical private law setting, suppose that one employee instructs another to start a machine while, known to the former but not the latter, a third party is in dangerous proximity to it. The instructed employee starts the machine and the third party suffers physical injury. The instructed employee causes the harm, the blame for it may lie with the instructor, while the burden of making repair to the victim will lie with their common employer. Here too we have no difficulty in seeing that there is a principled distinction to be made between persons who participated in causing the relevant harm, persons who may be to blame for it, and persons who may be required to bear the burden of repair for it.

This distinction is easy to draw because the concerns that underlie each of those questions differ. When we ask questions of blame, we are primarily concerned with deciding whether a person's conduct is of such a character that calls for moral criticism and, sometimes, for reconsidering the terms of our relationship to that person. Questions about the allocation of practical burdens and duties are different, not least because very often such burdens and duties need to be allocated even when no one is to blame for anything.[3] That is most obviously the case in respect of what I have called 'original burdens', like the burden of keeping one's promises or of driving safely, but it can be true in respect of the burden of repair too. It may easily happen that no one is to blame for an accident, but it cannot happen that no one will have to deal with the cost of repairing the damage, or of leaving it unrepaired. The concerns underlying questions of causation are harder to pin down, but that is because such questions are typically shorthand for questions of blame and the allocation of practical burdens, so the answer to questions about whether a person has 'caused' some outcome will generally depend on the particular purpose for which one makes that enquiry. Lord Hoffmann has illustrated this 'common sense' view about causation using the example of a man

> who forgets to take the radio out of his car and during the night someone breaks the quarterlight, enters the car and steals it. What caused the damage? If the thief is on trial, so that the question is whether he is criminally responsible, then obviously the answer is that he caused the damage. It is no answer for him to say that it was caused by the owner carelessly leaving the radio inside. On the other hand, the owner's wife, irritated at the third such occurrence in a year, might well say that it was his fault. In the context of an inquiry into the owner's blameworthiness under a

---

[3] *cf* J Raz, 'Responsibility and the Negligence Standard' (2010) 30 *OJLS* 1, 13–14, referring to the need to break 'the mesmerising fascination with responsibility as a condition of nothing but praise and blame'.

non-legal, common sense duty to take reasonable care of one's own possessions, one would say that his carelessness caused the loss of the radio.[4]

I think that something similar is true of questions about whether some conduct is properly *yours*, or whether you may be held *accountable* for that conduct. Asking whether some conduct is 'properly' yours equivocates amongst the various purposes for which that question might be posed. Again, you could ask back: 'properly mine in which sense, or for which purpose?', and that question may receive a different answer depending on whether the purpose is to decide whether you deserve moral criticism, or whether a given practical burden ought to fall on you or on others. Similarly, saying that someone may be held 'accountable' for some conduct leaves unspecified who that person will be held accountable to, and for what purpose. It is plausible that the conditions of accountability differ depending on whether we are talking about accountability to oneself or accountability towards others, and, in the latter case, whether the purpose of such accounting is to determine whether one's conduct deserves moral criticism, or to decide whether one ought to bear some practical burden.

As noted earlier, TM Scanlon calls 'attributive responsibility' the sense of responsibility involved in questions of blame and other forms of moral assessment of a person and their conduct. He calls 'substantive responsibility' the sense involved in questions about the allocation of practical burdens or duties.[5] That is the usage I will adopt here. Judgements of substantive responsibility so defined are the moral equivalent of what lawyers call 'liabilities'. I will not be referring to them as liabilities because my current aim is to keep the moral difference between attributive and substantive responsibility at the forefront of our attention, and because the plural 'responsibilities' seems to me to convey the substantive sense very well, without much danger of 'are we talking about law or about morality?' confusion.

To amplify the distinction between the two senses of responsibility, consider some further differences between them. One is that allocations of substantive responsibilities often involve divisions of labour between different persons, whereas ascriptions of blame do not. If some practical burden does not fall on your shoulders, it will usually fall on someone else's. If the risk that the goods might be destroyed before delivery is not allocated to you, it will fall on me. If

---

[4] *cf Empress Car Company (Abertillery) Ltd v National Rivers Authority* [1999] 2 AC 22 at 29, *per* Lord Hoffmann: 'The first point to emphasise is that common sense answers to questions of causation will differ according to the purpose for which the question is asked. Questions of causation often arise for the purpose of attributing responsibility to someone, for example, so as to blame him for something which has happened or to make him guilty of an offence or liable in damages. In such cases, the answer will depend upon the rule by which responsibility is being attributed.'

[5] TM Scanlon, *What We Owe To Each Other* (Cambridge, Mass, Belknap Press of Harvard University Press, 1998), ch 6.

the burden of taking care not to injure me falls on you, I will have less to do by way of looking out for myself, and so on. Ascriptions of blame do not work like that. They can be, and often are, comparative ('A is to blame for the accident a lot more than B is'), but they are not allocative, as there is no such thing as a given amount of blame to be divided in some way between different persons. That is why Perry's suggestion that, when a plaintiff's claim has deservedly failed, 'no one is liable'[6] for the resulting loss can be appealing if we understand it as 'no one is to blame for that loss', but makes no sense if we understand it as 'no one is to bear the burden of dealing with it'. This difference seems to me to reflect the fact that our assessment of whether A is to blame for something does not generally depend on our attitude towards B, even when A and B are co-participants in a situation. While we might sometimes say 'if A is not to blame for the accident, the blame lies with B', we do not think that we are justified in blaming B *because* we would not be justified in blaming A. If our blaming attitude towards B is justified at all, it is justified directly by the facts of the situation in which A and B feature, eg that B saw that A had passed out behind the wheel and failed to get out of the way of A's vehicle despite having had ample opportunity to do so. To put it differently, we can decide whether to take a blaming attitude towards B without necessarily deciding what attitude to take towards A. By contrast, we cannot decide whether B ought to bear some proportion of the burden of repair for the accident without also deciding which proportion, if any, of that burden ought to lie with A.

A further aspect of that difference is that we have reason to want ascriptions of substantive responsibilities to be generally prospective, and ascriptions of blame to be retrospective. As with any division of labour, we have an interest in allocating burdens and duties to people in ways that allow them to know in advance the extent and nature of their respective responsibilities, and to plan their lives accordingly. Blaming is different because it involves taking a critical moral attitude towards an agent in the light of their actual response in certain situations. It requires us, as Scanlon puts it, to assess whether 'a given action did or did not reflect that agent's judgment-sensitive attitudes'.[7] So while allocating burdens prospectively is very much the moral norm, prospective blame makes moral sense only as a (sometimes usefully motivating) counterfactual.[8] This difference affects, in turn, what goes into each kind of judgement. The prospective character of judgements of substantive responsibility comes with certain

---

[6] Perry, above n 1, at 89.

[7] Scanlon, above n 5, at 290.

[8] 'Listen Loddfafnir and listen well. Learn the words I speak and follow the wisdom you gain. Make shoes and arrows for no one but yourself. If the shoe should hurt or the arrow be untrue, the blame will be yours' from the Norse myth 'The Deception of Gylfi' in HY Grimes, *The Norse Myths* (Boston, Mass, Hollow Earth Publishing, 2010), 174.

epistemic limitations in the range of considerations that may justifiably figure in those judgements. Divisions of labour are often tough to get right because we may not be well placed to tell how things will turn out, eg how likely it is that some event will occur, how demanding a given burden is likely to be on a person, and so on. Sometimes the proper response to this 'epistemic horizon' problem is to hold back on the allocation until we are able to make safer projections. However, that concern is usually outweighed by our interest in achieving a degree of certainty over our respective responsibilities, and by the fact that deferring an allocation of burdens can often involve serious practical costs for us and others. We therefore make a second-order decision about who ought to bear the risk that our projections may turn out to be mistaken, eg who ought to bear the risk of performance costing more than expected, or of one's non-negligent use of land causing harm to others and so on. Blame does not work like that. When we are uncertain about the material facts of a person's conduct and its results, we suspend judgement. While we may sometimes blame a person for creating or not preventing some uncertainty about the material facts (eg because they are not forthcoming about their contribution to events, or because they could have easily clarified the situation but did not), we do not consider it appropriate to blame a person simply because of such uncertainty.

The differences between allocating practical burdens and ascribing blame go beyond issues of epistemic access. They also affect which facts are *material* in each kind of judgement. When we consider whether to blame others, we may sometimes be required to make our judgements sensitive to a wide range of aspects of their particular situation, including facts about their personality, history, upbringing, natural abilities or incapacities and so on. By contrast, when we make allocations of burdens, we have to bear in mind the situation of every person whose position may be affected by that allocation. This necessarily calls for substantive choices about the *degree of attention* that we ought to pay to each person's situation. Suppose that for reasons having to do both with your natural capacities and your driving history, your driving abilities fall below those of the average driver. It is plausible that, when we consider whether to adopt a blaming attitude towards you, we ought to take account of the complexities both in the history that led to you having limited driving abilities, and in the history of how you got to acquire a driving license. This will often be a complex exercise, but it does not require anyone else to make some sacrifice or to undertake any burden for your benefit. Things are different when it comes to substantive responsibilities. The more significance we attach, say, to the history of your limited driving abilities when we allocate responsibilities between road users, the greater the burdens that others will have to bear in the form of looking out for you, or of footing the bill in case your limited driving abilities cause an accident. And others may reasonably refuse to shoulder those burdens in your stead, if that would demand too much of them by way of care or costs.

Note that the difference in the concerns that blaming and allocating practical burdens respectively involve is consistent with certain complex possibilities. For instance, it allows that sometimes our moral assessment of a person's character can change *because* that person has taken on a practical burden. We may sometimes praise a person because they 'stepped up to the plate', or 'took responsibility' for dealing with a problem (eg protected a person against an attack by thugs) despite the fact that others could not have required them to do so.[9] Sometimes we may even blame or take a negative attitude towards a person who failed to 'step up to the plate' (eg effect a rescue that *seemed* easy, but may not have been), while accepting that we could not have required them to do so (perhaps 'this person is no hero' does not count as blame, but it is certainly an unflattering assessment of that person's character). This shows that substantive judgements can be a baseline for certain attributive judgements, in that they help determine what conduct is required and what is superogatory. However, this does not challenge the general separation between the attributive and the substantive, as each kind of judgement still proceeds on its own grounds, and attaches different significance to the fact that this person 'took responsibility'.

II. PRIVATE LAW PRINCIPLES AS ALLOCATIONS OF SUBSTANTIVE RESPONSIBILITIES

Private law is clearly concerned with questions of substantive responsibility. Whatever else they might do, the rules and principles of contract and tort law allocate practical burdens and duties (as well as benefits and rights) to people. Indeed, the typical ground on which we criticise those rules and doctrines is that they get that allocation wrong, ie that they ask too much of some people and too little of others. The core claims of the major models of private law themselves purport to be claims about the proper allocation of burdens between persons. They take the fact that one is a wrongdoer, or the fact that one is the cheapest cost-avoider and so on, as significant for private law in the sense that such a fact justifies allocating the burden of repair to one person rather than another. By the same standard, models of private law fail when they do not match our considered ideas about who ought to bear substantive responsibility for what. For example, the reason we do not take mere harming, understood as the causing of a setback to someone's interests, as a good justification for imposing the burden of repair on a person is that requiring a person

---

[9] On the value of 'taking responsibility', see D Enoch, 'Tort Liability and Taking Responsibility' in J Oberdiek (ed), *Philosophical Foundations of the Law of Torts* (Oxford, Oxford University Press, 2014) 250.

not to cause setbacks to the interests of others would be asking too much of that person, and not enough of those who suffer such setbacks, or third parties who ought to be protecting them in that regard.

This way of describing what private law does may not appeal to everyone. Stephen Perry thinks that deciding who ought to deal with some harm and determining who is responsible for it are very different matters:

> We do not ordinarily think that one or the other of the parties to a harmful interaction must be regarded as responsible for the harm, any more than the law insists that one or the other of the parties must be held liable for it. If the defendant is not held liable, we do not impute liability to the plaintiff; it is just that the plaintiff must bear the loss because, as a matter of contingent fact, that is where it fell. Under those circumstances, no one is liable... [A]s an empirical matter, someone must indeed bear the costs. But this does not mean that the plaintiff is necessarily *responsible* for the costs[10]

I think that Perry underestimates the possible varieties of meaning in the claim that deservedly unsuccessful plaintiffs are or are not 'responsible' for the loss that they suffer. That claim can be understood in at least two ways, each corresponding to the different senses of responsibility we have been exploring. We might say that deservedly unsuccessful plaintiffs are not necessarily 'responsible' for the loss they have suffered in the sense that they are not to blame for it. But we might use the same phrase to say something different, namely that those plaintiffs should not have to bear the burden of paying for that loss, or that this loss ought to be someone else's problem. These two possibilities are mutually independent, as we can affirm one and deny the other. Moreover, this is something that the language of responsibility is perfectly capable of expressing. For example, we could say, with minimal risk of misunderstanding, that deservedly unsuccessful plaintiffs may not be *responsible for* the relevant loss, but that dealing with that loss is *their responsibility*. Perry's point makes sense as a word of caution against thinking that a person who gets to bear a practical burden under private law principles must also be attributively responsible (ie that he or she must be to blame) for it. But it does not give us any reason to refrain from describing that person as substantively responsible for that burden.

Semantics aside, it seems to me that Perry relies on a poor account of what private law principles signify about the position of the deservedly unsuccessful plaintiff. Those principles do not tell us simply that the burden of repair may not be imposed on the defendant. They also tell us that, as far as certain persons—including the defendant—are concerned, the plaintiff *has nothing to complain about*. This is a normative claim, not an empirical

---

[10] Perry, above n 1, at 89, 90.

claim about 'where the loss fell', because it sets out what parties may or may not require of each other. In that regard, principles that allocate the burden of repair have precisely the same character as principles setting out original rights and duties between road-users, doctors and patients, contract partners, and so on. Say that a doctor does not owe patients a duty to warn them about infinitesimal risks of a certain operation. If that is a substantive normative claim about what patients may or may not require of a doctor, so is the claim that patients may not require the doctor who failed to warn them about such risks to make repair for the harm they suffered when those risks materialised.

The difference is admittedly somewhat blurred in private law litigation, where courts appear to be sitting in judgement of 'how the parties acted'. Even there, however, the purpose of the court's enquiry is not to pass judgement on the parties' respective conduct, but to resolve disagreements about the interpretation and application of whichever allocation of burdens the applicable private law principles have already made. The question is not 'may the parties be justifiably subject to moral criticism?' but 'what do the principles that aim to allocate burdens prospectively in situations of this sort say in this instance?' The reasons why private law litigation tends to have a retrospective feel are mostly logistical. In the absence of a harmful event, or a concrete disagreement about the content or validity of a contract, parties are simply unlikely to want to incur the expense of time, effort and money involved in asking courts for advance clarification of the burdens that private law requires each to bear. Questions about the timing of litigation raise important issues about the administration of private law and the adjudication of private law disputes (eg whether these matters are best left to courts or to other, more specialised agencies), but they do not throw doubt on the prospective character of the way private law principles allocate burdens.

III. SOME IMPLICATIONS OF THE ATTRIBUTIVE/ SUBSTANTIVE DIVIDE

A. No Carry Over

I have been arguing that the questions that private law principles address are questions of substantive rather than attributive responsibility, ie that they are concerned with the allocation of burdens and duties rather than ascriptions of blame. I think that this has two practical implications. The first is that arguments do not simply 'carry over' from attributive to substantive responsibility and vice versa. Influential or illuminating accounts of one sense of responsibility may not yield plausible insights applied to the other. Consider the ongoing philosophical debates about whether responsibility requires choice, or control over one's conduct, whether control requires regression (ie control over the causes of the conduct) or the practical ability to do otherwise, whether it is enough for one's response to be reason-responsive, and so on.[11] To the extent that those competing views aim to identify *necessary* conditions of responsibility, it is clear that we must understand them as being concerned with attributive responsibility only.[12] Those claims may well be correct in that domain, ie it may indeed be the case that control, or the ability to do otherwise, and so on, are necessary conditions for ascribing blame.[13] But they would not sound any-where near as convincing if they were understood as claims about substantive responsibility, because they are not equipped to answer questions about the role of choice, control or reason-responsiveness in determining what people may require of each other. For a start, those claims would obviously come up short when the conditions of control or reason-responsiveness are satis-fied either by all participants in events (if everyone had control, how are we

---

[11] From a vast literature, see H Frankfurt, 'Alternate Possibilities and Moral Responsibility' (1969) 66 *Journal of Philosophy* 828; JM Fischer and M Ravizza, *Responsibility and Control: A Theory of Moral Responsibility* (Cambridge, Cambridge University Press, 1998); S Hurley, *Justice, Luck, and Knowledge* (Cambridge, Mass, Harvard University Press, 2003); S Wolf, *Freedom Within Reason* (New York, Oxford University Press, 1990); B Waller, *Against Moral Responsibility* (Mass, MIT Press, 2011); RJ Wallace, *Responsibility and the Moral Sentiments* (Cambridge, Mass, Harvard University Press, 1994).

[12] As an illustration, consider David Shoemaker's essay 'Attributability, Answerability and Accountability: Towards a Wider Theory of Moral Responsibility' (2011) 121 *Ethics* 602. Shoemaker criticises what he calls a two-part view of moral responsibility that he attributes to TM Scanlon: 'According to the first part, for some agent to be morally responsible for some action or attitude Φ is for it to be attributable to the agent in the way necessary to render moral appraisal of the agent appropriate (where the sort of appraisal rendered appropriate depends on the evaluative quality of Φ). According to the second part, to hold some agent morally respon-sible is to respond in a certain way to the judgment that she is responsible, and Scanlon's own recent work has focused on developing a detailed and nuanced view of holding responsible with respect to negative actions—blaming, in other words—that builds insightfully on the account of being responsible. This two-part theory purports to provide a comprehensive account of our moral responsibility practices' (at 603). The last statement is accurate only if we understand it as referring to our practices for attributing actions to agents for the purpose of moral appraisal. Shoemaker is indeed only concerned with attributive responsibility, not with its substantive coun-terpart, and accordingly does not consider Scanlon's account of the latter. But the title of his paper and the last statement in the quoted passage may unwittingly encourage the impression that the former is all there is to responsibility.

[13] *cf* Hurley, above n 11, at 4, noting that the competing views that she discusses (by Fischer and Ravizza, Wolf, Klein, van Inwagen and Watson, respectively) all use responsibility 'in the full-blooded sense that licenses praise, blame, and reactive attitudes and that implies account-ability in principle'.

to allocate burdens?), or by none of them (if no one had control, who does the burden fall on?). More importantly, even when those conditions are satisfied by some participants only, the appeal to control, reason-responsiveness etc would still fail to determine the appropriate *stakes* for those persons of the fact that they were responsible for their conduct in the attributive sense.[14] Say that you punched someone because you did not like the look of their face. The fact that what happened was the result of your choice, you had control over your conduct, and so on, is part of the case for why you have no moral complaint against others' requiring you to make repair for the injury you caused, or against the state subjecting you to criminal punishment. But it is equally clear that sometimes you *will* have such a complaint despite having had control over your conduct and the outcome. Suppose that someone threatens to punch a third party unless you stop your speech at a public rally, and goes through with the threat when you decide to go on speaking. The difference between the examples turns not simply on whether you had control over your conduct and the resulting harm, but on certain familiar substantive judgements about what the parties in each situation owe to each other. It is those judgements (in this last variation, your right to free expression, the injured party's right to be free from physical harm, and the thug's duty not to blackmail and not to injure others) that determine how much attention, if any, we ought to pay to the fact that you had control over your conduct, and whose control—yours or the thug's—matters more.[15]

The point applies even in situations where you are the *only* person with control over the events. Such situations are a staple of discussions about the significance of people's choices for their entitlements under theories of distributive justice. Writing in that context, Gary Watson notes:

> When people discuss whether the poor are responsible for their stations in life, the judgments of responsibility involved go beyond attributability; they are substantive conclusions about whether or not these folks have moral complaints or entitlements of certain kinds. Often, individuals' (reason-responsive) choices will play some non-trivial role in their becoming or remaining poor; they will be in various ways responsible in the attributability sense. However, it is a matter of moral/political deliberation

---

[14]   Serena Olsaretti makes a similar point against luck-egalitarianism: to say that distributions produced by choices for which an agent is responsible are just, we need not just some account of what choices an agent is responsible for, but also an account of the *stakes* for that agent of choosing poorly, S Olsaretti, 'Responsibility and the Consequences of Choice' (2009) 109 *Proceedings of the Aristotelian Society* 165.

[15]   *cf* A Ripstein, *Equality, Responsibility and the Law* (Cambridge, Cambridge University Press, 2001) 13, urging that 'there is no way to retreat to equating responsibility with control'. Perry, above n 1, at 89 quotes Ripstein's passage, but misunderstands it as saying that 'responsibility cannot depend upon control'. It seems to me that Ripstein says simply that control is not all there is to substantive responsibility.

how much of the brunt of their choices they should bear, or whether they have some claims against other members of their society, and if so, of what sort.[16]

In a passage that I will be returning to, TM Scanlon spells out the general parameters of that moral deliberation in greater detail:

> The fact that an action resulted from a person's conscious choice may be sufficient to establish that that action can be attributed to him or her in the sense that is presupposed by moral appraisal. But a judgement of substantive responsibility depends on more than this. To justify the claim that a person who has done A has a certain obligation, or that someone who has done A has to bear the consequences (and that others are not obligated to share this burden), it is not enough to point out that this person chose to do A. One must also consider the costs that this assignment of responsibility imposes on a person who does A, the alternatives to A that are available to a person in this situation, and the implications, for this person and others, of assigning responsibility in some other way.[17]

Of course, the frequency with which the practical upshots of judgements of substantive and attributive responsibility happen to coincide, or the degree of overlap in our responses to the questions 'Whose problem should this be?' and 'Who is to blame?', suggests that those answers will often turn on similar considerations. For example, the fact that a person was at fault in causing an accident looks a plausible basis both for imposing on that person the burden of making repair, and for regarding them as blameworthy. Perhaps the same goes for the fact that a person could have avoided causing harm, or the fact that the conduct that caused the harm was under that person's control and so on. However, those occasional overlaps can be explained without positing some kind of deeper relationship of dependence or priority between the two senses of responsibility under discussion. Perhaps the elements of fault or avoidability or control matter for both substantive and attributive responsibility not because the questions underlying each sense of responsibility are somehow dependent on each other, but because those questions happen to attribute significance to similar elements.

---

[16] G Watson, 'The Problematic Role of Responsibility in Contexts of Distributive Justice' (2006) 72 *Philosophy & Phenomenological Research* 425, 431. *cf* GA Cohen, 'Expensive Taste Rides Again' in *On the Currency of Egalitarian Justice and Other Essays in Political Philosophy*, M Otsuka (ed), (Princeton NJ, Princeton University Press, 2011) 109: '[T]he mere fact that you made a choice, and could have chosen otherwise (for example, not to buy that steak), no more shows that subsidy is out of order than does the *mere* fact that you could have chosen not to buy that wheelchair shows that subsidy is out of order. In each case, facts in the background to the choice, facts about degrees of control, and about the cost of alternatives, affect the proper allocation of responsibility for the consequences of the choice.'

[17] TM Scanlon, 'Justice, Responsibility and the Demands of Equality' in C Sypnowich (ed), *The Egalitarian Conscience: Essays in Honour of G.A. Cohen* (New York, Oxford University Press, 2006) 70, 76–7.

I say 'perhaps' because a robust defence of this claim requires a worked out account of substantive responsibility, which I have yet to provide. But it seems to me that even when a certain element or idea appears to matter for both attributive and substantive purposes, the similarity is not likely to be deep, because attributive and substantive questions will be focusing on different aspects of the element or idea in question. Consider fault in some more detail. The fact that one is at fault matters for the purpose of moral criticism and blame insofar as it indicates that one failed to reason well in a situation, or to act upon one's assessment of the applicable reasons, or both. That is, one is to blame because of the way one responded in a situation, or the choices that one made in it. It is possible (and, in the view I will defend in the next chapter, the case) that the role of fault in judgements of substantive responsibility is very different. Perhaps its role there is to indicate that one had the *opportunity* to avoid the burden of repair for some harm by exercising due care. In that view, fault matters for substantive responsibility not as a quality of the choice that one *made*, but as an element in the description of the choice one *had*. If something like this is correct, then the claim that 'fault' is a condition of both attributive and substantive responsibility may not be flatly mistaken, but it is misleading insofar as it suggests that the significance of fault remains constant across these two contexts.[18]

B. 'Basic' Responsibility

A further implication of the cleavage between attributive and substantive responsibility is that the attempt to trace a root common to both in a single sense of responsibility is not likely to yield helpful results. I believe that this cuts against a number of important claims about the place of responsibility in private law. One is John Gardner's suggestion that a precondition of holding

---

[18] Susan Hurley's argument in *Justice, Luck and Knowledge*, above n 11, strikes me as another apt illustration of the point. The first half of Hurley's book discusses what I have described as theories of attributive responsibility, the second discusses theories of distributive justice. However, despite Hurley's stated conviction (at 129ff) that advances in the theory of attributive responsibility matter for distributive justice, her eventual position (at 233ff) is that what theories of justice ought to attend to is not certain claims about attributive responsibility, but agents' *beliefs* about what they are attributively responsible for (in that those beliefs affect agents' incentive-seeking behaviour and their conception of their well-being). The difference is important and, I think, undermines Hurley's stated thesis: if Hurley is right that theories of distributive justice ought to attend to agents' beliefs about attributive responsibility, that will be true whether or not those beliefs match the conclusions of the best available theory of attributive responsibility. On this point, see Watson, above n 11 at 426, who notes that 'the conclusions of Part II of the book seem to be more or less independent of what [Hurley] describes as the distinctive contributions of the new work on responsibility'.

a person responsible in the senses we have been discussing is that this person must be responsible in the 'basic' sense of having 'the ability to explain oneself, to give an intelligible account of oneself, to answer for oneself as a rational being'.[19] Gardner contrasts this basic sense of responsibility with what he calls 'consequential' responsibility, under which 'those who are responsible are those who are singled out to bear the adverse normative consequences of wrongful or otherwise deficient actions'.[20] In these terms, both attributive and substantive responsibility fall on the side of consequential responsibility, in that they are both concerned with the normative consequences of a person's conduct (wrongful or not; I return to the significance of this below). Gardner's claim is that ascriptions of consequential responsibility can only be justified on the assumption that a person is 'basically' responsible. And he suggests that this 'rudimentary link' between basic and consequential responsibility is conceptual in character: 'for there to be wrongdoing that has normative consequences there must (conceptually) be a wrongdoer. And a wrongdoer ... must (conceptually) be a basically responsible agent'.[21]

I think that Gardner's claim illustrates the importance of disaggregating the normative consequences that he groups under the heading of consequential responsibility. Whether a normative consequence obtains only when one is able to respond to and to offer reasons in accounting for oneself depends on the particular normative consequence we have in mind. Gardner could be right that this ability may be a necessary condition for ascriptions of blame. Blame involves the exercise of moral criticism towards others in the light of the way they have responded to the applicable reasons, so it makes sense that the relevant appraisal would be appropriate only on the assumption those persons had the basic ability to respond to reasons in the first place. But perhaps things are different when it comes to allocations of practical burdens. The capacity to respond to reasons could matter in that context too, but its significance may have a different explanation. Perhaps the possession of that capacity matters for substantive responsibility because people have general reason to want the burdens and responsibilities that they are required to bear to depend on their choices and other responses.

The difference is important because sometimes one can reasonably want one's responsibilities towards others to be *independent* of whether one is able to form and proffer a response to the applicable reasons. Consider the situation of a person suffering from 'unresponsive wakefulness' syndrome (what is still

---

[19] J Gardner, 'Hart and Feinberg on Responsibility' in M Kramer et als (eds), *The Legacy of H.L.A. Hart: Legal, Political and Moral Philosophy* (Oxford, Oxford University Press, 2008) 121, 123.

[20] Ibid at 132.

[21] Ibid at 138.

typically referred to as a 'persistent vegetative state').[22] That person lacks the capacity to respond to reasons, and may do so for a very prolonged period of time. However, if one of her elder relatives dies while she is in that condition, and leaves her a property in his will, she can reasonably want to have the same entitlement to receive that benefit and its fruits (eg any rental income that the property generates) as anyone else. In fact, she would have a very reasonable complaint against a principle that took her unresponsiveness to reasons as a ground for denying her that benefit. She could simply say that sometimes people can attach value to being able to receive certain benefits without *having* to make a choice or to form a certain response in a situation. Of course, that claim would have certain limits. For example, there is good reason why we would not extend it readily to the imposition of burdens.[23] Burdens constrain us, in a way that benefits do not, so it is much more important to us to have those constraints depend on the opportunities we have to avoid those burdens. But sometimes a person who lacks the capacity for reason-responsiveness will still have an interest in incurring certain burdens, say, inasmuch as those flow from the same relationship that entitles that person to benefits that this person has reason to want to receive. In the property example, suppose that the property bequeathed to the unresponsive wakefulness syndrome sufferer was under lease to a tenant, and that it now requires some repairs in order to be safe to live in. It seems obvious that the new owner should stand to bear the cost of those repairs, just as she stands to reap the benefit of the rental income. By the same token, suppose that the water tank in the back garden of the property that this person inherited collapses, and floods a neighbouring property. That person will be liable to pay appropriate compensation to her neighbours, just like anyone else. The fact that she lacked 'basic' responsibility, not just at the point when the harm occurred, but before she even came to own the property, will not shield her from liability. One might object that any allocations of benefits and burdens to a person in that condition ought to be made only on a provisional basis, until she recovers the capacity for reason-responsiveness and affirms them through her choices, or until she expires and those benefits and burdens pass on to other persons who possess that capacity. This could conceivably be correct, but it does not necessarily speak in favour of regarding 'basic' responsibility as a condition for conferring those burdens and imposing those burdens on that person. It may suggest instead that a person in that position can reasonably want more than the opportunity to incur those

---

[22] For a call to change the standard medical terminology from PVS to UWS, on both ethical and descriptive grounds, see S Laureys et al, 'Unresponsive wakefulness syndrome: a new name for the persistent vegetative state or apallic syndrome' (2010) 8 *BMC Medicine* 68.

[23] I discuss some further aspects of the asymmetry between benefits and burdens in ch 3.

benefits and burdens without having to make a choice or form a response to the applicable reasons. She may also want some further opportunity to *reverse* that state of affairs in the event that she should regain consciousness.

Regarding 'basic' responsibility as a condition for requiring a person to bear burdens would put us in further difficulty in situations where it seems justifiable to impose some burden on a person *because* that person is not reason-responsive. Suppose that, under certain clear and tightly controlled conditions, we justifiably withdraw state-funded medical support for a person with unresponsive wakefulness syndrome, on the ground that continuing such support beyond a certain point in time requires the commitment of medical resources that can be used to meet more urgent needs, or allocated to patients with greater prospects of recovery. That person's family then moves her to a private medical facility, where she makes a miraculous recovery. I think that this person will not be entitled to complain against the state for exposing her to the burden of the medical bills for private treatment. Determining the appropriate allocation of the burden of treatment in these situations might be a tough exercise. My point is that the fact that this person is not responsible in Gardner's 'basic' sense does not decide either whether the state ought to allocate medical resources to her in the first place, or whether the state would be entitled to withdraw those resources at some further point in time, and leave that person to bear the cost of private care.

Gardner is sensitive to these points. Having laid out his 'simple answer' about why basic responsibility is a precondition of consequential responsibility, he continues:

> This simple answer, however, does not stay simple for long. Aren't there cases in which a fiction of basic responsibility may, with moral propriety, be sustained in the law (or in other institutional settings), so that the advertised precondition of consequential responsibility may be treated as satisfied when really it is not? And what about the fact that consequential responsibility, unlike basic responsibility, may be vicarious? Here F is the wrongdoer but G is consequentially responsible. Whose basic responsibility, F's or G's, is supposed to satisfy the advertised precondition in such a case? These are troublesome questions. *But they are questions about the justification of particular norms.*[24]

This last phrase seems to me spot on. The allocation of burdens in the examples that Gardner gives must depend on the justification of the particular norms that determine what we owe to each other, eg how much sacrifice our health service must undertake for patients with unresponsive wakefulness syndrome, or how much employers ought to do for their employees and the victims of their employees' workplace torts.[25] In the view I will develop in the next chapter, we

---

[24] Gardner, above n 19, at 138 (emphasis added).
[25] I take up this question in chs 4 and 7.

should think about that justification in terms of the opportunities that those persons have in each situation, and the value of those opportunities for them. But even if that is not the right way to go about things, we have no warrant for thinking that the justification in question must rely on 'fictions' about basic responsibility, or that instances where one person has to bear the burden of dealing with the consequences of another's wrongdoing are somehow special or particularly troublesome. The need for those 'fictions' and the incidence of such 'troubles' are artefacts of the claim that consequential responsibility requires basic responsibility, and will fall away with it. To adapt Gardner's phrase, we should instead accept that *all* questions of substantive responsibility are questions about the justification of particular norms, and address them accordingly.

I think that Gardner is led astray here by his decision to limit his conception of consequential responsibility to wrongful conduct.[26] It may well be true that wrongdoing requires capacity for reason-responsive action, and therefore that examples involving patients with unresponsive wakefulness syndrome, or vicarious liability settings, pose difficult problems that could be dealt with in the ways Gardner suggests. But it is clearly not true that the normative consequences that Gardner has in mind accrue only when one has behaved wrongfully. Praise can be a normative consequence of one's conduct, but its proper incidence requires anything but wrongful behaviour. Even the determination that one's conduct deserves neither blame nor praise is a normative consequence, but that too does not depend on wrongdoing. The same goes for the allocation of substantive burdens. The allocation of very many familiar original burdens, from keeping one's bargains to driving carefully, is not at all contingent on wrongdoing or wrongful conduct (the direct account I have outlined suggests that this is true of the burden of repair too). So we have little reason to think that the conditions for characterising a person's conduct as wrongful match the general conditions of *either* attributive or substantive responsibility.

C. Agency

One of the most vibrant traditions in the philosophy of private law purports to trace a root common to attributive and substantive responsibility in a particular

---

[26] Gardner purports to adopt the term 'consequential responsibility' from Ronald Dworkin. However, Dworkin uses that term to refer not to responsibility for the consequences of one's wrongful or otherwise deficient conduct, but to responsibility that is consequential upon the advantages or disadvantages of one's situation. See R Dworkin, *Sovereign Virtue: The Theory and Practice of Equality* (Cambridge, Mass, Harvard University Press, 2001) 287: 'In this book we have been concerned with … consequential responsibility. When and how far is it right that individuals bear the disadvantages or misfortunes of their own situation themselves, and when is it right…that others … relieve them from or mitigate the consequences of those disadvantages?'

conception of the conditions of our agency as acting, rational beings (I will refer to accounts that are part of that tradition as 'agency' accounts). Agency accounts begin from the idea that we understand ourselves as rational agents, who possess a distinct identity and are capable of being authors, rather than mere causes, of actions and events in the world. They then try to identify with more precision the physical and mental conditions that are necessary for some conduct or some outcome to be attributable to a person's agency, and take those conditions as a threshold or basis for attaching certain normative consequences to that conduct or outcome, including the ascription of blame and the allocation of practical burdens. Tony Honoré, Stephen Perry, and Joseph Raz have offered accounts that follow this general strategy.

Honoré and Perry have referred to their accounts as accounts of 'outcome-responsibility', but it seems to me that this name does not identify the distinctive feature of the story they have in mind. Any account of responsibility will ascribe responsibility for outcomes. What differentiates one account of responsibility from another is the ground on which each justifies those ascriptions. For Honoré and Perry, that ground is the fact that the outcome may be properly ascribed to that person as an acting, rational agent, rather than as a mere cause. Honoré explains the normative consequence of this fact for responsibility as follows:

> In the real world ... human bodily movements and their mental accompaniments are with some exceptions interpreted as actions and decisions. They are ascribed to authors, who accordingly count as persons; and it is by virtue of those ascriptions that each of us has a history, an identity and a character. But there is a price to be paid for being a person. As the counterpart of this status, we are responsible for our actions and their consequences, and sometimes this responsibility exposes us to legal sanctions. To ascribe personhood and responsibility to people in this way is to apply normative principles. It is not merely that others attribute to us an identity and a character, but that we are entitled to claim for ourselves and ascribe them to others. Others in turn not only hold us responsible for our actions and their outcomes, but are entitled to do so.[27]

Stephen Perry's account develops a broadly similar general argument, though he differs from Honoré as regards the conditions for regarding a person as the author of an outcome.[28] Honoré believes that those conditions are satisfied

---

[27] T Honoré, 'Responsibility and Luck: The Moral Basis of Strict Liability' (1988) 104 *Law Quarterly Review* 530, 543. Honoré's other argument for outcome-responsibility was that a system governed by that principle would be fair. I discuss this in ch 3(I).

[28] Perry, above n 1, at 92–3: '[T]he exercise of a person's positive agency, under circumstances to which a harmful outcome could have been avoided and foreseen, leads us to regard her as the author of the outcome. Others can appropriately say of her, and she can say of herself, that she did it, and this is true even if others factors ... also causally contributed to the harm. The agent

when a person possesses the capacity to act in the world, and has made a choice in the situation.[29] Perry thinks that this is not enough, and argues that a person counts as the author of an outcome for the purposes of responsibility only when that person could have avoided causing that outcome. To illustrate the significance of avoidability, Perry uses the example of a young child who turns off the bath tap and thus avoids the outcome of the bath overflowing. Suppose that the child was too young to have the cognitive capacity to appreciate the connection between what it did and what happened. This, Perry says, would make us hesitate to regard the child as the author of the bath's not overflowing. While the child was the cause of that outcome and the child possessed, at least in *some* respects, the capacity to act in the world, the attribution of the outcome to the child's agency requires something more than that.[30] Perry thinks that this additional element is the capacity to foresee the outcome, and the ability and opportunity to take steps to avoid it.[31] Insofar as the child is not capable of understand that turning off the tap will prevent the flooding, we could not justifiably attribute that outcome to the child's agency and, therefore, hold the child responsible for it.

There is a clear reason why the story cannot end there. People's capacities to foresee things and avoid harm differs, sometimes considerably. In any given situation, you may be able to foresee things and avoid outcomes that I cannot. Maybe the reason I am less able than you to do those things is that I lack your experience, or that I don't have all the facts, or that I am generally slower on the uptake. It seems clear that only some of those reasons make it the case that I am not responsible for my failure to foresee and avoid certain outcomes. The challenge for agency accounts is to explain how we can pick those reasons out. Honoré and Perry agree on the answer here. They claim that the reasons that ground responsibility are distinguished by the fact that they point to my possession of a *general* capacity to foresee and avoid outcomes in a given type of action. What matters for the purposes of responsibility, in this view, is not whether I was able to foresee and avoid a particular outcome

---

acted and caused harm under circumstances in which she had a sufficient degree of control to avoid its occurrence, and for that reason she has a special responsibility for the outcome that other persons do not have. That we view outcome-responsibility as reason-affecting in this way is part of our deepest self-understanding of what it means to be a moral agent capable of both acting in the world and acknowledging responsibility for what one has done.'

[29] Honoré, above n 27, at 545. Also at 552: 'a person's character, aims and general capacity plus the circumstances of which he is aware normally determine his choice; his choice normally determines his conduct; and his conduct plus the circumstances in which he acts normally determines the outcome. If we are to be responsible for the outcomes of our actions, we are likely to find these loosely framed hypotheses reassuring rather than alarming.'

[30] *cf* S Perry, 'Honoré on Responsibility for Outcomes' in P Cane and J Gardner, *Relating to Responsibility—Essays for Tony Honoré* (Oxford, Hart Publishing, 2001) 61, 77–8.

[31] Ibid at 77; Perry, above n 1, at 91.

in a particular situation, but whether I am generally capable of doing those things in my life.[32]

This still needs some elaboration. A person who is generally good at something may make the odd mistake. When that happens, that person can plausibly say that their capacities *failed* them on that occasion. They can say 'that day I blanked out, but generally I am a good driver!', or 'that day I forgot to inform the patient about some risks of the treatment, but generally I am a good doctor!'.[33] The idea that what matters is the possession of a general capacity to foresee and avoid outcomes in those activities asserts that *occasional* failures in the exercise of that capacity do not absolve those persons from responsibility, but agency accounts owe us an explanation of what makes that assertion true.

Joseph Raz has proposed such an explanation in the context of his work on responsibility for negligence. He says that our general capacities are a measure of what we are good at, or which activities we have secure competence over. To that extent, they are part of how we recognise ourselves, and of our conception of our place in the world as acting, rational beings. When people hold us responsible for the outcomes of our actions, they are extending a similar recognition to us, by treating us as persons who possess those capacities and competences. The crucial point, Raz notes, is that this *remains* the case even when those capacities and competences fail us on particular occasions. Raz's insight is that we are not due any *less* recognition, both in our own eyes and in the eyes of others, just because our capacities failed us on some occasion. If that is correct, then, in holding us responsible for the outcomes of *both* our successful and our failed exercises of capacities that we normally command, others are doing nothing more and nothing less than to accord us the recognition we are due as persons.[34]

I am presenting Raz's argument as part of the same story that Honoré and Perry try to tell, and I want to justify this by explaining why a couple of differences between their respective accounts are not really fundamental. For a start, I do not think it matters greatly that Raz puts forward an account of responsibility for negligence, while Honoré and Perry are putting forward general accounts of responsibility in private law. The reason is that the core idea of Raz's account can be easily elaborated to fit contexts outside negligence too (that is, by focusing on negligence, Raz has done the hard part of the job). Consider nuisance or defamation. We see the use we make of our property, and the statements that we make to others, as part of our acting agency. Normally, we are able to do these things well, ie to serve our ends satisfactorily through our property use, and through our statements. In holding us responsible for

---

[32] Ibid at 78–9; Honoré, above n 27, at 550–1.
[33] I discuss the force of similar complaints in ch 5(IV).
[34] Raz, above n 3, at 17.

the results of our conduct in those situations, others are clearly giving us the recognition we are due as persons. But others owe us the same recognition in the occasions where the pursuit of our ends through our use of our property or through the statements we make to others leads to harmful outcomes, and so on. The story is even easier to tell outside negligence because it does not have to face problems of capacity to meet a given standard of care or advertence. A second apparent difference is that while Honoré and Perry attach significance to whether a person is generally able to foresee and avoid harmful outcomes in the context of an activity, Raz focuses on whether that person has secure mastery over that activity. This could be a more demanding test, depending on one's understanding of what it takes for a person to have such 'secure mastery' or 'command'. Again, however, the difference is small, because the way Raz applies the 'secure mastery' test brings it very close to that of the possession of general capacity to foresee and avoid. Raz says, for example, that parents who could have easily found out about certain social conventions regarding childcare and have failed to do so are responsible in case they fail to follow those conventions and their child suffers harm as a result. The parents may not have 'secure mastery' over the particular activity of childcare, but they have secure mastery over the more general activity of picking up and acting on social conventions.[35]

Honoré, Perry and Raz are, therefore, telling a substantially similar story. Differences of emphasis aside, their accounts all share the idea that a person's responsibility for some outcome turns on whether that outcome is connected with that person's agency in the right way. This sounds appealing, but I hope to show that agency accounts suffer from the same problem as Gardner's idea of 'basic' responsibility. While they distinguish between the conditions of attributive and substantive responsibility,[36] they assume that the 'right' connection between an outcome and one's agency stays constant across the two contexts.

---

[35] Ibid at 18, n 35. Raz says that whether the parent is responsible depends on 'whether not being aware of the duty is due to a malfunction of the parent's powers of agency. If the parent has normal competence and he lives in a society in which such a duty is widely understood, then he ... will be responsible for the ignorance (which is due to a malfunction of his rational powers) and derivatively responsible for the omission which arises out of that malfunction.' I discuss the point in some more detail in ch 5(III).

[36] Honoré, above n 27, at 541: '[R]esponsibility for a harmful outcome should not automatically involve a legal duty to compensate. An extra element is needed to ground the legal sanction'; Perry, above n 1, at 88: 'The avoidability conception of outcome-responsibility ... treats outcome-responsibility as a necessary but not a sufficient condition for the existence of an obligation to compensate ... [O]utcome-responsibility is best conceived ... as a potential basis for, rather than equivalent to, a moral obligation to compensate'; Raz, above n 3, at 3: 'I labour to emphasize that responsibility should not be identified with liability. Rather liability is—sometimes—a consequence of responsibility'.

This is not the case. What counts as the right connection between an outcome and an agent will differ depending on the question that we have in mind.
As Bernard Williams has shown, sometimes it may be both natural and appropriate for a person to feel regret for an outcome *simply* because they caused
it.[37] In Williams's example, the lorry driver who, through no fault of his, runs
over a small child considers it enough of a connection between the event and
his agency that it was he, rather than any other driver, who brought about the
child's death. The fact of his causal involvement is enough to explain both
why he may feel compelled to explain himself to others, and why others may
reasonably require him to supply such an explanation (eg to recount the situation so that others may form a view about whether or not he was at fault).[38]
At the same time, the fact that we would neither *blame* the lorry driver nor
hold him *liable* to pay compensation or to suffer criminal punishment shows
that this element is not sufficient to constitute the 'right' connection in other
contexts. We therefore have reason to require accounts of responsibility to
do more than simply point to the fact that all those questions are linked to a
person's agency. We should expect them to have enough resources to explain
how the 'right connection' may differ depending on the sense of responsibility
that our questions invoke. Agency accounts do not seem well-equipped to discharge this function. In that regard, consider this passage from Raz's account
of responsibility for negligence:

> Actions due to the malfunction of our capacities of rational agency result from fail-
> ure to perform acts of which we are masters. In acknowledging our *responsibility* for
> these unintentional acts and omissions we affirm our mastery of these abilities, deny
> that we are disabled in the relevant regards. When others attribute to us *responsibili-
> ties* for such actions they acknowledge our mastery of those abilities, and hold us
> *responsible* for these results of their use.[39]

Raz may be right that requiring a person to bear certain substantive responsibilities is a form of recognising this person's agency. Nevertheless, it seems

---

[37] B Williams, 'Moral Luck' in *Moral Luck: Philosophical Papers 1973–1980* (Cambridge,
Cambridge University Press, 1981) 34.

[38] *cf* C Schroeder, 'Causation, Compensation, and Moral Responsibility' in D Owen (ed),
Philosophical Foundations of Tort Law (New York, Oxford University Press, 1997) 347, 357: 'Authors
of actions have access to privileged information with respect to those actions that others lack.
They can frequently reconstruct the practical reasoning that preceded the action, almost always
better than external observers can. In so far as we must acknowledge a sense of authorship in
order to sustain agency, the responsibility of discharging the burden of explanation that falls
uniquely within an author's competence seems to suffice. Simply answering for one's actions
by "owning up"—saying that is mine, and this is yours—permits each person to continue to
construct and maintain an evolving personal history, which Honoré says is a prerequisite for
personal identity and character. If this is so, then outcome-responsibility as a duty to answer is
too thin a concept to bridge the gap from agency to the duty to compensate. Something more
is required.'

[39] Raz, above n 3, at 17 (emphasis added).

to me that his move from the (successful or failed) exercise of one's capacities, to the recognition by others that one possesses those capacities, and finally to the imposition of substantive responsibilities on that person, is too quick and ends up justifying too much.[40] It does not explain why a person can sometimes reasonably say that, although they are blameworthy for their mistake, someone else ought to pick up the bill for it. Or why that mistake should figure in the narrative of their life, but still not license others to blame them for it, or to impose on them any substantive burden on that account. More generally, it seems to me that both the ascription of blame and the imposition of substantive responsibilities on a person can be uncoupled from the recognition by others of that person's mastery of certain activities. Others can express such recognition in other, less invasive, ways too, eg they may console that person, and give them advice about how to avoid similar failures in the future. We therefore need a way of telling which of those modes of expressing such recognition are appropriate in a given situation. Raz's account does not show us how to do this.[41]

One might say that this does not really cast doubt on agency accounts, as much as it shows that those accounts do not take it upon themselves to do all the work that needs doing. Perhaps agency accounts set themselves the more modest aim of identifying certain shared aspects of attributive and substantive responsibility, while remaining very open to the possibility that the particular requirements of each kind of judgement will diverge at some further point. This way of thinking seems to me misguided. Appealing to agency to explain one's responsibilities assumes that our self-understanding as acting, rational agents is the horse, and responsibility is the cart. This misses that our conception of our agency and our identity are *themselves* shaped by particular truths about what burdens we and others ought to bear in relation to each other. Consider an example. You are a keen trumpeter, and you practise at certain times during weekdays. I am your neighbour, and have to put up with the disturbance. Let it be true that sometimes you play too loudly or too late in the evening. I suffer as a result. Suppose that we want to find out whether you should be subject to moral criticism. Honoré, Perry and Raz would say that a threshold matter for deciding that question is whether the conduct in question

---

[40] *cf* O Herstein, 'Responsibility in Negligence: Discussion of *From Normativity to Responsibility*' (2013) 8 *Jerusalem Review of Legal Studies* 167, 182: 'When assessing their inadvertent failures at φ-ing, people—due perhaps to information shortage or some psychological tendency—often focus on the single occurrence at hand rather than on their overall success rate at φ-ing over time. This tendency may lead to an overestimation of one's capabilities, resulting in one expecting near constant success and, therefore, to reacting with self-criticisms when confronted with occasional failures, thereby over expanding one's ascriptions of responsibility for negligence.'

[41] I return to this point in ch 4(V).

may be properly attributed to your acting, rational agency. It obviously can. The same story would explain why I am not to blame for that conduct. Your trumpet playing is not an exercise of my own acting, rational agency.

So far so obvious. But now let it be true that you keep your trumpet practice under control, eg that you do not practise too late in the evening, that you keep the volume down, and so on. Let is also be true that your interference with my use and enjoyment of my property does not cross the threshold of action-able nuisance, and therefore that the burden of living with the disturbance caused by your trumpet-playing lies with me. For Honoré, Perry and Raz, the threshold for that assessment is the same that it was when the question was the attribution of blame. The only agent to whom the trumpet playing has the 'right' connection is you. But suppose that some theorist thinks differently. Suppose that she claims that, because we are now talking about allocations of substantive burdens rather than about blame, and because some of those burdens lie with me and some with you, the conduct in question is attributable to *both* your agency and mine. This sounds heretical, I know. The description of your agency is supposed to be something more basic than your description of your substantive responsibilities towards others. But the theorist I have in mind does not agree. She claims that my agency is constituted, at least in part, by my relations to others. I am related to you as a neighbour. When the law of nuisance tells me that I have to bear the disturbance, it is not simply telling me how I ought to behave towards you. It is also giving me an insight into *myself as a neighbour*. Depending on the conception of neighbourliness that I had, that insight might require me to change some aspects of my self-understanding, and to affect the way I see my own conduct in the situation. For example, having realised that I ought to bear with you, perhaps I will now begin to see myself as a joint author of the sounds ringing across our building block on weekday afternoons. The outcome is now something we author together: you author it by playing, I author it by tolerating you.[42]

Maybe the heretical theorist's appeal to the idea of 'joint authorship' will give you the warm, fuzzy feeling it gives me. Or maybe it will strike you as mistaken. My point is that Honoré, Perry and Raz cannot explain what might be wrong with that idea. And the fact that this idea remains arguable gives us reason to think that our understanding of our agency may itself be con-text-specific. Just as we cannot rely on a 'basic' or portmanteau understand-ing of responsibility, applicable to both questions of blame and questions of

---

[42] *cf* AJ Julius, *Reconstruction*, forthcoming (Princeton, Princeton University Press, 2016), ch 10§6: 'The two persons are the subjects of a single standard calling for both actions and grounded on both reasons because each person depends for her normative success on both actions and both reasons.' As Julius has put the point elsewhere, 'walking by myself is something that I do with other people if I do it freely', id, 'A form of unfreedom', manuscript, §8.

substantive responsibility, maybe we cannot rely on a core understanding of agency either, but must instead tailor our enquiry into who we really are, and what we are really like, to the particular purpose for which we are asking those questions.

A similar point has been made in relation to other concepts too. As we have seen, Lord Hoffmann appreciated its significance in relation to causation.[43] Stephen Perry himself has argued against the libertarian fallacy of thinking that there is a single, portmanteau concept of factual causation that determines who is responsible for some outcome. Perry pointed out something very simple: on such a concept of causation, when I shoot you and you die, your death has been caused by both of us. I caused it by shooting you, and you caused it by being there. Remove either of those contributions and your death would not have occurred. The reason we focus on my contribution rather than yours is thoroughly substantive, namely that my actions violated my moral duty not to kill other people. It follows, Perry says, that any theory that grounds responsibility on mere factual causation lands its advocates in a dilemma: 'If the theory relies on a standard account of causation, it will give rise to significant indeterminacy. If it relies on a non-standard account that is specific to tort law, that account will inevitably extend beyond causation proper to include normative elements of some kind.'[44]

Contrast this with a claim Perry makes in reaction to Arthur Ripstein's suggestion that the allocation of responsibilities in private law is really a matter of determining who should bear the cost of certain activities. Perry thinks that this way of thinking about responsibility is misguided. When we think about responsibility in private law contexts, he says, we are not thinking about the proper allocation of burdens in general. Rather, we are thinking about how we should allocate burdens in the light of what one person has *done* to another. He writes:

> The trouble is that a conception of responsibility that underwrites this possibility seems unable to account for our intuitions about personal responsibility for causing harm. Our concern in the latter context is not with the allocation of loss on the basis of norms of equality, but rather with the fact that one person has *done something* to another for which he is potentially morally accountable. The blame-based, libertarian and avoidability-based conceptions of outcome-responsibility all provide different answers to the question of when one person has, in the appropriate moral sense, done something to someone else.[45]

---

[43] Above n 4.

[44] Perry, above n 1, at 86. See also S Perry, 'The Impossibility of General Strict Liability' (1988) 1 *Canadian Journal of Law & Jurisprudence* 147, 169; J Coleman and A Ripstein, 'Mischief and Misfortune' (1995) 41 *McGill LJ* 91, 101–8.

[45] Ibid at 90 (original emphasis).

In one respect, Perry is tapping on a strong intuition: whatever else it does, private law imposes responsibilities on people on account of their *responses* in a situation, rather than because of, say, who they are. Left at that, however, the claim suffers from the exact same fallacy that Perry exposed in libertarian accounts of causation. If it is substantive considerations that determine who counts as the 'cause' of some harm for the purposes of responsibility, it will be substantive considerations that determine what counts as having 'done something' for the same purposes. In a perfectly familiar sense, all of us are *always* doing something. What we need is a sense of 'doing' that is appropriate to the question that motivates our enquiry. The sleeping person is doing nothing in one sense, and failing to perform an agreed task or failing to take care in another. The former sense will be appropriate if the task at hand is to describe that person's physical movements. The latter senses will be appropriate if our aim is to determine whether that person may be saddled with some practical burden under the principles of contract or tort law. Similarly, employers may not be 'doing something' to the victim of their employee's carelessness in a physical sense, while they are 'doing something' in the sense of setting the tasks that the careless employee carries out. But whether setting those tasks is enough for us to say that employers are the authors of the victim's harm is a thoroughly substantive question about what employers owe to people injured in the course of the enterprise that employers have set up and direct. We do not work out the answer to that question starting from a fixed idea of what counts as acting, doing, or authoring.

IV. A PROGRESS REPORT

We can use the language of responsibility to express an array of different judgements. However, the distinction between those judgements and the corresponding senses of responsibility is intuitive, and it is not hard to clarify what we mean if we speak in full prose rather than in labels. Sometimes we may blame a person for some harm, and still say that it is not their responsibility to deal with it. And sometimes we may require a person to bear the responsibility of dealing with some harm, despite the fact that someone else, or no one at all, is to blame for it.

The distinction matters because it requires us to separate the discussion of whether a person may be blamed for their conduct from the question of how their conduct ought to feature in an account of the burdens that we may require them to bear. Getting that separation in place is important for private law, but it also has broader political significance. Scanlon notes how some of the most divisive political issues are often debated, across the political spectrum, in terms that fail to separate the two senses of responsibility:

It is said, for example, that there are two approaches to issues such as drug use, crime, and teenage pregnancy. One approach holds that these are the result of immoral actions for which individuals are responsible and properly criticized. The remedy is for them to stop behaving in these ways. The alternative approach, it is said, views these as problems that have social causes, and the remedy it recommends is to change the social conditions that produce people who will behave in these ways. Proponents of the first approach accuse proponents of the second of denying that individuals are responsible for their conduct. But this debate rests on the mistaken assumption that taking individuals to be responsible for their conduct in the sense of being open to moral criticism for it requires one also to say that they are responsible for its results in the substantive sense, that is to say, that they are not entitled to any assistance in dealing with these problems.[46]

It seems to me that, as private lawyers, we are ideally placed to avoid relying on the mistaken assumption that Scanlon points to. We are accustomed to see the law ascribing to people the responsibility to deal with harms that they are not to blame for, and to see people avoid legal liability for clearly blameworthy conduct. Private law theory too registers the point reasonably clearly. All theoretical accounts of responsibility in private law appreciate the principled difference between the conditions that justify blaming someone and the conditions that justify imposing some practical burden or responsibility on that person. Even those accounts that entertain the idea that substantive responsibility for some practical burden depends on a person being blameworthy eventually refrain from endorsing it outright.[47]

But while private lawyers are alert to the difference between the attributive and the substantive, it seems to me that accounts of responsibility in private law have often tended to rely on assumptions and claims that obscure rather than highlight that difference. Recall the claim that the language of responsibility is not apt for describing the position of deservedly unsuccessful claimants ('the claimant is not responsible for the loss; he must simply bear it because that is where it fell'); the claim that both attributive and substantive responsibility require capacity for reason-responsiveness or the authorship of certain outcomes; or the claim that situations where the author of an outcome and the bearer of the substantive responsibility are different do not

---

[46] Scanlon, above n 5, at 293. *cf* A Williams, 'Liberty, Liability and Contractualism' in N Holtug and K Lippert-Rasmussen, *Egalitarianism: New Essays on the Nature and Value of Equality* (Oxford, Clarendon Press, 2007) 241, 256: 'Taking for granted that culpability renders ... individuals liable to various penalties, right-wingers then advocates harsh prison sentences and cuts in welfare payments. Various leftists appear to endorse the right-wing inference as valid, but nevertheless abhor those conclusions. So, turning a conservative *modus ponens* into a progressive *modus tollens*, they try—often unsuccessfully—to convince others that the individuals concerned are not really blameworthy.'

[47] *cf* the discussion by W Lucy, *Philosophy of Private Law* (Oxford, Oxford University Press, 2007) 110ff.

raise general but only particular issues. I have argued that these assumptions and claims are largely mistaken, not because they conflate substantive with attributive responsibility, but because they encourage the thought that the link between a person, their actions, and the resulting outcomes remains constant between the two senses. That thought is mistaken. Judgements of attributive responsibility are expressions of moral criticism. Judgements of substantive responsibility are divisions of labour. Each kind of judgement raises a different range of questions and assesses facts about a person, their actions and the resulting outcomes in a different light.

This completes my ground-clearing exercise. I have concluded that private lawyers need an account of substantive, not attributive responsibility, and that this account needs to be specific to questions about the allocation of practical burdens. The next chapter lays out an account that meets that bill.

3

Choice and Responsibility

S AY THAT, IN a certain situation, you lacked the capacity to respond to reasons, eg because you were unconscious. Or that you lacked control over what you did and what happened. Or that you lacked the opportunity to do otherwise. Or that you could not have avoided acting in a certain way or causing a certain outcome. Does it follow that others may not impose on you a certain substantive burden or responsibility in that situation? I have argued that the answer is 'not necessarily'. Some or all of the elements of reason-responsiveness, control, or ability to do otherwise may generally be necessary for the attribution of blame or other moral criticism to you, but they are not generally necessary for the ascription to you of substantive responsibilities. Unlike expressions of moral criticism, judgements of substantive responsibility are divisions of labour. Sometimes others may require you to undertake part of that labour even if none of the above elements is present. At the same time, there is no denying that things like capacity to respond to reasons, control, choice and avoidability do matter when we allocate substantive burdens to people. While sometimes we may justifiably impose burdens on persons who lack the capacity to respond to reasons, this is something we may do only on a few occasions, and only in relation to a few burdens. Control over the production of some harm may not be a necessary condition for imposing on a person the burden of repair, but the fact that this person lacked such control will generally be something that we should address when we give a story about why that imposition is nevertheless justified. 'I could not have avoided what happened', or 'I could not have done otherwise', or 'I had no choice' can be similarly powerful complaints. It seems clear that the power of such complaints is related to the fact that it is important for people to have what happens to them, including what they owe to others, depend on how they respond in situations of choice. But given that none of those complaints has the force of a veto against the imposition of a substantive responsibility, we need to find some other way of accounting for their moral significance.

That account will necessarily have several moving parts, for three reasons. First, the importance for people of having what happens to them depend on their choices and other responses may differ between different persons, as some will be better choosers than others. It may also differ between different aspects of the same activity, as a person may be a good chooser when it comes to attaining the benefits of the activity, but not so good when it comes to avoiding or containing the risks and burdens that the activity involves. Secondly, the force of complaints like 'I could not have avoided this' will vary depending on the context or practice that we have in mind, and on the kind of burden involved. The fact that your medication causes you to fall asleep during an event may matter little, or not at all, for your substantive responsibilities if the event in question is a play that you paid to see. You cannot claim your money back just because your medication made you sleep through the play. Things may be different if the event you sleep through is a business meeting that lays out the details of your duties in a new job. There we may need to raise more detailed questions about whether the instructors knew or ought to have known about your condition; what you could have done to stay alert, to schedule the doses of the medication differently, or to notify the instructors of your condition; whether what you missed was material; whether your duties are laid out sufficiently clearly in other forms too, the other party has taken reasonable steps to bring those forms to your attention, and you had adequate time and opportunity to consider them. Thirdly, any assessment about the 'context' or the 'kind' of burden involved must be sensitive not just to your position (understood to include your circumstances, alternatives, capacities and so on), but also to those of others. After all, there is a limit to how much instructors ought to do to bring stuff to your attention, and ensuring that you are awake and alert at all material times, or that you read every document you are supplied with, will sometimes go beyond it.

My aim in this chapter is to outline an account of responsibility that is sufficiently sensitive to those parameters. To that end, I follow TM Scanlon's 'value-of-choice' account of the significance of choice in judgements of substantive responsibility.[1] I draw three related claims from that account. One is that the significance of choice for people's substantive responsibilities is directly connected to the general reasons people have for *valuing* opportunities to affect what happens to them through their choices. The second claim follows from the first: whether people ought to bear some burden or responsibility in a situation depends not on the choice they *made* in that situation, but on the choice they *had* in it. That is, what matters is not that one chose to act in a certain way (and ostensibly forfeited any complaint against being treated

---

[1] TM Scanlon, *What We Owe To Each Other* (Cambridge, Mass, Belknap Press of Harvard University Press, 1998), ch 6. Scanlon first laid out the value-of-choice account in his Tanner Lectures, see infra n 16. See also *Moral Dimensions: Permissibility, Meaning, Blame* (Cambridge, Mass, Belknap Press of Harvard University Press, 2008) 198ff; 'Forms and Conditions of Responsibility' in R Clarke, M McKenna and A Smith, *The Nature of Moral Responsibility: New Essays* (Oxford, Oxford University Press, 2015) 89.

in certain ways) but that one was favourably positioned to have what would happen to one depend on one's choices and other responses. The third is that sometimes putting one in such a favourable position may require others to offer one not just more or better opportunities, but also some degree of *protection* against the consequences of choosing poorly.

These claims carry important implications for private law theory, or so I will argue. For a start, they give us a clear reason to reject wrongfulness-based accounts of the burden of repair. If the substantive responsibilities others may require one to bear depend on the choices one has rather than the choices one makes, then those responsibilities are in place before one makes a choice, wrongful or not. What justifies imposing the burden of repair on that person is not the wrongful character of their eventual response in the situation (eg their failure to take due care, or to avoid causing some harm, or to live up to a voluntary undertaking), but the fact that they had the opportunity to affect those responsibilities through their choices, and that opportunity was something that they had reason to value. The same point illustrates the limitations of the main rivals to wrong-based models of private law, namely models based on the idea of maximising the efficient use of social resources, or of containing the social cost of accidents. We can agree with those models that a person's responsibilities turn on how that person is placed in a situation, without subscribing to their broader claim that the aim of private law is the maximisation of social benefit, or the reduction of social cost. That is, we can say that that person's responsibilities turn on the value of the opportunities that this person has, and take the measure of that value to be whether having those opportunities is likely to lead to better consequences *for that person*, rather than whether it is likely to have positive society-wide consequences.

The value-of-choice account is an account of the significance of choice for substantive responsibility, but it plays a further role as part of Scanlon's overall formula of moral contractualism. According to that formula, an action is wrong if and only if it would not be allowed under a principle that no person could reasonably reject, insofar as that person is aiming to find principles for the mutual governance of conduct. One obvious objection to Scanlon's formula is that it puts the cart before the horse: surely the reason why a person could reasonably reject a principle that allows, say, theft or killing is that those things are wrong, not vice versa. The value-of-choice account is part of Scanlon's defence against this objection. If a person may reject a principle on the ground that it is not sensitive to the opportunities that this person had in a situation, then the reason why the actions that this principle allows would be wrong lies precisely in that insensitivity, rather than in some independent criterion of wrongness. While I have no stake in showing that the value-of-choice account supports Scanlon's general case for moral contractualism, I will address some aspects of that debate, insofar as they relate to claims about the significance of choice for substantive responsibility. Another question I will set aside is whether accounts that make a person's responsibilities contingent on their choices are threatened by the thesis that our choices are causally determined by factors outside our control.[2] However, I will discuss the importance of causal factors to the extent that they affect the value of a choice for a person, by making it less likely that a person will choose well in a given situation.

My discussion follows the general strategy of Scanlon's account. Section I outlines the various reasons why having a choice can be valuable for a person. Section II discusses how the value for a person of having a choice affects the substantive burdens others may require that person to bear in a situation. To that end, it compares two accounts of the significance of choice for substantive responsibility, the will-based (or forfeiture) account and the value-of-choice account, and argues for the latter. Section III defends the argument against certain objections. Section IV shows how this argument cuts against the accounts of responsibility considered in the previous chapter, and against a range of different models of private law.

I. THE VALUE OF CHOICE AND THE ASYMMETRY
BETWEEN BENEFITS AND BURDENS

Having a choice is, generally speaking, a good thing. It is most obviously good in an instrumental sense. Much of the time things are likely to go better for a person in a situation if what happens depends on that person's choice. You are far more likely to enjoy your meal in a restaurant, or a new pair of shoes, if you pick them yourself rather than if someone else picks them for you. Of course, there will be occasions when that is not true, ie when you will be much better off if someone else chooses for you, eg if a person both knows your tastes and has a better grasp of the particular cuisine, or the quality of some types of footwear. But even in those situations it will generally be the case that

---

[2] For a classical statement of this view, see G Strawson, 'The Impossibility of Moral Responsibility' (1994) 75 *Philosophical Studies* 5. Scanlon's response is that this 'Causal Thesis' does not threaten our judgements of responsibility because the fact that causal factors operate *on* us does not make it any less true that they operate *through* us, ie those causal influences are still part of who we are, rather than external impositions on our true, causally unencumbered selves, Scanlon, above n 1 at 261–2. *cf* HLA Hart, 'Legal Responsibility and Excuses' in *Punishment and Responsibility: Essays in the Philosophy of Law*, 2nd edn (Oxford, Oxford University Press, 2008) at 48: 'The choices remain choices, the satisfactions remain satisfactions, and the consequences of choices remain consequences of choices, even if choices are determined and even if other "determinants" beside our choices condition the satisfaction arising from their being rendered effective …'. For another defence of responsibility against the Causal Thesis see R Dworkin, *Justice for Hedgehogs* (Cambridge Mass, Belknap Press of Harvard University Press, 2011), ch 4.

things will go better for you if it is yourself, rather than anyone else, who gets to decide whether to let another person choose on your behalf on account of their expertise, or of some other feature that makes them a 'better chooser'. Maybe that day you feel like choosing a dish or a pair of shoes that you would not normally choose, or want to experiment with things you have not tried before, if only to test your hunch that you would not enjoy doing them. Having the choice to do something 'out of character', even at the risk of disappointment, is valuable for you as it allows you the opportunity to stretch your preferences when you feel like it.

The last example suggests that having a choice may sometimes be valuable for a person in a non-instrumental sense too. Its value may lie in the fact that this person's choices say something about, or represent, their personality, tastes and attitudes. You want to be able to choose your wardrobe, your home furnishings, or the way you wear your hair, because these are ways of expressing who you are and what you like. Similarly, when you make a gift to a friend or relative, you may care not just about getting them something that is likely to please them, but also about expressing something about yourself and your feelings about that person. Sometimes the fact that you wrestled with the perennial 'what should I get them?' problem will carry greater significance both for yourself and the receiver of the gift than the sheer benefit the latter gets from the gifted item. The receiver will perhaps never listen much to the Bill Evans bootleg that you spent ages trying to locate, but still feel very grateful for the effort you put into finding it, and for your thinking that they might enjoy listening to it. By the same token, sometimes a person will value being able to exclude their tastes, attitudes or preferences from playing that representative role. For example, you may have to recuse yourself from a recruitment panel if one of your close friends is a candidate. Or you may think it fit that your students' exam papers be anonymised before you get to assign marks to them, so as to avoid your assessment of their class performance during the year spilling over into your assessment of their exam efforts.

Sometimes persons value having a choice in a situation because *not* having a choice would signify to others, and to themselves, that those persons are not as capable as others in making certain decisions. Adolescents are acutely aware of this symbolic aspect of the significance of choice. The transition from having your clothes bought, or your daily routine determined for you, to choosing those things yourself tends to be a charged affair precisely because it signifies that you are no longer a child who cannot be trusted to take care of itself but a full adult with an adult's powers and moral standing. Conversely, sometimes it can be symbolically important for a person not have a choice that is available to everyone else. The Queen not having the ability to vote or to stand for public office as a matter of UK constitutional custom is one example. In the monarch's own eyes, having either choice would not be consonant with her institutional role as a symbol of national unity, or with the exercise of certain of her constitutional functions.[3]

As advertised, I follow TM Scanlon in picking out the various reasons for which having a choice may be valuable for a person, and my examples mirror his own.[4] Scanlon goes on to say that this variety matters in two ways. First, it matters when we consider the grounds on which that person might complain against not being given a choice in a certain situation. For example, restrictions on the ability of a female to marry will run against different objections, or against no objection at all, depending on what they imply about her moral standing and worth, as opposed to her ability to represent herself through her choices, and the likelihood of her choosing well. That is why we cannot reasonably insist that an adult woman obtain her parents' consent before she marries, or arrange a marriage against her wishes, but we can tell an eight year-old girl that she cannot marry her sweetheart just yet.[5] In a crude sense, both restrictions are paternalistic. However, that sense is crude precisely because it fails to distinguish between restrictions that treat an adult woman as socially inferior and subordinate, on the one hand, and time-bound and gender-neutral restrictions based on the assessment that things are less likely to go well for a person if they are allowed to make the sort of commitment that marriage involves at the age of eight, on the other. The same goes for other examples of regulation of individual choice, from health and safety legislation that limits working hours, or requires the use of helmets and goggles in the workplace on pain of criminal sanction, to laws that prohibit certain transactions and set minimum wages. As Scanlon puts it:

> These laws can both diminish and augment workers' ability to shape their lives to suit their preferences … But they need not involve the kind of interference with representative values that gives paternalism its bad name, nor do they involve treating the workers they protect as foolish or incompetent. So it is useful, in weighing the force of objections to policies on the ground that they are 'paternalistic', to identify and distinguish between these various kinds of reasons rather than simply appealing [sic], in a general way, to the value of making one's own choices.[6]

---

[3] *cf* the Official Website of the British Monarchy, at https://www.royal.uk/queen-and-government: 'As Head of State The Queen has to remain strictly neutral with respect to political matters, unable to vote or stand for election'. The older version of the text, reproduced at www.britpolitics.co.uk/the-powers-of-the-british-monarchy, went on: 'The Queen's role is to provide continuity and the focus for national unity, and the Royal Family's public role is based on identifying with every section of society, including minorities and special interest groups. Although the law relating to elections does not specifically prohibit the Sovereign from voting…, it is considered unconstitutional for the Sovereign and his or her heir to do so'.

[4] Scanlon, above n 1 at 251–6. Hart focused on the instrumental (or, in his terms, 'predictive') value of choice, above n 2 at 47.

[5] Ibid at 256–7.

[6] Ibid at 254–5.

A second reason why this variety in the value of having a choice matters is that a given choice will have 'different instrumental value for people with different levels of knowledge, self-control, and discrimination, different representative value for people with different aims and attachments, and different symbolic value for people in different groups or societies'.[7] This makes the job of accounting for the significance of choice in judgements of substantive responsibility difficult, because it exposes that account to two sources of pressure. On the one hand, there is pressure to make assessments of the value of having a choice more and more 'individualised', in order to take account of the particularities of each person's preferences and circumstances. On the other hand, there is pressure to pitch the relevant principles of substantive responsibility (and the significance they accord to choice) at a certain level of generality, so that they can serve as simple and clear practical guides in governing relations between different persons. The resulting tension between 'individualised' and 'generic' reasons is obviously a feature of all moral reasoning, rather than a problem special to questions about the significance of choice for responsibility, but it presents itself in a particularly acute form in that context.[8]

The instrumental value of a choice, in particular, may differ not just from one person to another but also between different aspects of a single person's activity.[9] This asymmetry can be easy to miss because much of the time we think of the benefits and burdens that an activity involves as a package. One cannot want both to win the lottery and to avoid the risk of losing the price of the ticket. If one wants the winnings, one has to accept to pay the cost of the ticket too, because that is how lotteries work. Similarly, having the choice of driving their own car allows people to go where they want to, but it also saddles them with the burden of negotiating road traffic and complying with traffic rules. Minimum wage legislation allows workers to shop

---

[7] Ibid at 255. In Jean Renoir's film *The Rules of the Game* (1939), Octave (played by Renoir) offers a less sanguine version of the point: 'The awful thing about life is that everyone has their reasons'.

[8] See Scanlon's discussion of this problem of 'standpoint', ibid at 202ff, especially 204–6.

[9] Scanlon's discussion of the symbolic value of a choice could be read as implying that there is some such asymmetry there too. As he describes that value, having a choice is symbolically significant for you because of what it allows you to avoid, namely being regarded as less competent than others, or as having lower standing in relation to them, rather than in what it allows you to achieve. The point is that this value has no exact flipside to it. The 'normative opposite' of being considered less competent by not having a choice is not being considered more competent by having it, but being considered as competent as anyone else who has it. That seems to me true, albeit in the reverse form, in the example of the Queen's being unable to vote. The Queen achieves the symbolism of being perceived as standing outside political affairs by not having the choice to vote. However, there are situations in which the symbolic value of a choice for a person lies precisely in the fact that this person is credited with a special status or achievement, eg when the winner of a sports tournament gets a choice of prizes etc.

around for work in the safety that their remuneration will not fall below a certain level, but it also restricts their ability to compete with other workers on the price of their services, and so on. In those situations, the opportunity to derive some benefit goes together the assumption of certain burdens or the imposition of some restrictions because people cannot have one without the other. Drivers cannot both enjoy the benefit of being able to drive where they please with a modicum of safety, and still avoid the burden of complying with traffic rules, just as workers cannot both avoid the danger of having to work for a pittance, and retain the opportunity to out-price each other below a certain level.[10]

Things are different when the package of benefits and burdens that comes with having a choice in a situation can be designed in different ways. Consider the risk of liability for car accidents. One might say that, like the burden of dealing with traffic, this risk comes as a package with the freedom to drive where one wants: one must take the 'bad' with the 'good'. That would not be correct. The benefit of driving and the burden of obeying traffic rules will remain a package until our technology is advanced enough to split them, but the benefit of driving and the burden of liability for traffic accidents can be relatively easily disassociated. It is perfectly possible for people to have the opportunity to drive where they want, and still be protected from the burden of liability in case they cause an accident while driving. The 'bad' part of the package can instead be a requirement on drivers to take out insurance against the risk that they might cause a traffic accident, or the lighter requirement to contribute to a community fund that covers all personal injury costs.

The existence of such practical alternatives raises substantive questions about which package of choices ('freedom to drive + unlimited personal liability'; 'freedom to drive + compulsory car insurance'; 'freedom to drive + compulsory general insurance' etc) drivers would have reason to value most. But it also raises questions about the *specific aspect* in which drivers might want that package to be sensitive to their choices. It suggests the possibility that, other things being equal, drivers may place more value in being free to choose where and how to drive than in being able to choose their own method for protecting themselves against the consequences of their driving mistakes. This asymmetry seems to me to have a relatively straightforward explanation. People who are licensed to drive are, on the whole, good at that activity. Almost all of the time, they get where they want to go, and they get there safely. At the same time, the fact that driving mistakes tend to occur relatively infrequently and without much advance warning makes it more likely

---

[10] My point is not that benefits and harms or burdens are *morally* asymmetrical, though I agree with Seana Shiffrin that they are, see S Shiffrin, 'Harm and its Moral Significance' (2012) 18 *Legal Theory* 357.

that a driver will underestimate the probability that they will make such a mistake.[11] This, in turn, entails that such a driver is likely to miss the true value of obtaining appropriate protection against the burden of liability. So while both the benefit of going where one wants in safety and the burden of liability for traffic accidents arise in the course of the same activity, drivers may be good choosers in respect of reaping the benefits, and bad choosers in respect of protecting themselves against some of the burdens, especially when a certain rational bias impedes their understanding of the likelihood that they will incur them.

Something similar seems to me to hold more generally. A person may often value having a choice that allows them to derive benefits from some activity, and still value having *less* of a choice with regard to how they might protect themselves in case they make harmful mistakes in the course of that activity.[12] That will tend to be the case when the harms or burdens involved are serious and very hard to bounce back from, the nature of the activity makes it less likely that one will be a good chooser when it comes to protecting oneself against the risk of bearing the burden of dealing with those harms, and the cost for one of having some safety net in place is likely to be low. This asymmetry in the respective value of attaining benefits and avoiding burdens through choice matters in two ways. For a start, it shows that we cannot always take the fact that one wants the benefits that one derives from the activity to be choice-sensitive as an indication that one wants the same of the burdens that the activity in question might involve. Sometimes one can reasonably want *both* to be able to have a choice when it comes to how to derive certain benefits in a situation, and to be able to rely on others to give one some protection against the consequences of one's poor choices. This suggests that the argument as to why others may require that person to bear a burden in a situation may need to be similarly bifurcated. When we allocate substantive responsibilities to that person, it is not enough to ask whether their life will be better if we leave it up to them to choose whether and how to engage in some activity. We must also ask whether we ought to do something to *lower the stakes* for that person of choosing poorly, or of underestimating the consequences of doing so. Sometimes we will answer both questions in the affirmative.

---

[11] From a long literature on risk perception, see P Slovic, B Fischhoff and S Lichtenstein, 'Facts versus fears: Understanding perceived risk' in D Kahneman, P Slovic and A Tversky, *Judgment Under Uncertainty: Heuristics and Biases* (Cambridge, Cambridge University Press, 1982) 463; P Slovic, *The Perception of Risk* (London, Sterling VA, Earthscan Publications, 2000).

[12] *cf* TM Scanlon, 'Reply to Zofia Stemplowska' (2013) 10 *Journal of Moral Philosophy* 508, 511: 'The instrumental value of being warned of [a] danger, and thus given the choice of avoiding it, is a function of the value of the alternatives that would result from the actions one might choose when presented with this choice and the likelihood that one will choose the action with the more favorable outcome'.

This asymmetry seems to me to reconcile two apparently conflicting aspects of Tony Honoré's account of the significance of choice for responsibility. Famously, Honoré makes two claims in favour of a system of 'outcome-responsibility' for tort law. One is that the ascription to us of responsibility for both the good and the bad outcomes of our actions is a constitutive part of our personhood and agency.[13] The other is that a system of 'outcome-responsibility' is fair as long as people stand to 'win' more often than they 'lose' under it.[14] The two arguments are not co-extensive, because the second draws the bounds of responsibility more tightly than the first. The fairness argument allows 'I lose more often than I win' as an objection to a system of outcome-responsibility, while the personhood argument does not. If my fore-going discussion is right, though, perhaps Honoré's two arguments respond to different aspects of the same core intuition. Maybe the cleavage between the two arguments is a reflection of the asymmetry between the value of having a choice in relation to the benefits of some activity and the value of having such a choice in relation to the burdens that that activity may carry. While we value the opportunity to be able to achieve things through our choices, we can still want some protection against the adverse consequences of those choices, especially when we are more likely than not to underestimate the need for such protection. Honoré seems to think that it is enough of such protection that, most of the time, our choices tend to pan out well for us. In Chapter 4, I will argue that this is not the case, both in cases where the stakes of even a rare and small slip are very high, and in more run-of-the-mill cases. However, this disagreement arises precisely because both views attribute significance to the fact that the stakes of 'losing' and 'winning' as a result of our choices are not symmetrical.

II. MAKING A CHOICE VS HAVING A CHOICE

How does the value of a choice for a person affect the responsibilities others may require that person to bear? It seems obvious and intuitive that there should be some connection between the two. When you get to choose what happens, you have the power, so you must bear the responsibility. If the dish you chose in a restaurant turns out to have been a terrible match for your tastes, you still have to pay for your meal. If the team you chose to bet on

---

[13] T Honoré, 'Responsibility and Luck: The Moral Basis of Strict Liability' (1988) 104 *LQR* 530, 543.
[14] Ibid at 541. On the difference between the two arguments, see S Perry, 'Honoré on Respon-sibility for Outcomes' in P Cane and J Gardner (eds), *Relating to Responsibility: Essays for Tony Honoré* (Oxford, Hart Publishing, 2001) 61, 62–4; id, 'The Moral Foundations of Tort Law' (1992) 77 *Iowa LR* 449, 488ff.

loses the match, you cannot claim your money back. If you chose to drive like a maniac, you cannot complain when others require you to make repair for any harms that you have caused. If you decided to ignore a 'danger of electric shock' sign, tampered with an appliance and were electrocuted in the process, you cannot complain about your injuries.

There are at least two ways to explain how a person's choices affect their responsibilities in these contexts. One view is that this person ought to bear the relevant responsibilities because, in each of those examples, they *made* a choice. This account attributes significance to the fact that what happened was the result of that person's response in the situation, ie their decision to select one of the alternatives on offer and to pass up others. A different view is that this person ought to bear those responsibilities because, in each of the above examples, they *had* a choice. This account grounds that person's responsibilities not on the fact that they responded in a certain way, but on the fact that they were placed in a favourable position to have what happens depend on their response. In the first view, responsibilities turn on how a person chose; in the second, they turn on how they were placed to choose.[15]

Both accounts fit the examples I have used. However, each relies on different assumptions. The first assumes that it is the act of choosing, ie of selecting some alternatives and passing up others, that legitimates the imposition of substantive responsibilities on a person. There are several ways of explaining what gives the act of choosing its legitimating force, and of describing its effect on a person's responsibilities. Maybe choosing has that force because it involves the exercise of a person's will, or autonomy, or freedom, or powers of rational agency. And maybe the effect of the fact that a person made a choice in a situation is that, having chosen, they are thereby 'accepting' the imposition of certain burdens on them, or are 'forfeiting' any complaint they might otherwise have had against bearing them. In earlier statements of his views on the significance of choice for responsibility, Scanlon placed emphasis on this last description of the effect of making a choice, and called the view described here the 'forfeiture view'.[16] In later versions, his emphasis has shifted to the explanation of what gives choosing its legitimating force, so

---

[15] Here I am glossing over the fact that having or making a choice affects a person's responsibilities, when it does, only because a moral principle attributes significance to this. It seems to me obvious that the standoff between the two views (and some others that I discuss in the next section) about the significance of choice for responsibility is a standoff precisely about the content of that principle.

[16] TM Scanlon, 'The Significance of Choice' in S McMurrin (ed) *The Tanner Lectures on Human Values*, vol 8 (Salt Lake City, University of Utah Press, 1988) 192ff; above n 1 at 258–9.

he now refers to this view as the 'will-based' view,[17] and that is the name I will be using for it here.[18]

The second account—which Scanlon calls the 'value-of-choice' account—works differently. It assumes that the significance of choice for a person's responsibilities is determined by the reasons that make having a choice something valuable for that person. If having the opportunity to choose is something a person has reason to value, say, because this will make it more likely that things will go well for them, that person could not reasonably object to a principle that made their responsibility to bear some burden contingent on whether they had that opportunity. This account therefore approaches questions of responsibility by asking whether, and under which conditions, a person would value having that opportunity. Its two main objects of attention are, accordingly, the range and quality of the options that were available to that person in the situation that called for their choice or response, and the conditions under which that person was called to choose among those options.

A rough way to illustrate the difference between the will-based and the value-of-choice accounts is to ask at which moment in time they each regard the justification for imposing some responsibility on a person as complete. Under the value-of-choice account, the critical moment is the moment in which the available alternatives are at that person's disposal and the situation awaits for their response. Under the will-based view, the critical moment is the moment of the choice itself. So in the example where you suffer an electric shock when you tamper with an appliance, the value-of-choice account says that you are responsible for what happens as long as you had sufficient information about the nature and the seriousness of the danger in question,

---

[17] TM Scanlon, 'Responsibility and the Value of Choice' (2013) 12 *Think* 9, 9–10.

[18] Scanlon appeals to the notion of forfeiture to capture the idea that the act of choosing has the effect of *laying down* an objection that a person would otherwise have. This idea is, indeed, characteristic of the view in question. Under the value-of-choice account persons either have an objection on the ground that the relevant moral principle fails to make the imposition of a burden sensitive to their choices, or they do not. The idea that those persons had an objection, which they then laid down is not part of its general explanation (though the account can explain why that idea is more appealing in the context of voluntary undertakings; I discuss this at the end of this section). That said, I think the name 'will-based' is both a better fit for the view that it describes, and a better match for the name of its counterpart. After all, the value-of-choice account is named after the reason that makes it the case that a person ought to bear some substantive responsibility. It is therefore appropriate to name the opposing view too after the reason (ie the exercise of the will) that explains why the act of choosing has a certain effect (ie forfeiture), rather than after the effect itself. On similar grounds, Andrew Williams calls the view in question 'agency-based'; A Williams, 'Liberty, Liability and Contractualism' in N Holtug and K Lippert-Rasmussen, *Egalitarianism: New Essays on the Nature and Value of Equality* (Oxford, Clarendon Press, 2007) 241 at 246.

practical alternatives that would have allowed you to avoid exposure to that danger (eg you could have called a technician to look at the appliance), and you had reasonably favourable conditions for choosing among those alternatives. The fact that these circumstances were in place is sufficient for others to require you to bear the responsibility for the injury you incurred when you tampered with the appliance, even if your tampering was never the result of a conscious choice on your part.[19] By contrast, the will-based view says that you are responsible for your injury because you chose the course of action that brought it about, namely to tamper with the appliance, and your choice was in an appropriate sense free, or voluntary, or autonomous, and so on. Whereas the value-of-choice account holds you responsible because you were well placed to avoid a risk, the will-based view holds you responsible because you took that risk.

The difference may still seem rather small fry. In fact, one might, reasonably intuitively, think that the two views are really aspects of the same overall idea. If you had to choose from within a constrained range of alternatives or under unfavourable conditions, maybe your choice is not really free or voluntary or autonomous, and therefore others may not regard you as having accepted certain burdens or as having forfeited any objections you might have against their imposition on you. I think that there is something right in this suggestion. It is certainly common ground between the will-based and the value-of-choice account (and perhaps any plausible view about the significance of choice) that the circumstances under which a person was called to make a choice matter in the assessment of that person's responsibilities. However, the claim that this common ground shows the two views to be part of the same idea runs against an obvious problem: it does not explain the justificatory usefulness of the appeal to freedom, voluntariness, autonomy, and the notions of acceptance or forfeiture. To put it schematically, why should the justification go 'poor range of options/conditions of choice → no free/voluntary/autonomous choice → no acceptance/no forfeiture → no responsibility' instead of 'poor range of options/conditions of choice → no responsibility'? If, as the value-of-choice account holds, being presented with an unfavourable range of options or conditions of choice is enough to allow one to object to the imposition of the relevant responsibility, the story could stop there. We would gain nothing by referring to the (possibly true) further fact that this person's actual response in the situation does not count as a free, voluntary, autonomous choice, or that responding in this way does not entail that this person accepted the relevant burden, or forfeited their objections against having to bear it.

---

[19] Scanlon, above n 1, at 258: '[i]f a person has been placed in a sufficiently good position, this can make it the case that he or she has no valid complaint about what results, whether or not it is produced by his or her active choice'.

At the same time, the problem with the attempt to merge the two views helps illustrate the core difference between them. The will-based view says that having a valuable choice in a situation does not suffice to make a person responsible for the burdens that a certain option might lead to, unless that person *goes on to choose that option*. The value-of-choice account denies this.

Scanlon claims that we should endorse the value-of-choice account over its rival. He builds his argument for this around a rich example that involves the exposure of members of a community to a serious but avoidable danger to their health. The purpose of the example is to allow us to compare the positions of various persons in that community, and to assess the significance for their respective responsibilities of the fact that, to a greater or lesser extent, those persons were presented with the opportunity to have what happens to them depend on their choices.

> [S]uppose that the officials of a city need to remove and dispose of some hazardous waste that has been found near a residential area. Apparently it has lain there for years, and they want to move it to a safer spot some distance away. Digging it up and removing it will inevitably release some hazardous chemicals into the air, but this is much less dangerous than leaving it in its present location, where it will in the long run seep into the water supply. Obviously they must take precautions to reduce the risks involved in this operation. They need to find a safe disposal site, away from where normally people have to go. They should build a fence around the new site, and another around the old one where the excavation is to be done, both of them with large signs warning people to keep away. They should also be sure to have the material wetted down and transported in closed trucks to minimize the amount of hazardous material released into the air. Inevitably, however, some of it will be released—enough to cause lung damage to those who are directly exposed if, because of past exposure or genetic predisposition, they are particularly susceptible, but not enough to pose a serious threat to anyone who stays indoors and away from the excavation site. Given that this is so, the officials should be careful to warn people, especially those who know they are at risk, to stay indoors and away from the relevant areas while the work is being done.[20]

Scanlon then asks us to suppose that, despite all the precautions taken, some people are exposed to the hazardous material and suffer lung damage as a result. The question he wants to ask is how the fact that those persons were duly warned about the danger, and therefore had the opportunity to avoid injury by choosing appropriately, makes it the case that they cannot complain about the result. To separate that question from concerns about the overall justification of the community's response to the problem of removal, Scanlon asks us to take as stipulated that the officials did all that they could have been expected to do to warn and protect people in the situation (eg that evacuation

---

[20] Ibid at 256–7.

of everyone in the affected area was not a reasonable alternative), and that a principle that allowed the officials to act as they did was one that no one, including the persons who were in fact injured, could reasonably reject.[21] This stipulation allows us to focus not on whether the community has failed those persons, but on what makes it the case that the community did enough for them when it gave them the opportunity to avoid exposure by choosing appropriately (in the next section I will address some implications of relaxing Scanlon's background stipulations).

The value-of-choice account gives a straightforward answer to this question. The community has done enough for those persons by making their health and safety dependent on their choices, because having the choice to protect themselves by choosing appropriately is something that those persons have instrumental reason to value in the situation. That is, given that things are more likely to go well (or less likely to go badly) for them if they have the opportunity to decide how to protect themselves, they cannot reasonably object to a principle that made holding them responsible for what happens to them contingent on them having this opportunity. The answer is straightforward because it treats giving people the choice in question as just another way of protecting them, and assesses its significance in the same way one would assess the significance of other protective measures.[22]

Scanlon argues that this remains true despite the fact that the value of that choice varies from one individual to another, ie that some people will be better than others at heeding the various warnings officials have issued. One reason for this is that, as moral principles must govern relations between different persons, questions about the value of choice will need to be discussed at a certain level of abstraction:

> Appeals to the value of choice arise in moral argument chiefly when we are appraising moral principles or social institutions rather than when we are discussing particular choices by specific individuals. In these contexts we have to answer such general questions as: How important is it to have the selection amongst these alternatives depend on one's choice? How bad a thing is it to have to choose under these conditions? When we address these questions, fully individualized values are not known. We argue instead in terms of what might be called the 'normalized' value of a choice: a rough assignment of values to categories of choice when we take to be a fair starting point for justification.[23]

---

[21] Ibid at 257.

[22] Ibid: '[L]ike the fences, the careful removal techniques, and the remote location of the new site, "giving people the choice" is just another means through which the likelihood of injury is reduced'.

[23] Scanlon, above n 16 at 182–3. I return to the tension between 'individualised' and 'normalised' reasons for valuing a choice in the next section.

It follows that what matters for the purposes of justifying the significance of the fact that a person had a choice is not so much whether having the choice in question will necessarily be advantageous to every person, but whether having that choice is something that even persons who are less likely than others to choose well have reason to value as a general matter (I return to this point in the next section).[24]

A second reason is related to, and qualifies the first. The fact that some persons are likely to make poor choices in the situation suggests that the community would not be doing enough if it simply warned people of the risks and left them to fend for themselves. On the contrary, the value of the warnings for people lies in part in the fact that the community has also taken *further* protective measures, the force of which is independent of the warnings, such as fencing the excavation and removal sites, selecting a remote location for the new site, wetting down the waste etc. In other words, part of the case why people have reason to value having a choice about acting on the warnings is that the community put in place enough of a 'safety net' to lower the risk of them coming to harm in case they choose poorly.[25] As Scanlon has put the point:

> Even if we know that actions avoiding a certain unwanted outcome will be available to us in a given situation, we also know that our processes of choice are imperfect. We often choose the worse, sometimes even in the knowledge that it is the worse. Therefore, even from the point of view of an agent looking at his own actions over time, situations of choice have to be evaluated not only for what they make 'available' but for what they make it likely that one will choose. It is not unreasonable to want to have some protection against the consequences of one's own mistakes.[26]

Scanlon then asks whether this basic account of how choice matters for substantive responsibility works in certain variations of the example. In particular, he considers whether there is some special quality, which the value-of-choice account misses, in cases where a person actually *decides to respond* to the warnings in one or another way. Scanlon develops this objection by contrasting the positions of three persons: one never got word of the danger, despite all the warnings; the other was made aware of the danger but did not take it seriously; the third got word of the danger, but decided to venture out regardless in order to complete a scientific project that was very important to her. Under the value-of-choice account, none of those persons may complain about what happened to them, insofar as they all would value receiving warnings that would put them in a favourable position to avoid risk to their health by choosing appropriately and staying indoors. The only difference is that, in the

---

[24] Scanlon, above n 1 at 263.
[25] Ibid at 263.
[26] Scanlon, above n 16 at 195.

case of the first person, the warnings did not actually succeed in putting that person in the favourable position both he and the community wanted him to be in. This may seem to miss an important difference between the three persons' responses. The last two persons involved actually chose to take the risk involved. We can say of them, but not of the first person, that *they brought their injury upon themselves*. The will-based view offers a natural way of making this differentiation. If what matters for responsibility is the choice a person makes, then we can easily justify why we should treat the second and the third person differently. By contrast, the value-of-choice account has no way of registering that assessment, as it does not attribute significance to a person's actual response in the situation.[27]

Scanlon's reply to this objection has two parts. He points out, first, that, were we to attribute special significance to the fact that the latter two persons 'chose to take the risk', we would not be able to account for the position of a fourth person, who got word of the danger but then forgot all about it. It seems clear that, as long as the community did enough to put that person in a favourable position to avoid harm by choosing appropriately, he cannot complain about the injury he suffered when he unwittingly exposed himself to the hazardous substance, despite the fact that he never made a conscious decision to 'take the risk'.[28] Of course, it is true that in some contexts being well placed to choose from a certain range of options is not enough for a person to incur a certain responsibility. It must also be the case that this person actually made a choice, by selecting one of those alternatives, and passed up others. Contracts are an example in point.[29] The mere fact that a person is favourably placed to consider whether to enter into a legally binding agreement is not enough for that person to incur any contractual responsibilities; that person must also signify their assent to the deal. However, and in the second part of his response, Scanlon notes that the value-of-choice account has enough resources to explain the special significance of making a choice in those settings. What is special about contracts is precisely that they reflect voluntary commitments, so there are good and obvious reasons why a person would want the additional safeguard of being able to avoid incurring contractual obligations by withholding assent. Having a choice would not be valuable for a person in this situation, unless the package of options that the choice came

---

[27] Scanlon, above n 1 at 258–9.

[28] Ibid at 259.

[29] Scanlon notes that actual choice is also generally necessary for realising the representative value of a choice for a person, eg to represent my feelings to my partner on our anniversary, it is not enough that I am able to choose a gift for her, but also that I do go on to choose a gift. By contrast, the symbolic value of choice lies precisely in having that choice, not in actually exercising it; TM Scanlon, 'Reply to Serena Olsaretti' (2013) 10 *Journal of Moral Philosophy* 484, 485.

with included the option of avoiding incurring contractual duties by not sign-ing the deal, or not saying yes to a request for their assent.[30]

Scanlon goes on to note that the impression that the 'will-based' or 'forfei-ture' view offers a better explanation of the force of voluntary commitments is a mere artefact of the *stage* at which assent is typically sought and given in those contexts:

> In cases … such as voluntary agreements, the fact that a person chose to do some-thing, or gave his or her consent to its being done, appears to have distinctive importance in part because it is the last justifying element to be put in place. If the conditions are right, then the person's choice or consent is sufficient (and in these cases generally necessary) to make the result morally legitimate. When we focus on this last step, the fact of choice appears to have the distinctive moral force that the Forfeiture View suggests. The conditions which must already have been in place in order for the choice to have this force recede into the background, or seem impor-tant only insofar as they affect the 'voluntariness' of that choice.[31]

Scanlon argues that the problem with this line of thought is that it packs too much into the idea of 'voluntariness' (or the neighbouring ideas of 'free' or 'autonomous' choice). Even when the making of a conscious or explicit choice is necessary for the justified imposition of some responsibility, the explanation of that necessity cannot be plausibly tied to whether the relevant choice was voluntary. The choice of a person who enters into a contract because the other party concealed from them a better alternative that it ought to have disclosed is as voluntary as the choice of a person who simply ignored a better alternative. The difference between the two situations lies precisely in the fact that only the first person could object to the background conditions of the choice that they were presented with. By focusing on those background con-ditions separately from the fact of choice itself, the value-of-choice account allows those conditions 'to be given the independent significance appropri-ate to them'.[32] The point is not that actual choice never has the effect of forfeiting objections that a person would otherwise have. It is, rather, that the effect of forfeiture 'is a creature of particular institutions and relatively specific principles such as those governing promising … It is not a moral fea-ture of choice in general.'[33] A similar argument explains why it does not help

---

[30] *cf* Scanlon, above n 16 at 211; Hart, above n 2 at 34–5, 45.

[31] Scanlon, above n 1, at 260. *cf* Scanlon, above n 29, at 486: 'In some cases, … it may seem as if the fact that a person actually made a choice has special justificatory significance beyond what I have described. I believe that this is an illusion, due to the fact that this actual choice comes last in the sequence of events. Because it comes last, it therefore seems to be the decisive factor. But it is decisive only because the other relevant factors are already in place, and because giving the person the choice under those conditions constitutes doing enough for him or her'.

[32] Ibid at 261.

[33] Ibid at 265.

to tie responsibility to a requirement that a person must have been able to 'do otherwise'. The person from whom a better alternative was objectionably concealed could have done otherwise. They could, at the very least, have refused to assent to the contract. This does not make it the case that, by choosing to enter into that contract in these circumstances, they have forfeited their complaint against being saddled with duties under it.

The advantage of the value-of-choice account over will- and voluntariness-based alternatives becomes clearer when we consider the several familiar exceptions to the general principle of contract law that agreement requires an explicit acceptance of an offer. For example, it is generally accepted that a person may be bound by a contract, despite the fact that they never gave assent to it, if that person's conduct was such as to induce a reasonable person to believe that such assent was given.[34] Similarly, a person can be bound by a contractual clause despite the fact that they clearly did not read it,[35] and may in certain cases be considered to have accepted an offer by mere silence.[36] One feature common to these situations is that the person in question had the opportunity to avoid becoming contractually bound. But another feature common to them is that this person could not have reasonably required other parties to take further steps to obtain that person's explicit assent. Unlike will- and voluntariness-based accounts, the value-of-choice account can explain why this matters, as it makes a person's responsibilities depend in part on whether others have done enough for that person by giving them the opportunity to read the agreement and express their attitude towards it. I discuss these questions, and the variety of constraints on a person's transactional opportunities, in more detail in Chapter 6.

III. TWO SETS OF OBJECTIONS

Scanlon's value-of-choice account has been the target of two objections. One questions whether the appeal to the value of a choice for a person is enough of a ground on which to base judgements of substantive responsibility. The other worries that the appeal of the value-of-choice account might be an artefact of the stipulations that Scanlon makes in the waste disposal example that animates his discussion.

---

[34] The principle of the 'objective' interpretation of parties' intentions in English law is laid down in *Smith v Hughes* (1871) LR 6 QB 597 at 607 *per* Lord Blackburn. See also *First Energy (UK) Ltd v Hungarian International Bank Ltd* [1993] Lloyd's Rep 195 at 201.

[35] *L'Estrange v Graucob Ltd* [1934] 2 KB 394.

[36] *Vitol SA v Norelf Ltd* [1996] AC 800 at 811 *per* Lord Steyn; *Rust v Abbey Life Insurance Co* [1979] 2 Lloyd's Rep 335, where the offerees were held to have accepted by silence an offer made at the instigation of the offerees themselves.

Andrew Williams has pursued both objections. With regard to the first, he begins by noting that the value-of-choice account leaves unclear whether our reasons to value having certain opportunities are sufficient in themselves to explain why we may be required to bear certain substantive responsibilities, or whether those reasons are simply to be counted alongside others in assigning responsibilities to people.[37] He then argues that neither of those options (which he terms, respectively, 'ambitious' and 'modest') looks very convincing.

Williams's objection to the more ambitious reading of the value-of-choice account is straightforward. Thinking about the value for a person of having a choice gives us a clue about the options and conditions of choice that this person would want to have available in a situation. However, we do not reach judgements about substantive responsibility simply on the basis of what people could reasonably want. We also need to ask questions about how much others may be required to do in order to offer people their desired options. As the value-of-choice account seems to focus only on the position of the person who has the choice, it seems poorly placed to explain this dimension of those judgements. Williams writes:

> [A]rguments that address questions of substantive responsibility primarily from the decision-maker's standpoint are unlikely to provide convincing answers across a suitably wide range of cases. For we normally respond to these questions by treating the perspective of agents other than the decision-maker as at least as important in deciding how liability should be assigned.[38]

The more modest version of the account, Williams says, fares no better. If a person's reasons for wanting to have a choice are just one of several inputs to the moral calculus that determines that person's substantive responsibilities, then we cannot reach any firm conclusions about the significance of choice for substantive responsibility until we identify the additional reasons that go into that calculus. In the waste disposal example, the fact that people had a choice about how to protect themselves may carry the significance that Scanlon thinks it does precisely because he has fixed many *other* morally significant parameters of the example, by stipulating that the officials have done all that could be reasonably required of them. Maybe if the officers could have put in place more (non-warning-based) protection, and at little cost, the value for the persons involved of being able to protect themselves through their choices would have been diminished. Unless we know more about the costs

---

[37] Williams, above n 18 at 249 n 5 points out that Scanlon prevaricates between the claim that a person's having the choice can 'make it the case' that he cannot reasonably reject a principle that ascribes that burden to him (eg Scanlon, above n 1, at 251), and the claim that having a choice 'weakens' that person's grounds for rejecting a principle (Scanlon, above n 1, at 256).

[38] Ibid at 250.

and benefits of alternative policies for the persons affected by them, we cannot reach safe conclusions about how giving those persons the choice affects their substantive responsibilities. As Williams puts it: 'Construed more modestly as an explanation only of why certain factors are relevant when arriving at conclusionary judgments, [Scanlon's] account is unsatisfactory because so incomplete'.[39]

It seems to me that the distinction between the 'ambitious' and 'modest' versions of the value-of-choice account misunderstands the overall purpose of that account. The value-of-choice account is not an account of substantive responsibility. It is an account of the significance of *choice* for substantive responsibility. The difference matters because, as Scanlon himself notes when he first lays out the distinction between attributive and substantive responsibility, 'judgments about what a person's substantive responsibilities are can be used very widely, to express judgments about almost any duty, or at least the duties connected with any role'.[40] We should therefore expect complete accounts of substantive responsibility to track the structure of our preferred general account of what we owe to each other. For example, according to Scanlon's contractualist formula, the answer depends on whether a principle that imposes certain responsibilities on certain persons is one that those persons could not reasonably reject. A corresponding theory of substantive responsibility should therefore be sensitive to all the grounds of reasonable rejection that those persons might be able to put forward. The value-of-choice account is an account of the significance of one such ground. Its purpose is not to supply a general explanation of who ought to bear which substantive responsibilities in every context, but to explain what makes it the case that the fact that a person was given the opportunity to choose bears on that question.

But while the value-of-choice account does not purport to be as ambitious as Williams makes out, it is not quite as modest either. As Williams notes early on in his discussion, Scanlon believes that the fact that people were placed in a sufficiently good position to avoid certain burdens by choosing appropriately entails that those persons may not 'make morally compelling demands on others to relieve them of [those] burdens'.[41] The value-of-choice account is Scanlon's explanation of why that is so. In reply to a similar criticism by Serena Olsaretti, Scanlon has said:

> My aim is to explain why having had a choice is one element in making it the case that a person can't complain in this sense. This does not seem to be an overly modest or trivial aim. The explanation I offer is just that having a choice is one thing, among others, that an individual has reason to want in such cases ... I sometimes

---

[39] Ibid at 252.
[40] Scanlon, above n 1 at 248–9.
[41] Williams, above n 18 at 245.

have said that the fact that a person had a certain choice can *make it the case* that he or she has no valid complaint about the result. This is not a stronger claim than the one I have just stated—that having a choice is one factor among others that can render an outcome legitimate—because these other factors are meant to be included in the 'sufficiently good conditions'.[42]

The point is that, under the value-of-choice account, the significance of the fact that the officials gave people the opportunity to protect themselves by staying indoors is not *simply* additional to the other protective measures that they put in place. The implementation of those other, non-warning-based, measures is part of the case for why people had reason to value the opportunity to protect themselves by responding appropriately to the warnings. Absent the non-warning-based measures, that opportunity would have been less valuable to them. Williams is right to suggest that we cannot estimate the moral significance of choice without considering what other protective measures could be taken for the benefits of those persons, the costs involved in doing this and so on. But leaving the point at that misses that, under Scanlon's account, the value of the choice itself changes with the availability of those other protective measures.

The second objection suggests that the value-of-choice account explains that relationship in some situations but not in others. Advocates of that objection worry that Scanlon's account does not match our intuitions about the significance of choice when we relax his stipulation that no reasonable alternative protection policy was available to officials. They say that when alternative policies are in fact on the table, as they very often will be, Scanlon's account may not do such a good job of explaining how considerations of choice affect the selection of one such policy over others. If this objection succeeds, then the value-of-choice account would be more or less useless in practice, as it would not help us settle any of the familiar debates about whether the conditions of responsibility, including the conditions of legal liability, in particular situations should be more or less demanding.

Alex Voorhoeve, Zofia Stemplowska and Andrew Williams have pressed this objection in broadly similar terms.[43] Voorhoeve proposes a variation of Scanlon's waste disposal example in which officials have a choice between two different policies. One is to conduct a very thorough information campaign, which will ensure that everyone in town gets a standard warning about the risks involved and the ways in which they can protect themselves. Voorhoeve calls this policy 'Inform Everyone', and asks us to suppose that almost every

---

[42] Scanlon, above n 29 at 485–6.
[43] Williams, above n 18; A Voorhoeve, 'Scanlon on Substantive Responsibility' (2008) 16 *Journal of Political Philosophy* 184; Z Stemplowska, 'Harmful Choices: Scanlon and Voorhoeve on Substantive Responsibility' (2013) 10 *Journal of Moral Philosophy* 488.

person will act prudently and protect themselves. However, there will be one person, though we cannot know in advance who that will be, who will impetuously visit the excavation site despite being aware of all the risks, just because the warnings have excited her curiosity about the nature of the hazardous material and the process of excavating it. That person ('Curious') will suffer a severe and incurable case of emphysema as a result. The alternative policy is to spend more money on the information campaign in order to impress on people the effects of exposure by means of vivid images. However, since those images will be more costly to produce, this campaign, which Voorhoeve calls 'Vivid Warning', will be somewhat less extensive in its coverage of the community despite the officials' best efforts to reach everyone. As a consequence, one person ('Walker'), whose identity we cannot tell in advance, will remain uninformed and, as he goes about his daily stroll on the day of the excavation, become exposed to a harm as serious as that which threatens Curious.[44]

Voorhoeve, and Stemplowska who builds on his variation of the hazardous waste example, argue that Inform Everyone seems intuitively the correct policy but that the value-of-choice account cannot help us decide between that policy and Vivid Warning. The reason is that, under that account, both policies would be reasonably rejectable. Walker could reasonably object to Vivid Warning because that policy fails to give him the choice of protecting himself, as he stays uninformed about the removal of the hazardous waste. But Curious could reasonably object to Inform Everyone since, given her curious disposition, the warnings issued did not make it more likely that she would be protected from harm.[45]

Scanlon agrees with the intuition that Inform Everyone is the right policy. But he argues that the value-of-choice account has enough resources to explain this. The choice between Inform Everyone and Vivid Warning raises concerns not so much about whether responsibility turns on the value for a person of the opportunity to choose in a situation, as about the way in which risks should figure in the assessment of each person's position in that situation. More specifically, the objections that Curious and Walker might have against one or another policy certainly appear equivalent when we consider their respective position ex post. However, the knowledge that Curious (rather than anyone else) would not be made safer by the warnings, and that Walker (rather than anyone else) would remain uninformed would not be available at the time when the community must decide which of the two policies to adopt. Given this 'natural veil of ignorance' about the risks run by each particular person, the outcomes of each policy may only be assigned probabilities, and

[44] Voorhoeve, above n 43 at 184–5.
[45] Ibid at 186; Stemplowska, above n 43 at 495–6.

that assessment must be made ex ante. In turn, adopting this ex ante perspective allows us to note a significant difference in the force of the respective objections of Curious and Walker:

> A principle permitting the adoption of Vivid Warning permits a policy that, at the time it is acted upon, involves failing to give certain people the protection of a warning. Such a principle is therefore open to objection from those who are in this situation. By contrast, a principle permitting the adoption of Inform Everyone requires us to give everyone the benefit of a warning. The value of this benefit is reduced by the likelihood that it will not be effective, but an objection based on this is weaker than the objection to Vivid Warning.[46]

I find this response broadly right, but I think that more needs to be said to explain why Curious has the weaker objection. After all, we do not need to amend the example radically to make it the case that the ex ante value of the warning for Curious would be not only lesser, but *negative*. As Andrew Williams has proposed, we could simply stipulate that some persons are by disposition so impetuously curious that putting their health in their hands in such situations will risk making their position much worse than it would have been, as it will make it more likely that they will suffer great harm by choosing poorly. Persons in that position could therefore reasonably argue that, given their decision-making tendencies, protecting them from harm in this situation requires us to deny them the opportunity to choose.[47]

I think that we can elaborate on the general strategy of Scanlon's response and say that the ex ante value of the warning for a person in the position of Curious depends also on the means and options that Curious has, as a general matter, for containing her curiosity, or for preventing herself from acting on it. In fact, it seems to me that the force of her case against Inform Everyone turns largely on the assumption that persons like Curious cannot do much about their general disposition. Accordingly, the more we relax that assumption, the weaker the grounds Curious has to object to that policy. Consider two persons: Curious A is naturally curious, but she is mindful of the bad decisions that this can lead her to. She therefore calls on her friends and relatives to be on the

---

[46] Scanlon, above n 12 at 511. In his discussion in ch 5 of *What We Owe To Each Other* at 235–8, Scanlon had implicitly accepted that, as a general matter, the appropriate perspective from which to assess the position of the parties was the ex post one. In his reply to Stemplowska, he corrects that mistake (at 510–11), which he attributes to his concern that adopting an ex ante perspective would, at least in some cases, license a kind of aggregation that his contractualism aims to resist. For defence of the ex ante perspective in Scanlon's contractualism, see A James, 'Contractualism's (not so) Slippery Slope' (2012) 18 *Legal Theory* 263.

[47] Williams, above n 18 at 254. As Voorhoeve, above n 43, at 189 notes, the stipulation is anything but arbitrary. Very often, public decision-making takes into account ex ante the likelihood that certain classes of persons will come under greater risk if given a choice of protecting themselves.

look-out so that when she declares that a certain dangerous situation excites her curiosity, they will take some measures that will keep her from acting on that disposition, eg they will keep her occupied with conversation, or organise a trip for her on the day of the removal. Suppose that the incidence of such situations is rare enough that at least a few of her friends and relatives agree to play the shipmates to her Ulysses. Curious B has the same natural disposition and self-awareness, but she has no friends or relatives to support her in this way, and is too proud to ask strangers for help. I think that neither person would have a reasonable objection to Inform Everyone, but that the reasons will differ in each case. Curious A may not object to the policy, as giving her a warning actually makes it more likely that even persons in her position will remain healthy. The only qualification is that this will hold true as long as those persons have the opportunity to rely on other people to keep them from acting on their natural curiosity (it seems to me that the same qualification explains why young children could not reasonably object to Inform Everyone). The significance of this qualification emerges even more clearly in a silly counterfactual in which there is an easily available and affordable pill that 'cures' people of their curiosity for a whole day, with no significant side effects. It seems to me that the availability of that pill would affect the value of the warnings for those persons in much the same way as the availability of friends or relatives who could help keep Curious A from acting on her natural curiosity. That idea also explains why the position of Curious B is not quite the same. Silly counterfactuals with pills aside, Curious B lacks the options that Curious A has to keep herself from acting on her curiosity. The reason why Curious B too cannot object to Inform Everyone even ex ante is, rather, that her complaint is based on 'individualised' rather than 'generic' reasons. Her complaint is weaker because it must rely on the claim that, having no friends or relatives to protect her, and being too proud to ask strangers for help, she is not getting the benefit that people, *including* the naturally curious, would normally get from the warnings.[48]

IV. FROM THE VALUE-OF-CHOICE ACCOUNT
TO MODELS OF PRIVATE LAW

Private law principles impose burdens on people. They require them to drive safely, or to keep their bargains, and to make repair in case they do not. The value-of-choice account says that those principles are justified when the persons on whom those burdens fall have reason to value the opportunities

---

[48] Note that Curious B could not claim that being able to desist from approaching strangers for help has *symbolic* value for her, and nevertheless favour a policy that would not allow anyone to ask for such help.

to choose that those principles afford them. When that reason is instrumental, the justification of the relevant private law principles will depend on how likely it is that things will go better for those persons if they have the choice in question. So, we require people to observe the traffic code, and to make repair for accidents they cause when they do not, because they have reason to value the opportunity to drive where and when they please. We require people to keep their bargains, and to make repair when they fail to do so, because they have reason to value the opportunity to make and receive legally enforceable voluntary commitments. These, of course, are easy cases. In other cases, the value of an opportunity for a person may be harder to ascertain. Sometimes it may depend on whether others have done enough to make it more likely that a person will *choose well* in a situation, eg on whether a doctor has informed a patient about the risks of a treatment and its alternatives. Sometimes it may depend on whether others have offered that person a measure of *protection* in case they choose poorly, eg on whether others have given that person access to affordable insurance in case things go wrong. By the same token, sometimes giving people the choice will not have value for them, so the proper policy would be to *deny* people that opportunity altogether. Recall Scanlon's hazardous waste example: if the city could have ensured everyone's complete and absolutely safety through non-warning-based measures alone, giving people a choice on the matter would have been an awful policy, precisely because it would have exposed people needlessly to the risk of suffering harm in case they made the wrong call. The same goes for familiar private law situations. If some medicament is poisonous, we are justified in prohibiting its distribution and sale, precisely because (or to the extent that) people have no general reason to value the opportunity to purchase it. Needless to say, each of those ways of making a choice valuable for a person, or of ensuring that people do not have to make choices that are not valuable to them, may develop its own complexities. For example, in Scanlon's hazardous waste case, it was stipulated that officials had actually done all that citizens could reasonably have required them to do on both of those fronts. They had undertaken an information campaign to make it more likely that people would choose well, and they had put in place non-warning-based protective measures in case, despite the warnings, some people had gone on to choose poorly. In other situations, all these questions about how much others ought to do for people will be up for discussion. Should doctors be allowed to prescribe any treatment they think is warranted, or should their discretion be limited by government standards? How much decision making should the traffic code leave to drivers? Should contract breakers be liable for the entire extent of the losses caused by their default, or should the victim of the breach be required to take certain measures to contain or mitigate those losses?

Chapters 4 to 7 apply the value-of-choice account to practical questions of this sort. Here I want to consider how that account should affect what we make of the accounts of responsibility I looked at in the previous chapter, and of wrongfulness-based accounts of the burden of repair. I also want to use this opportunity to explain how the value-of-choice account cuts against certain other models of private law, especially models that see the purpose of private law as the maximisation of social welfare or the minimisation of social cost.

A. Basic Responsibility and Agency Accounts

It seems to me an advantage of the value-of-choice account that it helps us appreciate what is right about the accounts of responsibility that I considered in the previous chapter. Gardner's claim that responsibility requires reason-responsiveness emphasises the importance for people of having their responsibilities depend on their choices and other responses. Honoré and Perry's claim that accounts of responsibility must attend to a person's 'general' rather than their 'specific' capacity to avoid outcomes captures the idea that the reasons why a choice is valuable for a person need to be pitched at a certain level of generality, and cannot be sensitive to every particular aspect of that person's situation. Similarly, Raz's more particular claim that others may hold a person responsible in negligence only when the activity which gave rise to the harm lay within that person's domain of secure competence highlights the importance of linking that person's responsibilities with the likelihood that they will be a good chooser in a situation. The same, I think, goes for Honoré's broader claim that a person's responsibility turns on whether their responses in situations of choice come out well a lot more often than they come out badly. The value-of-choice account does not necessarily understand those claims in the way their authors put them forward (eg in Gardner's case, as a conceptual claim about responsibility). However, it does present them as part of the explanation of the moral significance of choice for substantive responsibility.

At the same time, the value-of-choice account draws attention to the fact that sometimes a person may not value having a choice in a situation, despite the fact that they possess the general capacity to avoid certain outcomes by choosing appropriately, or have a reasonably secure mastery over the activity involved. That is one of the reasons why, in situations like that in Scanlon's hazardous waste example, the officials would not have done enough for people by simply warning them of the relevant risks. While most citizens would have had the general capacity to avoid harm, and would have possessed reasonably secure competence in self-protecting by staying at home, it was always possible that some of them would forget about the danger, or fail to assess properly its seriousness, or overestimate their ability to deal with it. A proper policy in that situation therefore had to attend not just to people's general capacity to choose well, or to their secure mastery over basic measures of self-protection, but also to the possibility that those people might fail to exercise that capacity or mastery on a certain occasion. That will be especially true when the stakes of people failing to do so are very high. The additional non-warning-based measures, like the fencing off of the site and the wetting down of the material, were there not just for the benefit of people who did not get the word, but also for the benefit of the fully informed persons, in case they failed to heed the warnings. The value-of-choice account has a straightforward explanation for this: the value for a person of having a choice in the situation depends in part on what *else* others have done for that person, besides giving them the choice, to make it more likely that things will go well for them. Moreover, that explanation is perfectly consistent with regarding the persons who failed to heed the warnings as blameworthy for their failure. Accounts that make responsibility turn on the possession of a general capacity to avoid harm, or the secure mastery over the appropriate measures of self-protection, have no obvious way of drawing this distinction between the conditions of substantive and attributive responsibility.

One might argue that those accounts simply cut the pie in a different way. Perhaps their claim is that reason-responsiveness, or the possession of a general capacity to avoid outcomes, or the secure mastery of some activity, are *pro tanto* reasons for ascribing a burden on a person, but that those reasons may be outweighed by countervailing considerations, including considerations about what others have to do for that person.[49] I think that this 'two-stage' view faces an important difficulty. Under the value-of-choice account, our *pro tanto* reason for ascribing responsibility for some substantive burden to a person is a function of the value for that person of having a certain choice. However, that value is itself dependent on what, if anything, others had to do to ensure that giving that person the choice would be likely to make things go well for that person in the situation. It follows that considerations about what others ought to do for a person besides giving them the choice are not additional to those concerning the value of choice. They partly determine that value for that person and, therefore, the content of the *pro tanto* reason we might have to ascribe responsibility to them. Another way of putting the point is to note that the two-stage view involves a certain degree of inflation about reasons. Suppose that, in the hazardous waste example, officials had chosen the policy of simply issuing the starkest warning possible to everyone. It seems to me that we would be giving a poor description of the applicable reasons if we said that we had 'basic' reason to hold those who failed to heed the warnings responsible for what happened to them because they had certain capacities or skills

---

[49] See citations from Honoré, Perry, and Raz in ch 2, n 36.

that would have allowed them to self-protect, but that this responsibility was then diminished in the light of the 'special' reasons officials had to put in place non-warning-based protective measures too. That description would be poor precisely because the 'basic' and the 'special' or countervailing reasons are more closely connected that the two-stage view acknowledges. What officials ought to do for people will already figure in an account of the reasons why people would value having the choice to self-protect.

B. Accounts of the Burden of Repair

I hope it is clear that the value-of-choice account of responsibility is bad news for wrongfulness-based accounts of the burden of repair. Those accounts say that one ought to bear the burden of repair when one has made a certain defective choice, say has driven carelessly, played music much too loud in the middle of the night, breached one's contractual duties, or made a misrepresentation.[50] If the value-of-choice account is right, this claim is mistaken. The reason why others may require one to make repair in those situations is not that one made a certain choice, but that one had a choice that one had reason to value, eg the opportunity to shape one's voluntary commitments to others, to choose how and where to drive, to control one's use and enjoyment of one's own land, and so on.[51] It follows that any theory that ties a person's responsibilities to wrongs and wrongdoing places the 'moment' in which that person incurs those responsibilities too late. This gives us all the more reason to reject the claim that the point of imposing the burden of repair on a person is to make that person suffer, or to allow the person harmed to 'get even'. The problem with that claim is not that it trades on certain strong claims about the morality of revenge. It is that it assumes that the imposition of the burden of repair on a person is a response to that person's wrongdoing. That is not the case. All the pieces of the responsibility puzzle are in place before that person goes on to wrong anyone else. That remains true even in contexts where the imposition of some burden (original or further) on that person depends on them making an explicit choice, eg in the case of contracts or other voluntary commitments. The only difference is that the value of the relevant opportunity lies in part in the ability to avoid becoming bound by withholding one's explicit assent.

---

[50] *cf* Honoré, above n 13 at 545: 'It seems possible, then, to justify both outcome-responsibility and the liability, strict or fault-based, which legal systems superimpose on it, if those held responsible have the proper capacity and made the relevant choice'.

[51] I discuss the significance of opportunities in typical negligence and stricter liability settings in ch 5.

This might seem to miss the obvious, namely that others cannot require one to bear the burden of repair *until* one has actually caused harm to another person, or breached one's undertaking and so on. This is correct, but it is no basis for an objection to the value-of-choice account. Saying that a person's responsibilities are in place even before that person causes harm, or breaches a voluntary commitment, is as straightforward as saying that, when you buy a lottery ticket, what happens, good or bad, is your responsibility even before we know whether you have the lucky number. What matters for responsibility is not the point at which one ought to *make* repair, but the point at which one *incurs the burden* to make repair, should such repair become due. At any rate, the fact that one must have caused harm, or committed a breach of contract, to be required to make repair does not justify the much stronger claim that one incurs that burden only when one's conduct has been wrongful.[52] It is simply saying that whether one will be called on to make repair, and the precise content of one's responsibilities in that regard, can be contingent on whether certain events do or do not occur.

If the value-of-choice is bad news for wrongfulness-based accounts, it is good news for the direct account I pitched against them in the first chapter. The basic idea of the direct account is that there is nothing special about the justification for imposing the burden of repair. Just as you need not be a wrongdoer for us to require you to bear the burden of driving safely or of keeping your promises, you need not be a wrongdoer for us to require you to bear the burden of making repair for some harm. The value-of-choice account backs up this claim in two ways. For a start, it allows us to see that the burden of making repair is just one element in the 'package' of opportunities that particular principles present people with. Principles that allocate the burden of repair for traffic accidents are part of the package of opportunities that the law provides drivers with. It should therefore be justified on terms similar to those that we would apply in respect of other burdens that people undertake in the course of the same activity, eg the burden of driving safely or of having insurance. Secondly, the value-of-choice account can explain why we should not draw conclusions about who the burden of repair should fall on simply on the basis that a person ought to bear an original burden, eg to drive safely. The reason is that one may value the opportunity to reap the benefits of some activity, and still want some protection in case one makes mistakes that require repair in the course of that activity.

---

[52] Accordingly, the case for the particular principles Scanlon has proposed about the enforceability for voluntary undertakings is meant to be independent of the fact that breaching a promise is wrong: TM Scanlon, 'Promises and Contracts' in *The Difficulty of Tolerance: Essays in Political Philosophy* (Cambridge, Cambridge University Press, 2003) 234, 252–3. I discuss the principles proposed by Scanlon in ch 6.

Sometimes one can be a good chooser when it comes to discharging the original burden (eg given the opportunity, one will likely drive safely by far most of the time) and a poor chooser when it comes to discharging the burden of repair (eg given the opportunity, one will likely fail to take adequate protection against the consequences of a driving mistake). This asymmetry suggests that when we think about imposing the burden of repair on a person, it may not be enough to show that this person was well placed to discharge the original burden and that others had put sufficient measures in place to make it likely that this person would do so (eg by checking that this person has had proper training, and that their vehicle is roadworthy). Sometimes we will also need to show that others have done enough to allow that person to avoid the burden of repair for avoidable mistakes (eg they have put in place a safety net that, given human fallibility, would lower the stakes for drivers of being liable for traffic accidents). All this fits well with the direct account's claim that our conclusions about the imposition of the original burden do not necessarily preoccupy our conclusions about the imposition of the burden of repair.

This becomes clearer when we turn to details. As an illustration, consider how the value-of-choice account might explain why, as the direct account recommends, we should relax the requirement that repair must always take the form of doing the 'next best thing'. Recall that in *Ruxley Electronics v Forsyth* the cost of repair was grossly disproportionate to the value of that repair for the customer (Forsyth). Should the contractor be required to make such repair? The value-of-choice account would begin to answer this question by noting that building pools was part of the contractor's business. He had far more expertise than Forsyth as regards the cost of doing the job and of repairing it in case it was done poorly. This suggests that a principle that required the contractor to cure the pool's defect (or do the 'next best thing') would be sensitive to him having had an opportunity that he had reason to value in the situation: to do the job according to his own assessment of what it would take to do that job well, and, if appropriate, negotiate an exclusion or limitation of his liability in case of poor performance.

However, leaving things at that would miss two further points. One is that while the contractor has clear reason to value the opportunity to decide how to perform, he may *also* value having in place some protection in case he messes up when performing. The other is the assessment of both the value for the contractor of having the benefit of such a 'safety net', and the burden for Forsyth of providing that benefit, must proceed at a certain level of generality, ie attend to the general reasons that persons in the parties' position would have for wanting that protection, and for objecting to being required to provide it. I think that these points supply a prima facie justification for the decision of the House of Lords in *Ruxley*, which can be understood as making two corresponding substantive claims. One is that, when the nature of the work that the contractor is undertaking involves a significant risk that the cost of curing defects in that work will be particularly high, the contractor may reasonably value the opportunity to have some protection against the burden of having to bear that cost. The other is that, unless the parties have made explicit their preference to the contrary, the level of sacrifice that providing such protection would involve for Forsyth must be assessed by reference to the 'generic' rather than the 'individualised' value of that sacrifice, ie to the disvalue that persons in Forsyth's position would attach to its deep end being safe but shallower than they wanted to be.

I say that this way of justifying *Ruxley* is only prima facie because the second of those claims needs serious qualification. The court's decision does not say that Forsyth could never be entitled to require the contractor to cover the cost of building the pool to the agreed specification. What it suggests is that if Forsyth wanted to have that option, he ought to have made special provision for this in the original agreement, or sought special assurance by the contractor to that effect. The problem is that a person in Forsyth's position will sometimes not be well-placed to appreciate that telling the contractor how he wants things to go may not be sufficient for that purpose. In fact, it is a fair bet that many persons in Forsyth's position would be surprised to hear that, in order to be able to insist that the contractor pay for the cost of re-building the pool to the agreed standard, they would have to specify not only what they want the pool to be like, but *also* that the deep-end measurement is central to the value that they attach to having the pool. For those persons, the value of the opportunity to negotiate a 'this really means a lot to me' clause may, accordingly, be diminished: people do not value the chance to bargain for things that they have reason to believe they are already entitled to.

This suggests that, under the value-of-choice account, sometimes a person could reasonably object to a principle that required them to do more than state their preferences clearly in order to be able to require the contractor to make full repair in case of poor performance. Suppose that a customer has ordered a rather pricey suit from a tailor. The customer has specified that he wants the inseam of the trousers to be 32 in long. Let it be true that hardly any persons who wear suits in that society, and are of the same built as the customer, would want their suit trousers to be 32 in long. The fashion is, and has long been, that people wear their trousers in a way that leaves their ankles showing. The customer wants his suit trousers to be longer because he does not like his ankles to be visible. In the event, the tailor delivers trousers that are only 30 in long and, as it happens, he has not left enough cloth in the seam to be able to extend the trousers to a length of 32 in. To deliver trousers of the agreed measurement, the tailor would have to put together a completely new pair.

I think that here the tailor should be required to cover the cost for the customer of buying a suit with the agreed length of trousers, ie that he should *not* be allowed to escape the obligation to do the 'next best thing'. In particular, he should not be allowed to invoke the fact that, in the eyes of everyone but the customer himself, the 30-in-long trousers fit the customer just fine and, say, get away with giving the customer some courtesy vouchers. The reason is that, even if the customer had the opportunity to insist on a 'perform as agreed, or pay full cost of repair' clause in the agreement, that opportunity may not have been valuable to him. To determine whether it was, we would need to ask whether the customer had reason to believe that exercising the opportunity to insist on such a clause would make it more likely that he would receive the trousers he wanted. It seems to me that, in the present example, the answer would be 'no'. A request for the extra reassurance of that clause could easily be perceived by the tailor not simply as excess caution on the customer's part, but also as mistrust for the tailor's skill. A customer could therefore reasonably believe that asking for such reassurance might not be worth incurring the risk that the tailor would take the customer's request badly and resolve not to put any more than the absolutely necessary effort into making the suit. This conclusion gains support when we consider that, once measurements are taken and the order is in, the customer may have no further opportunity to inspect the tailor's work and to point out that it falls short of the agreed specifications. If the opportunity to seek extra assurance has no value for the customer at the point of order, it may have no value for him in the context of the transaction as a whole either.

A full justification of *Ruxley* should be able to explain how that case differs from the tailoring example. In particular, it should focus on two questions. First, whether a person in Forsyth's position had reason to believe that insisting on an explicit 'perform as agreed, or pay full cost of repair' clause would make it more likely that he would receive the pool he bargained for. Secondly, failing that, whether a person in Forsyth's position would have had further and easily available opportunities to inspect the work and point out any shortfall from the agreed standards. It seems to me that, on the facts of *Ruxley*, one could make a good, though perhaps not irrefutable, case that Forsyth indeed had reason to value the opportunity to insist on the extra assurance of a 'perform as agreed, or pay full cost of repair' clause. Part of that case would be that *Ruxley* involved an extended building project, rather than just a typical consumer transaction, and that the higher the stakes of the transaction, the more reason a person in Forsyth's position has to seek the extra assurance of the relevant clause. Perhaps it also matters in that respect that, unlike the situation in my tailoring example, Forsyth had sufficient reason to doubt the contractor's skill, as the contractor had made serious mistakes at earlier stages of the project, and had agreed once already to restart it from scratch without charge.[53]

Note that this way of justifying *Ruxley* does not lay stress on the *disproportion* between the burden to the contractor and the benefit to Forsyth. Rather, it focuses on the significance of those sums in the assessment of the value of the opportunities that each party had in the situation. To see this, suppose that we scaled down the relevant costs, as accepted in *Ruxley*, by a factor of 100. That would bring the cost of repair to £215.60, Forsyth's loss of amenity to £25, and his damages for inconvenience to £7. The proportion between the numbers would remain the same. What would change would be the stakes for the contractor of not enjoying protection against the burden of repair. Since the value of the opportunity to avoid that burden is determined, in part, by those stakes, the contractor could not object to a principle that required him to make repair in this variation (the same would probably apply in the tailoring example). I return to this issue, and how it bears on questions about the significance of distributive considerations on responsibility, when I discuss consumer and employment agreement contexts in Chapter 6.

The value-of-choice account also explains why the direct account is right to say that the justification for imposing the burden of repair on a person may turn on considerations other than rights. Consider the example of a doctor who prescribes the wrong drug because a patient chose to withhold information about an allergy that they were suffering from. It seems clear that the doctor could object to a principle that made them responsible for the cost of the harm that the patient suffers as a result of taking the prescribed drug. The reason is that the opportunity to choose a treatment for one's patients has value for the doctor only on the condition that patients do their part in providing doctors with information that is easily available to them, and not otherwise available to the doctor. That remains true despite the fact that the doctor does not have a right that the patient come forward with that information.

C. A Possible Accommodation?

Suppose you innocently knocked over someone in the street, because you stepped onto a transparent slippery substance you had no reason to believe was there. Let it be true that, under the value-of-choice account, you could reasonably object to a principle that made you bear the burden of repair for the harm you caused to the person you knocked over, because, having no knowledge of the lurking danger, you did not have the opportunity to avoid

---

[53] *Ruxley Electronics and Construction Ltd v Forsyth* [1996] AC 344 *per* Lord Lloyd at 361–2.

the accident. We could still square this conclusion with a wrongfulness-based account in two ways. We could say that, in causing harm to the other person, you violated that person's rights, or wronged them, but that this *pro tanto* reason to require you to compensate them is outweighed by the fact that you did not have the opportunity to avoid the accident in question. Or we could say that, because you lacked the opportunity to avoid the accident, you did not violate the victim's rights, or commit a wrong against them in the first place. Doesn't this suggest that the value-of-choice account and wrongfulness-based accounts of the burden of repair are not really at odds?

I think that the answer is 'no', because neither of the above methods of accommodation has great prospects of success. The first option puts wrong-fulness-based accounts in an awkward bind. If considerations of responsibility sometimes weigh more than considerations of rights or wrongs, perhaps sometimes they will also weigh *enough* to justify imposing a responsibility on you even when you have violated no right or committed no wrong. As a general matter, that should not be surprising. As we have seen, very many of the responsibilities people are required to bear have nothing to do with wrongdoing. One might, of course, insist that the violation of a right or the commission of a wrong has special significance for the burdens that one may be required to bear, eg it might create a special reason why a wrongdoer may be made to suffer on account of their wrong. The problem is that the more force one invests such special reasons with, the harder it becomes to explain how those reasons might be outweighed by considerations of responsibility.

The second option reads the conditions of your responsibility into the conditions of the injured person's rights, or the conditions for describing your conduct as wrongful. The problem with that option is that reading responsibility into statements about rights or wrongs robs those statements of their *pro tanto* explanatory force in relation to statements about responsibility, ie it makes it harder to make statements like 'you are responsible *because* you violated one's rights or *because* you committed a wrong'.[54] If we need to look at what you are responsible for in order to tell whether the person you knocked over had a right towards you, or whether you have committed a wrong against them, all the work we need is done by the relevant considerations of responsibility. Another aspect of the same problem is that sometimes there is clear value in distinguishing statements about rights/wrongs from statements about responsibility,

---

[54] *cf* JJ Thomson, *The Realm of Rights* (Cambridge, Mass, Harvard University Press, 1990) 82ff and J Feinberg, *Rights, Justice and the Bounds of Liberty: Essays in Social Philosophy* (Princeton NJ, Princeton University Press, 1980) 221ff. Thomson and Feinberg have also pointed out that, if generally adopted, a 'specificationist' strategy of folding considerations like those of responsibility into propositions about rights would end up making rights 'unknowable', ie it would complicate their accurate statement at the expense of their utility as guides to practical reason.

especially when we are thinking in a prospective sense, when all is still well and we are deciding how to conduct ourselves towards other people. Consider the statement 'she does not have a right to require you not to knock her over innocently'. One odd thing about that statement is that it would make a rather bad guide to your deliberations on how to conduct yourself towards that person, not because your innocence in knocking her over will be morally insignificant for your responsibility, but because your (lack of) responsibility in such an event should not be something that figures in your thoughts when you are considering how you should behave when you are in her vicinity. The point is not that you should be prospectively indifferent to the burdens that you might be required to bear in case an accident happens. It is, rather, that even the prospective knowledge that you will not be responsible for paying her medical bills in case you knock her over innocently should not make a difference to how you choose to conduct yourself when you are around her.

I would argue that the same difficulties undermine the attempt to read the conditions of responsibility into models of private law that do not focus explicitly on the idea of wrongfulness, but are similarly committed to the view that the ground of a person's responsibility is the choice they make, rather than the choice they have in a situation. This is clearest in respect of two familiar models of contract law, the model of promises and the model of consent.

The model of promises takes the core moral feature of the burdens that contract law places on people to be the existence of one or more promises between the parties.[55] Consider how that model might account for situations in which the promisor fails to do as promised, but should not bear responsibility for making repair, eg because the promise was extracted from them by misrepresenting some essential aspect of the deal to them. It might say that the *pro tanto* reason the promisor had to perform as promised is outweighed by whichever considerations make it the case that the promisor is not responsible for breaching that promise. Or it might say that the promise in question was never binding in the first place. As we saw in relation to wrongfulness-based accounts, both alternatives land the model of promises into some trouble. On the one hand, if considerations about what one is responsible for weigh more than considerations about one's promissory duties, they may sometimes weigh enough to impose on one a certain burden in the context of a voluntary transaction even when one has not made a promise to that effect, eg it might be enough that one voluntarily encouraged the other party to entertain certain expectations. On the other hand, reading the conditions of responsibility

---

[55] C Fried, *Contract as Promise: A Theory of Contractual Obligation* (Cambridge, Mass, Harvard University Press, 1981); A Ripstein, *Force and Freedom: Kant's Legal and Political Philosophy* (Cambridge, Mass, Harvard University Press, 2009), ch 5.

into the conditions of promising limits the capacity of statements about one's promissory duties to explain statements about one's substantive responsibilities. If we need to find out what one is responsible for in order to tell whether one made a binding promise, the appeal to the fact that one made such a promise will at best be only one aspect of explaining what one is responsible for. The same applies in respect of the model of consent, according to which the justification for imposing contractual duties on a person lies in the fact that this person gave consent to bearing those duties.[56] Take any consideration that limits what burdens others may require one to bear for breaching one's consensual undertakings and consider how the model of consent might account for that consideration. If it treats that consideration as outweighing one's consent, then it leaves itself open to the challenge that consent matters only insofar as an account of responsibility so dictates. If it treats that consideration as determining what counts as 'true' or 'genuine' or 'valid' consent, then it limits the explanatory force of statements about consent over statements about substantive responsibility.

D. Cost-based Models

They say that when you have a hammer, everything looks like a nail. To do my part in confirming this bit of popular wisdom, in this section I contrast the value-of-choice account with a family of private law models that I have not discussed at any length in earlier chapters. These are models that take the purpose of private law to be to maximise the efficient use of social resources, or to minimise the social cost of certain activities (I will refer to them as 'cost-based' models). One such model, proposed and elaborated by Guido Calabresi, says that it is your responsibility to make repair for an accident when you were best-placed to work out and act upon the measures worth taking to prevent its incidence, ie you are the 'cheapest cost-avoider', or the 'best decider'.[57] Another, advocated by Steven Shavell in tort and Richard Craswell in contract, says that you are responsible to make repair when a principle to that effect is socially efficient or optimific.[58] Many important debates in private law

---

[56] R Barnett, 'A Consent Theory of Contract' (1986) 86 *Columbia LR* 269.

[57] G Calabresi, *The Costs of Accidents: A Legal and Economic Analysis* (New Haven, Yale University Press, 1970). Calabresi distinguishes between the 'cheapest' and the 'best' cost-avoider, ie between the agent that the market picks out as being optimally placed to bring about primary accident cost avoidance, and the agent that the community's decisions about the desirability of certain activities pick out as optimally placed to do the same (at 174–5). My text uses 'best placed' to cover both of those senses.

[58] S Shavell, *Foundations of Economic Analysis of Law* (Cambridge, Mass, Belknap Press of Harvard University Press, 2003); AM Polinsky and S Shavell, *Handbook of Law and Economics*

theory have been organised around the stand-off between those models and their wrongfulness-based counterparts.[59]

My main reason for introducing those models to my discussion now is that I hope to use my conclusions on substantive responsibility to do two things: first, to point out a number of respects in which cost-based models seem to me to work particularly well, and to highlight some areas of affinity between them and the value-of-choice account; and secondly, to identify some respects in which those models and the value-of-choice account part ways, and to explain why I believe that the latter captures better the character and content of the justification for imposing the burden of repair on a person.

The value-of-choice account and cost-based models are in broad agreement in two respects. One, which comes out most clearly in respect of Calabresi's 'best decider' model, is that one's responsibilities turn on how one was *positioned* to decide, rather than on how one decided. Moreover, both accounts accept that whether one is well positioned for that purpose turns in part on the range of options available to one, and the conditions in which one is called to choose among them. The other respect, which is more pronounced in Shavell's and Craswell's models, is that one's responsibilities are a function of the value for one of having a choice in a situation. Cost-based models express that value in terms of the expected utility for that person of having a certain choice, and how this utility affects one's practical incentives. This idea is clearly wide enough to include what the value-of-choice account refers to as the instrumental and representative value of a choice. It does not seem equally able to account for the symbolic value a choice may sometimes have for a person, but I will not pursue this point here.

At the same time, cost-based models and the value-of-choice account have different understandings of the ideas that they share. The significance of being in a favourable position in Calabresi's model is a *relative* matter. That is, the fact that one has a choice affects one's responsibilities insofar as it makes one a

---

(Burlington, Elsevier Science, 2007), chs 1 and 2; R Craswell, 'Efficiency and Rational Bargaining in Contractual Settings' (1992) 15 *Harvard Journal of Law & Public Policy* 805. See also C Goetz and R Scott, 'Liquidated Damages, Penalties and the Just Compensation Principle: A Theory of Efficient Breach' (1977) 77 *Columbia LR* 554.

[59] Jules Coleman's *Risks and Wrongs*, Reprint (New York, Oxford University Press, 2002) was written partly as a general response to Calabresi's cost-based model, while Ernest Weinrib's *The Idea of Private Law*, Rev edn (Oxford, Oxford University Press, 2012) was meant as an alternative to views that see private law as having 'external' aims, such as maximising utility. See also S Hershovitz, 'Two Models of Tort (and Takings)' (2006) 92 *Virginia LR* 1147; id, 'Harry Potter and the Trouble with Tort Theory' (2010–1) 63 *Stanford LR* 67; M Geistfeld, 'Economics, Moral Philosophy, and Positive Analysis of Tort Law' in G Postema (ed), *Philosophy and the Law of Torts* (Cambridge, Cambridge University Press, 2001) 250; R Craswell, 'Contract Law, Default Rules, and the Philosophy of Promising' (1989) 88 *Michigan LR* 489; G Fletcher, 'Fairness and Utility in Tort Theory' (1972) 85 *Harvard LR* 537.

better or a worse decider than other persons involved in the situation. In a lot of contexts, this makes good sense. Putting responsibility on the shoulders of the best decider, rather than dispersing it amongst all well-placed deciders in the situation, may be more likely to avoid wasteful duplication of precautions. What is less clear is why we would want to commit to a principle that allocates responsibility, as a general matter, *solely* to the best decider.[60] As the hazardous waste example shows, sometimes the stakes involved will be high enough to justify a wider distribution of responsibilities, even if that leads to some 'over-shooting', or duplication of precautionary effort. The value-of-choice account can accommodate that possibility because it does not treat placement as a relative question. It treats it as a question about the options and conditions of choice that *each* person would generally value having in a given situation. The fact that B is better placed than A matters for A's responsibilities only insofar as it suggests that A would not value having a choice in that situation. For example, this explains why the responsibility to choose one or another physical treatment ought to lie with the physiotherapist that the patient consults, rather than with the patient themselves, even if the patient has the opportunity to do some basic online research about their condition and even to undertake certain measures of self-care. By contrast, a pedestrian may be worse placed that a driver to avert a traffic accident involving the two, but may still bear responsibility to take care, and perhaps to pay some of their own bills in case they fail to do so and an accident occurs. The reason is that, while worse placed than drivers as a general matter, pedestrians still have reason to value the opportunity to look out for their own safety.

If under the 'best decider' model the significance of having a choice is always relative, under Shavell's and Craswell's models that significance is always *mediated* by considerations of efficiency. While the value-of-choice account makes a person's responsibilities contingent on the value for that person of having certain opportunities in a situation, those models make those responsibilities contingent on whether their imposition is socially efficient. This difference is important in principle, and I will turn to it in a moment, but it should not overshadow the extent of agreement between efficiency models and the value-of-choice account. For a start, note that under the value-of-choice account too, one may sometimes have to bear burdens that one did not have sufficient opportunity to avoid, as long as it would be too costly for others to take measures to put one in a more favourable position for that purpose. The situation of the person who, despite the extensive information campaign, did not get

---

[60] *cf* Shavell, above n 58, at 189–90. Shavell argues that the 'least-cost avoider' model is unsuited to contexts of 'bilateral' accidents (ie accidents in which one party's conduct affects the other party's conduct). It seems to me that, on Shavell's own terms, this criticism succeeds on the assumption that the overshooting can be efficient.

word of the danger in the hazardous waste example illustrates this clearly. The reason why officials could not have been required to spend more time and effort to ensure that absolutely everyone had received and understood the warnings was that doing this would not have been worth the cost to public health of putting off the excavation.

Efficiency models can also explain why one may sometimes require others to lower the stakes of one's mistakes in a situation. In that regard, consider the four parameters that Shavell has proposed for assessing whether the state ought to regulate some activity with the aim of preventing accidents from occurring, or to allow that activity to proceed without government regulation and provide appropriate rules of tort liability in case the activity causes harm to others.[61] These are: any difference in knowledge about risky activities as between the parties and the regulatory authority; the ability of private parties to pay fully for any harm done; the probability that a private party would not face the threat of a law suit for such harm (eg because the harm will be sufficiently diluted amongst potential claimants that none will bother to seek repair), and; the magnitude of administrative costs of different policies on the parties and the community. Shavell claims that sensitivity to those parameters helps identify the most efficient policy response in a situation. However, it seems to me that those parameters may also identify particular complaints that persons left to deal with the cost of an accident might have under the value-of-choice account. Suppose that the state fails to regulate a reasonable but risky activity even though it is better placed to assess the relevant risks. The fact that this failure puts private parties in the position of having to fend for themselves may give rise to an objection *both* from the point of view of the private party who caused harm and gets to bear liability for it, and from the point of view of the harmed party. The harming party could plausibly object to having to bear responsibility on the ground that the state did not do enough to lower the stakes for that party of making a mistake. Similarly, the harmed party could object to the requirement of having to sue the harming party in order to obtain repair, both because the state's failure has made obtaining such repair contingent on the ability of the harming party to provide it, and because suing the harming party may be a very costly affair.

There are, of course, important respects in which all cost-based models and the value-of-choice account diverge. To some extent, that divergence is a direct effect of the difference between the general moral ideas that motivate each theory. The consequentialist perspective of cost-based models commits them to taking *aggregate* social costs and benefits as the proper test for the allocation of substantive burdens. By contrast, the contractualist perspective

---

[61] S Shavell, 'Liability for Harm Versus Regulation of Safety' (1984) 13 *Journal of Legal Studies* 357.

of the value-of-choice account commits it to considering costs and benefits only from the point of view of *each person* to whom they accrue. The practical difference between the two perspectives becomes clear in situations where a socially optimific principle of responsibility would impose very serious costs on particular persons. Suppose that you are blind and that the only practical way for you to process information about some complex and important financial decisions is to have that information converted into braille. The main options for converting that information are either for you to purchase a suitable converter, or for the bank to convert the information for you at its expense. Also suppose that buying a converter would, generally speaking, be a good investment for you because it would allow you to convert information without having to rely on others, but the cost of buying one is very serious for a person of your, let us say, average means. Still, that cost happens to be lower than the cost for the bank of having discrete documents converted, eg because the bank has to follow certain procurement rules and other regulatory requirements that increase its transaction costs. Whereas, on those facts, cost-based models would favour a principle that requires you to bear the cost of buying a converter, the value-of-choice account would ask whether a proposed principle could be justified to each person whom it affects, namely yourself, the bank and any affected third parties. In particular, it would ask whether each party on whom the burden of buying a converter might be placed has reason to value the opportunity to do so. In that regard, there is a difference between your position and the bank's. You may not be using braille all the time. In fact, most of the time you get by perfectly well with information conveyed orally or via audio systems. In that situation, the opportunity for you of purchasing the expensive converter just in order to convert the text of your mortgage agreement may not be something you have reason to value, as the converter is bound to remain largely unused for the rest of its life. Things are different for the bank, because many people are in your position, and some of them are bound to be its customers. The opportunity to purchase a converter may therefore be valuable to the bank. Details of that sort will affect the range of each party's options and, therefore, the value of the relevant opportunity to them.[62] The salient point for present purposes is that

---

[62] Here I glide over the issue of the possible grounds on which, under a contractualist account, people may object to principles. Scanlon believes that those grounds are basically *personal*, ie that persons may object to a principle only if the principle places a burden on them, Scanlon, above n 1 at 229: 'the justifiability of a moral principle [under contractualism] depends only on various *individuals'* reasons for objecting to that principle and alternatives to it. Derek Parfit argues that we can allow that only individuals may object to principles, and still say that the grounds on which they might do so are not restricted to personal reasons, but may also include reasons of priority of need between different persons: D Parfit, *On What Matters*, vol 2 (Oxford, Oxford University Press, 2011), ch 21 § 76.

while both cost-based models and the value-of-choice account agree that costs matter, each takes account of such costs in a different way. Cost-based models care about costs as social aggregates. The value-of-choice account cares about costs as considerations that affect the position of each person on whom those costs fall.

I draw two conclusions from this. The first is that several insights of cost-based models can be usefully accommodated within a value-of-choice account of responsibility (if you will, instead of rejecting those models, we can recruit them). In particular, those insights can enhance our imagination about alternative policies and allow us to form a more considered view of their practical implications. The second is that we can accommodate those insights without accepting the consequentialist starting point of cost-based models. We can accept that costs matter for responsibility, and still insist that they matter as grounds of individual objections to principles for the allocation of substantive burdens, rather than as aggregates.

4

Protection Against the Burden of Repair

I HAVE ARGUED that asking whether others may require one to bear the burden of repair is very much like asking whether they may require one to bear any other burden, eg to keep one's promises or to drive safely. And I have enlisted the help of Scanlon's value-of-choice account to claim that answers to such questions have two parameters. The first is whether the imposition of such burdens on a person is contingent on that person having valuable opportunities to affect how thing will go for them in the situation. The other is whether others did enough by giving that person such opportunities, or whether they ought to have done more to ensure that 'having a choice' would be likely to make things go well for that person. The value-of-choice account explains how the second parameter is related to the first. Whether a person has reason to value the opportunity to shape what happens to them by choosing appropriately depends on the quality of the 'background conditions' of that choice. It follows that the case for imposing some burden on that person will sometimes turn on showing that they could not require others to improve those background conditions, either by taking measures to make it more likely that this person will choose well (eg informing that person about the available options), or by lowering the stakes for that person of choosing poorly (eg by protecting that person against the consequences of making a poor choice).

In this and the next chapter I discuss in more detail how each of those parameters should affect the way we think about the burden of repair. For reasons to be explained, I will do things backwards and start from whether, besides giving a person the choice, others sometimes also ought to lower the stakes for that person of choosing poorly. I will refer to this as the parameter of 'protection', in order to register its affinity with certain features of the main example that animates Scanlon's defence of the value-of-choice account. In that example, you will recall, city officials are undertaking an operation to move some hazardous waste from a residential area to a remote site. Despite all precautions that have been taken, it is expected that, as the waste is being dug out, some of the hazardous material will be released into the air and cause lung damage to any persons who are in the vicinity and become exposed to it. However, it is also reliably estimated that people can protect themselves against that hazard by staying away from the excavation site. Scanlon asks us to suppose, plausibly, that the officials would not have done enough for people if they simply had warned them about the operation and gave them all the relevant information about the risk involved and how to protect themselves against it. The officials also had to put in place further, non-warning-based, protective measures (such as fencing the excavation site, wetting the material down, transporting it in sealed containers, moving it to a remote location, and so on) that would benefit not only those who, despite all reasonable efforts, did not get the word, but also those who might forget about the warnings, or fail to take them seriously. The value-of-choice account says that the two aspects of the operation are connected, because the non-warning-based protective measures affect the value for people of having a choice in the situation (recall that if the community could have ensured everyone's absolute safety through non-warning-based protective measures, giving people the choice about their safety would have been terrible policy). That is, part of the reason why those persons would value having the opportunity to protect themselves through their own choices is that the community had done enough to give them a good measure of protection against the consequences of them choosing poorly.

In the hazardous waste example, the relevant burden or responsibility that people are required to bear is the responsibility to self-protect. My aim here is to extend that idea to responsibilities that one owes to others, eg to take care, or to avoid certain dangerous forms of conduct. More specifically, I want to ask whether and when it is a condition for requiring one to bear certain substantive burdens in the course of an activity that others protect one against the burden of repair for one's mistakes in the course of that activity. I will not be concerned with what other people can do to improve one's chances of choosing well, eg to give one adequate information about available options, or to secure for one certain favourable conditions for selecting among those options. To isolate the question I am interested in, I will simply assume that one has nothing to complain about on those fronts, ie that one was well-informed and could have avoided the burden of repair by choosing appropriately. My enquiry will start from the fact that, in spite of all this, that person made an avoidable mistake.

I. WHY PROTECTION?

Sometimes we ought to protect people against the consequences of their poor choices. This claim certainly accounts well for some very plausible intuitions about the fate of the persons who suffer harm in the hazardous waste example. Let it be true that those persons could not reasonably object to the principle that allowed the city to expose them to risk of suffering harm while the removal operation went ahead. It is still arguable that the city ought to not leave those persons to bear the consequences of their mistake on their own. That is, even if the city did not owe it to those persons to refrain from creating the risk, maybe it does owe it to them to give them a degree of protection against the burden of dealing with the consequences of their avoidable mistake, eg to pay for their medical treatment.[1] We might support this claim in a number of ways. The removal operation carried a legitimate but extraordinary risk. Operations like that do not happen every day, so it was to be expected that some people's sense of danger would fail them, and that they would not perceive the true magnitude of the risk, or the seriousness of the consequences of exposure. Moreover, the present cost to those persons of paying for their own treatment may be unaffordable or crushing, especially for those who happen not to have health insurance. By contrast, having taxpayers bear that cost would not impose a great burden on any one of them. After all, if the protective measures that the city has taken were any good, the number of people exposed to the hazardous chemicals would likely be very small (if that number were projected to be large, then maybe officials should have postponed the operation, or called for the city to be evacuated).

Note two things about this claim. First, it calls for the city to protect those who suffered harm, but it does not make it any less the case that those persons had the original responsibility to self-protect, or that their failure to do so may be something for which they are blameworthy. Rather, the claim takes it as given that those persons failed to discharge that original responsibility, and then asks whether the city owes it to those persons to protect them against having to bear the substantive burden of making repair for the consequences of that failure. Secondly, some of the arguments that bear on how much the city ought to do for those persons now that they have failed to self-protect will already have featured in the discussion of how much the city ought to have done for them *in order* to be able to require them to self-protect. The claim I have in mind counts the extraordinary character of the operation and the seriousness of the danger to people's health as significant *both* for the assessment of what protective measures the city ought to put in place so that people may remain safe *and* for the assessment of whether the city ought to protect persons who were harmed from bearing the cost of their own poor choices.

This may look like double counting. If the city gave all due consideration to the extraordinary character of the risk, undertook all reasonable steps to warn

---

[1] *cf* S Olsaretti, 'Scanlon on Responsibility and the Value of Choice' (2013) 10 *Journal of Moral Philosophy* 465, 474; A Williams, 'Liberty, Liability, and Contractualism' in N Holtug and K Lippert-Rasmussen, *Egalitarianism: New Essays on the Nature and Value of Equality* (Oxford, Clarendon Press, 2007) 252.

people about it, and put in place additional non-warning-based measures to protect people against foolishly or unwittingly harming themselves by straying into the excavation site, should we not say that those considerations *have already been properly accounted for*, and that, in failing to do their own part to keep themselves safe, those persons 'brought it upon themselves' and therefore cannot require others to protect them against the consequences of their poor choice? The claim I am developing says that this is not necessarily so. Perhaps what the city ought to do to put people in a good position to avoid harm, and what it ought to do to protect them against the consequences of their poor choices in that regard are distinct questions, so the fact that some consideration bears on the former question does not block it from bearing on the latter too.[2] This line of thought still leaves open the possibility that the city owes nothing to those who were harmed because of their poor choices. It simply says that this debate is not settled by the fact those persons had no complaint against the city's decision to put an aspect of their protection in their own hands. Needless to say, some consideration would also need to be given to whether the harm involved is serious whether protecting those persons would cost the city too much, whether those persons could deal with the cost on their own, and so on. Depending on the facts, each of those concerns could counsel in favour of or against protection. But none of them would be blocked from bearing on the question just because the persons harmed had no complaint against being required to bear the original responsibility of self-protecting.

You may recognise this as the gist of the 'direct account' that I outlined in Chapter 1.[3] The direct account says that the fact that a person is a wrongdoer, in the sense of having failed to discharge an original burden owed to another person, does not decide whether that person ought to bear the burden of repair, and does not necessarily block or exclude certain considerations from bearing on that question. Here I will try to reinforce that claim by showing that sometimes others may owe it to a person to give them a measure of protection against the burden of repair for their mistakes in the course of

---

[2] This seems to be the tenor of Scanlon's position too. In reply to Olsaretti's point that persons exposed to harm may nevertheless be able to require others to compensate them, Scanlon notes that this is a separate question on which he took no stand, TM Scanlon, 'Reply to Serena Olsaretti' (2013) 10 *Journal of Moral Philosophy* 484, 487. It seems to me that Scanlon's overall account of the significance of choice gives him a good ground for answering that question in the affirmative. In fact, the following passage in *What We Owe To Each Other* (Cambridge, Mass, Belknap Press of Harvard University Press, 1998) at 265 supports this natural reading of that account: 'A person who recklessly chooses to enter the affected area does not lay down a right to further protection against contamination. She has, by assumption, already received all the prior protection she is entitled to, and she does not lay down her right to rescue or treatment unless this has been prescribed and the policy including this prescription is justified.'

[3] See ch 1(II).

some activity precisely *in order* to be able to require that person to bear the original burdens that the activity involves.

To make the case for this claim, I will need to do move beyond examples like the hazardous waste removal case. After all, the original burden that people had to bear in that case was a burden they owed to themselves. By contrast, private law is concerned with cases in which people ought to make repair for their failure to discharge some original burden they owed to others. There are several possible reasons for thinking that the difference might matter when we think about protecting people from the consequences of such failures, ie that we ought to do less for people whose failures cause harm to others than for people whose failures cause harm to themselves alone. I think that this is right in some situations, but not in others, and I will try to fashion a moral principle out of the value-of-choice account to explain the difference.

I go about this in five steps. Section II explains why it matters to talk about protection before we think about the significance of avoidability for responsibility. To that end, I distinguish protection that 'bails people out' of their responsibilities from protection that constitutes a condition for imposing such responsibilities on them in the first place. Section III lays out some basic aspects of how protection might function as a condition for imposing responsibilities on a person, and section IV focuses on three different contexts in which, in my view, protection has that function: contributory negligence, liability for workplace accidents, and certain activity- and hazard-specific schemes of compulsory insurance. Section V applies the value-of-choice account I have been developing, and puts forward a 'protection principle', which says that whether the supply of protection 'bails people out' of the responsibility to make repair for their mistakes in some activity, or counts as a condition for requiring them to bear the original burdens that the activity involves (eg to exercise care, or to avoid causing certain outcomes) depends on the relationship between such protection and the value for those persons of the opportunity to engage in the relevant activity. Section VI illustrates how the protection principle cuts against certain accounts of contributory negligence.

II. PROTECTION AS A 'BAIL OUT' AND AS A CONDITION OF RESPONSIBILITY

The argument I will develop says that sometimes one may require others to protect one against the burden of repair for mistakes that one could have avoided. In this section I want to explain why I think that we should address the question of protection before we address that of avoidability. Going about things in this way looks odd. It seems more natural to start from a discussion of the opportunities that a person had to avoid incurring the burden of repair in relation to some activity, and then move on to what, if anything, others might be required to do to protect that person against having to bear that burden.

I believe that thinking about protection before we think about avoidability helps us see the limitations of a very intuitive idea about the character of protection. That idea says that when others are required to offer a person protection against the burden of repair, they are 'lifting' or 'shifting' responsibilities from where they belong originally. Talk of protecting people against the consequences of their mistakes often carries that implication, sometimes justifiably. It suggests that the responsibility to deal with those consequences belongs to those persons, but that sometimes we should 'bail them out' of it. This sounds like a plausible description of the position of at least some of the persons harmed in the hazardous waste example. The person who knows all about the danger but chooses to go and check out what is going on in the removal site is doing something stupid, perhaps even in the knowledge that it is stupid. It certainly makes sense to say that, in paying for their medical treatment, the city is 'bailing that person out'.

Viewing protection as a sort of 'bail out' fits the way many discussions of protection in private law have tended to proceed. Protections against the burden of repair are typically discussed in the context of questions about what a community ought to do for victims of accidents, or about how the community could minimise the social cost of such accidents and other harm-causing events. Both of those enquiries are clearly sensible. Often the chief reason why others hold back from demanding that one make repair for one's mistakes, or why they feed the cost of repair into a given insurance structure, is to protect the victim of those mistakes, by ensuring that the victim obtains repair even if the person who made the mistake is not in a position to provide it. It also makes sense that sometimes the reason why others ought to offer that person a certain degree of protection against the burden of repair is that this policy is socially optimific. Under both arguments, any protection given to those who cause avoidable accidents is a side-effect of the pursuit of some other aim, be that the compensation of the victim or the optimal use of social resources. If such protection is due to those persons, it is not due to them *for their own sake* but for the sake of others. Just like big banks and other financial institutions in the post-2008 financial crisis, they are being 'bailed out' because to leave them unprotected would be to fail other persons who the community ought to protect (eg depositors) or other aims that the community ought to secure (eg financial stability).

Nevertheless, it seems to me that sometimes protecting people against the consequences of their mistakes is not a 'bail out', or a 'lifting' or 'shifting' of responsibilities from where they lie originally. We have already come across contexts that show this. In the hazardous waste removal example, when city officials put in place reasonable non-warning-based protective measures, they were not 'lifting' or 'shifting' responsibility for people's protection from where it originally fell. They were *making it the case* that people had reason to value the opportunity to self-protect and, therefore, that they could not object to a principle that required them to bear the corresponding burden.[4] If this is true of the imposition of the burden of self-protecting, perhaps it might be true of the imposition of the burden of repair too. Maybe giving a person affordable insurance options against the burden of repair, or allocating that burden to another person altogether, is part of what makes the opportunity to engage in a given activity something that this person has reason to value. And, as in the hazardous waste example, that may be true *even when* that person could have avoided mistakes in that activity by choosing appropriately (eg by being careful, or by avoiding certain activities in the first place). In those situations, the supply of protection is not a 'bail out', or an occasion of 'lifting' or 'shifting' the relevant responsibility from that person onto someone else. It is a condition for requiring that person to do certain other things, or to undertake certain other burdens in the course of an activity. To put it differently, it involves saying to that person: 'part of the reason why you ought to bear this original burden is that we got you covered in case you fail to discharge it'. If something like this makes sense, talking about protection before we talk about avoidability is important because seeing the provision of protection in those situations as a 'bail out' would not just misunderstand the significance of protection. It would also overstate the significance of avoidability.

Maybe this is small beer in practice. If we agree on the nature and the degree of protection that others ought to provide to a person against the burden of repair for mistakes that this person could have avoided, perhaps it does not matter much whether we see the provision of such protection as 'bailing that person out' of certain responsibilities, or as a further condition for imposing those responsibilities on that person in the first place. I think that this impression is mistaken. The way we cast the relationship between protection and responsibility makes a practical difference in three respects.

The first is presentational. People do not tend to think kindly of those who receive a 'bail out', even when it is clear that such a 'bail out' is necessary in the bigger scheme of things. It therefore matters whether protecting persons against the consequences of their poor choices in some activity is indeed a matter of 'bailing that person out' of their responsibilities, or a condition for imposing such responsibilities on them. The point is not just that 'bailing out' someone looks more demanding, or seems to require a greater sacrifice on the part of other people, than refraining from imposing some burden on that person in the first place. It is also that claims about 'what

---

[4] See also ch 3(IV)(A).

people are responsible for' have significant moral and political resonance. Such claims can be, and have been, used to vent fury towards bankers and speculators who gambled with other people's money before 2008 and were nevertheless 'bailed out' by taxpayers in order to save the economy. But the sword is double-edged. Similar claims can be, and often are, made in an effort to dismantle protections for some of the weakest of our fellow citizens. In that connection, consider the contrast between describing support payments to persons of lower income as 'benefits' or 'welfare' (as in the UK) or as 'social security' (as in the US). The degree of support those persons are entitled to should not hinge on the name we give to the policies that supply it, but our choices on that front can affect the way in which we frame the case for or against such policies.[5] Support for higher 'benefits' sounds a lot like support for subsidising people's 'lifestyle choices'.[6] Support for 'social security' sounds like support for providing people with a degree of assurance that their well-being will not fall below a certain basic threshold. It follows that cuts to the level of state support for the poor may become easier to defend if such cuts are described as restrictions of benefits rather than as restrictions in the provision of social security.

It seems to me that something similar is the case in respect of the burden of repair. Even if we agree that sometimes people ought to be protected against the burden of repair for their mistakes, the moral and political case for the provision of such protection may become more or less difficult to make depending on whether we count the supply of such protection as 'bailing people out' of their responsibilities, or as a condition for imposing on them the original burdens and responsibilities that the relevant activity involves. As an illustration, consider the way Rob Merkin and Jenny Steele make the case as to why we should incorporate insurance and its structures into our conceptions of private law:

> Market arrangements and private ordering have their place in the determination of tort duties, as of contract duties. So too do other ideas—including protection of the vulnerable, and deterrence; and the existence of social and political choices as to the ordering of risks. Welfarism and economic rationalism coexist as potential objectives

---

[5] On 'framing effects' see generally A Tversky and D Kahneman, 'Rational Choice and the Framing of Decisions' (1986) 59 *Journal of Business* 251. For a discussion of the effect of framing on our conception of what people are morally responsible for, see S Hurley, 'The Public Ecology of Responsibility' in C Knight and Z Stemplowska, *Responsibility and Distributive Justice* (Oxford, Oxford University Press, 2011) 187, 195ff. I return to this point in ch 6.

[6] On the Blair government's attempt to shift emphasis from 'welfare' to 'social investment', see A Giddens, *The Third Way: The Renewal of Social Democracy* (Oxford, Polity Press, 1998) 117ff; A Dobrowolsky and R Lister, 'Social investment: the discourse and the dimensions of change' in M Powell, *Modernising the Welfare State: the Blair Legacy* (Bristol, Policy Press, 2008) 125. See also R Lister, 'Benefit cuts: how the language of welfare poisoned our social security', *Guardian*, 1 April 2013.

in the law. These ideas do not replace moral argument; but equally, there is little basis on which to conclude that fault or responsibility are themselves sufficiently powerful ideas to displace concerns about these risk structures.[7]

Some (myself included, subject to what follows) will find this claim appealing, some not. But it seems to me that Merkin and Steele put themselves on the back foot by conceding that arguments from 'morality' and 'responsibility' speak, even *pro tanto*, against their position. This concession matters because it suggests that the 'moral default' is that responsibility lies with the person who has failed to discharge some original burdens. It therefore agrees by implication that the debate should be about whether and when such responsibility might nevertheless be 'lifted' or 'shifted' from that person and onto someone else, eg to increase social welfare, protect the vulnerable, achieve efficiency, and so on. The view that sometimes the provision of protection against the burden of repair is a condition for requiring people to bear those original burdens in the first place makes no such concession. It frames the debate as one about what we cannot justifiably do to people whose avoidable mistakes have caused harm to others, rather than about when we might be required to 'bail them out'.

A second implication concerns the delimitation of the domain of private law. The view that sees protection as a 'bail out' will be naturally friendly towards a division of labour between legal principles and institutions that ascribe responsibility for the burden of repair, and those principles and institutions that dispense (or require the provision of) various forms of protection against that burden. In turn, that division of labour supplies a handy criterion for distinguishing the domain of private law, which is in the business of telling us who ought to make repair to whom, from those of regulation, insurance, or insolvency, which are in the business of protecting people against the incidence of harms and, should such harms occur, against the risk of suffering financial collapse under the burden of liability.[8] The view that sees protection from the burden of repair as a potential condition for requiring people to bear the original burdens that an activity involves is less happy with this delimitation, because it sees some of the regulatory protections given, say, to workers, consumers or insurance policy holders as part of the case for requiring

---

[7] R Merkin and J Steele, *Insurance and the Law of Obligations* (Oxford, Oxford University Press, 2013) 249.

[8] *cf Lister v Romford Lice and Cold Storage Ltd* [1959] AC 604 at 627 per Viscount Simonds: 'As a general proposition it has not, I think, been questioned for nearly 200 years that in determining the rights *inter se* of A and B the fact that one or the other of them is insured is to be disregarded'; J Stapleton, 'Tort, Insurance and Ideology' (1995) 58 MLR 820: 'neither actual insurance nor insurability are or should be relevant to the reach and shape of tort liability'; R Stevens, *Torts and Rights* (Oxford, Oxford University Press, 2007) 109: 'Both the rights we have and their scope need to be determined without reference to insurance concerns'.

those classes of persons to bear certain original burdens in the course of their respective transactions with employees, businesses and insurers. Those regulatory protections can sometimes have a clear effect on the value for workers, consumers and insurance policy holders of the opportunity to engage in the relevant transactions or activities. For example, looser health and safety legislation may sometimes raise the stakes for workers of making a mistake in the workplace.[9] By putting more of workers' safety in their own hands, it may make it less likely that those workers will remain safe. Such legislation may accordingly diminish the value for workers of the opportunity to self-protect. The same goes for legislation that restricts a worker's ability to sue an employer for breaches of health and safety laws that cause harm to employees.[10] By putting more of the risk of bearing the burden of repair in employees' own hands, such legislation makes it less likely that those employees will be able to avoid the severe financial stress that having to deal with personal injury entails. It follows that changes to the relevant regulatory protections may require changes to the distribution of the original burdens that result from those transactions and situations.[11]

A third respect in which it matters whether we see protection as a 'bail out' or as a possible condition for requiring the protected person to bear the original burdens of an activity concerns institutional competence and design. That respect can be easy to miss when the question of who ought to protect whom and the question of who ought to make repair to whom are more or less symmetrical. Situations of mitigation and contributory negligence are the clearest examples of such symmetry. The defendant ought to make repair to the claimant, who in turn ought to provide the defendant with a measure of protection against the burden of repair. It therefore seems obvious and natural for the institution that decides questions about original burdens to decide the question of protection too. That symmetry will not obtain in other situations. To return to an earlier example, suppose that the state fails to provide drivers with affordable options for obtaining appropriate third-party

---

[9] On this point, see G Gray, 'The Responsibilization Strategy of Health and Safety: Neoliberalism and the Re-configuration of Individual Responsibility for Risk' (2009) 49 *British Journal of Criminology* 326, which looks at the effect on the incidence of industrial accidents of 'ticketing' individual workers for health and safety violations. Gray concludes (at 337) that 'ticketing' programmes fail to acknowledge that 'health and safety violations by workers (and frontline supervisors) are often the result of indirect pressure stemming from the economic climate of the work environment and the systems of production implemented by firms'.

[10] See, eg, s 69 of the UK Enterprise and Regulatory Reform Act 2013, which abolishes actions for breach of statutory duty for violations of health and safety regulations.

[11] For a discussion of the effect of the broader availability of insurance in restricting the range of duties of care in US tort law, see K Abraham, *The Liability Century: Insurance and Tort Law Reform from the Progressive Era to 9/11* (Cambridge, Mass, Harvard University Press, 2008), ch 6.

insurance coverage, and that this matters when we discuss whether drivers ought to bear the full burden of repair for accidents caused by their careless driving. Here the party who ought to supply protection and the party who is entitled to repair are not the same. This matters not just because the situation now involves three parties rather than two, but also because the justification of protection through a compulsory insurance scheme will generally require consideration of parameters broader than those that justified the imposition on drivers of the original burden to drive safely. In the present example, that broader range of considerations would include the structure of the insurance market, the nature of the pooled risks, the economies of scale to be achieved, the appropriate distribution of insurance costs between those insured, the ability of alternatives to compulsory insurance to deliver affordable premiums, and so on. This opens up the possibility that institutions that are well placed to decide questions of protection in symmetrical situations (most notably, law courts) may not be equally well placed to decide them in asymmetrical ones. Maybe the proper way to decide those questions in the latter type of situation is to assign them to an agency that has access to the relevant economic and actuarial expertise, and features consultation procedures that allow all affected parties to be heard (eg in the model of the New Zealand Accident Compensation Corporation). More generally, the view that sees protection as a possible condition for requiring a person to bear some original burdens in the course of an activity is committed to keeping an open mind about the design of the institution that decides questions about who ought to bear the burden of repair, as that design will depend, in part, on who ought to provide such protection to whom, and in what form.[12] By contrast, the view that sees protection as a 'bail out' can afford to take a more categorical position on that front, because it is not troubled by the asymmetries I have noted. It can simply say that questions of responsibility for the burden of repair should be decided by courts, and remain agnostic as to which government agency might be best placed to decide questions of protection.

III. PROTECTION AS A CONDITION OF RESPONSIBILITY: A PREVIEW

When might one require others to protect one against the burden of repair for one's avoidable mistakes in some activity, as a condition for requiring one

---

[12] Institutional alternatives to traditional tort litigation have been explored for different ends in economic literature, see, eg, S Rose-Ackerman, 'Tort Law in the Regulatory State' in P Schuck (ed), *Tort Law and the Public Interest: Competition, Innovation and Consumer Welfare* (New York, WW Norton & Co, 1991) 80. For the effect of mass torts on the development of the traditional tort litigation, and the 'shift from tort law to administration', see R Nagareda, *Mass Torts in a World of Settlement* (Chicago, University of Chicago Press, 2007) viii—ix, and Part II.

to bear the original burdens that an activity involves (eg the burden of taking care, or of avoiding some activity)? In a shameless effort to make the case for the provision of protection as a condition of responsibility more direct, I will cast you, the reader, in the position of that person.

I start from the fact that sometimes others are in a position to prevent your avoidable mistakes from leading to harmful outcomes.[13] For example, others may be able to take precautions so that your failure to take due care or to keep your end of a bargain does not cause harm to them or to third parties, or so that the extent of the harm is contained or otherwise mitigated. Sometimes others may also be in a position to protect you against having to meet the cost of repairing harms that result from your failures to discharge those burdens. For example, they may be able to feed the cost of repair into an insurance structure that you lack easy access to, so that you avoid having to pay for those costs yourself, and every end-payer bears a very small part of the total burden.

The fact that others can do these things for you does not mean that they owe it to you to do them. Maybe others ought to protect you against the burden of repair in those ways only when they have voluntarily undertaken to do so. This view is consistent with the idea that others ought not to make it *harder* for you to avoid the burden of repair by meddling with the 'background conditions' of your choice in a situation, eg by limiting the range of options that would otherwise be available to you for that purpose, or by making tougher the conditions under which you would otherwise be choosing among those options. This is a familiar idea from private law doctrines like duress, undue influence, misrepresentation, and the principle that people do not have a general legal duty to assist others but only a duty not to make it more difficult for them to be rescued (eg by botching a rescue attempt).[14] But all this is about others refraining from making life harder for you, not about owing it to you to make things easier. To be required to make things easier for you by protecting you against the burden of repair, the view in question goes, others must be under some special duty to do so, having undertaken such a duty voluntarily being the most obvious way. Note, incidentally, that this view also gives a natural explanation of why, in the hazardous waste example, city officials were required to warn people and to take further protective measures while removing the material. Officials had a duty to do all this precisely because of their status as

---

[13] I am not presently concerned with whether some of those outcomes may be properly described as the 'consequences' of your negligence or as its 'results' (ie the constituent elements of your being negligent). For a discussion of that distinction see J Gardner, 'Obligations and Outcomes in the Law of Torts' in P Cane and J Gardner, *Relating to Responsibility: Essays for Tony Honoré* (Oxford, Hart Publishing, 2001) 130–1.

[14] *cf Horsley v MacLaren ('The Ogopogo')* [1972] SCR 441 *per* Richie J.

officials, ie because their institutional position came with certain special duties towards citizens. The local private waste removal enterprise might have been equally well placed to transport the hazardous waste safely, but that would not have been enough of a ground for others to require that enterprise to undertake the removal, unless and until it had agreed to do so.

As advertised, I will argue that we should not take this view as expressing a general truth. Under conditions to be discussed, giving you a measure of protection against the burden of repair in relation to some activity is sometimes part of the reason why others may require you to bear the original burdens involved in that activity. That is because, absent that protection, the opportunity to engage in that activity will not be something that you have reason to value.

The broad idea that others may have to protect you against the burden of repair is familiar to private lawyers and theorists. It is certainly an aspect of discussions of contributory negligence in both tort and contract and of mitigation in contract. Protection also features in discussions about the justification of vicarious liability and various compulsory insurance schemes, from third-party insurance for motorists to general accident insurance models like that of New Zealand. However, each question seems to raise different concerns. For example, in contributory negligence our concern seems to be whether a wrongdoer may require the victim to share in the burden of repair. In relation to vicarious liability and various compulsory insurance schemes, we debate whether it is right or efficient that employers and consumers bear the burden of compensating the victims of careless employees, or whether it is right or efficient that diligent, safety-conscious drivers have to bear burdens for the benefit of more accident-prone ones, and so on.

There are other reasons to think that the concerns underlying each of those contexts are distinct. One is that there are many different things that other people may conceivably do to provide you with protection against the burden of repair for your mistakes. They might bear the whole burden of repair themselves; share the burden with you under some appropriate standard of apportionment; give you access to an insurance structure that covers you against that burden under reasonably favourable terms; grant you some form of debt relief in case you lack the resources to meet the cost of repair and so on. Another is that the identity of the 'others' who may have to protect you from the burden of repair will often differ depending on the sort of protection we have in mind. Sometimes the 'others' in question will be other persons involved in the accident, eg your victim, your co-defendants, or perhaps some more distal parties too, eg your employer. Sometimes, especially in relation to insurance schemes, they will be persons who can feed the cost of the accident into the relevant insurance structure, as well as any persons whose insurance policy is affected by the addition of the accident you have caused into the risk pool.[15] The task of justifying the imposition of those burdens on others will therefore need to be sensitive both to the nature of the burdens in question, and to the position of each person that those burdens might fall on. Maybe the contexts will display too much variation to be adequately captured under a single moral principle.

I will try not to lose focus on this complexity, though I will address only how much others have to do to make it the case that you have reason to value the opportunity to engage in a particular activity. I will not discuss situations in which the protection that others would provide you would help you in a more general way, eg prevent you from suffering financial collapse. This leaves out debt relief and various public and private protections for insolvent persons, inasmuch as these regimes are meant to protect those persons on account of their weak overall financial position, rather than on account of the fact that their mistakes in an activity have caused outcomes that require repair. Accordingly, I will be interested in the fact that the burden of repair may sometimes be very heavy only to the extent that this affects any protection that you may require of others in relation to that burden.

I will also leave aside situations where—rightly or wrongly—private law says that no repair is due at all, eg when the proper construction of a contract says that you did not assume responsibility over some particular consequences of your default,[16] or when your carelessness has caused a claimant purely economic loss, and there is no special relationship or other consideration that would entitle the claimant to repair for that loss.[17] It may be intuitive to describe the relevant rules as protecting you from the outcome of your mistakes, but that is true in the sense that those rules simply deny the claimant a right of repair. Instead, I want to focus on situations where it is clear that you owed certain original burdens, the failure to discharge which entitles the victim to obtain repair for the resulting harm, and ask whether you may still require others to make repair in your stead, as a condition for imposing the relevant original burdens on you. To keep things simple, I will use examples of personal injury and property harm in which a duty of care and a right of repair will be obviously present.

---

[15] For a description of the most important compulsory insurance schemes in the UK, see R Merkin and S Dziobon, 'Tort Law and Compulsory Insurance' in TT Arvind and J Steele (eds), *Tort Law and the Legislature: Common Law, Statute and the Dynamics of Legal Change* (Oxford, Hart Publishing, 2013) 303. The authors report (at 325) that about 90% of personal injury claims are made in the context of compulsory insurance schemes related to workplace and motoring accidents.

[16] cf *Transfield Shipping Inc v Mercator Shipping Inc ('The Achilleas')* [2008] 4 All ER 159 *per* Lord Hoffmann at [21]–[26].

[17] cf *Murphy v Brentwood District Council* [1991] 1 AC 398 at 408–10 *per* Lord Keith.

With those qualifications in place, I will suggest that, although they seem different, many contexts in which the law requires others to protect you against the burden of repair for your avoidable mistakes are morally similar. In particular, I will claim that contributory negligence, employers' liability and some compulsory insurance schemes are all instances in which you may require others to offer you some protection against the burden of repair as a condition for others to require you to bear the original burdens that the activity involves, eg to exercise a certain level of care or skill. And I will propose a 'protection principle' to capture the general features of the contexts in which that claim holds true. In line with the value-of-choice account, the protection principle says that the 'moment of responsibility' for both you and others is the moment when you are presented with the opportunity to engage in the relevant activity. If that opportunity was something you had reason to value at that point, mainly in the sense that having that opportunity made it more likely that things would go well for you, you may not require others to protect you against the burden of repair for your mistakes, no matter how well-placed they might be for that purpose. But if the value of that opportunity for you was contingent on you having some protection against the burden of repair for your mistakes, and others have not provided you with such protection, you may disclaim responsibility for some or all of that burden and require others to pick up the slack. The specification of what others have to do for you will, of course, be context-sensitive but, if the protection principle is correct, we should expect the justification in each of those contexts to proceed on the same broad terms.

The claim that sometimes you may require others to protect you against some burden even if they have not agreed to do so is not particularly novel. We teach it to first-year law students in the form of propositions about the protection one person owes to another, eg when the former has 'assumed or undertaken responsibility' or stands in a 'special relationship to' the latter.[18] The protection principle extends that idea to claim that sometimes assuming responsibility to make repair for another person's mistakes is part of the case for requiring that person to take on certain other substantive responsibilities in the first place.

IV. WORKING EXAMPLES AND VARIATIONS

Consider some situations in which you may require others to give you some protection against the burden of repair for your avoidable mistakes. In these

---

[18] *cf Hedley Byrne & Co Ltd v Heller & Partners Ltd* [1964] AC 465 *per* Lord Reid at 478–9 and Lord Devlin at 508–9 (emphasising the need for a special relationship); Lord Morris at 502–3 (emphasising the undertaking of a task that requires special skill).

examples, others owe you such protection even though they have not agreed or otherwise voluntarily undertaken to provide it. However, the form of that protection differs from one example to another, both in terms of who ought to provide it, and in terms of how its supply improves your position.

A. Three Examples

Garden: You have been careless in leaving a hole in your garden uncovered and unmarked, and this poses a risk to me as your visitor. I am in a position to take some obvious and easy measures to protect myself from falling into the hole, namely to watch my step a little. I fail to take those measures, I fall in the hole, and suffer harm. The fact that I failed to take easily available measures to self-protect matters in the distribution of the burden of repair for my injury, in the sense that you may now require me to pay part of my own medical expenses. That is a textbook application of the law on contributory negligence.[19]

Employment: You have been careless in the course of your employment for me and your carelessness has resulted in an injury to a fellow employee. I can implement a system of work that reduces the incidence of such accidents and take out insurance in case they occur, and spread the cost of both to my consumer base through adjustments in the price of the goods or services that I produce. By contrast, you can only take out similar insurance at a cost that is prohibitive to a person of your means and situation, and you have no way of spreading that cost to those who consume the goods or services that your work is producing. The fact that I am better placed than you to bear the burden of repair for the injury you caused seems central to the justification of statutory regimes of compulsory insurance for industrial accidents and, under some accounts, of the common law doctrine of vicarious liability too.

Car insurance: You are a driver and you use your car every day to drop the kids to school, commute to work, do your shopping and so on. Your means are not anywhere near enough to cover the cost in case you make a driving mistake and cause an accident, but the car insurance premiums are rather high. Our institutions can make car insurance affordable for you by requiring all drivers to take out a policy, thereby expanding the risk pool and lowering the insurance costs for each individual driver. The fact that our institutions can implement a scheme that has the effect of shielding drivers against unlimited

---

[19] The concept is referred to as 'comparative negligence' in US law, which uses 'contributory negligence' or 'pure contributory negligence' in situations where the victim's carelessness constitutes a complete defence against a claim. US jurisdictions have tended to retreat from the latter rule in favour of the former, *cf* American Law Institute, *Restatement (Third) of Torts (2000)— Apportionment of Liability* (St Paul, American Law Institute Publishers, 2000), Foreword.

personal liability on payment of an affordable premium seems relevant to the justification for mandating all drivers, no matter how skilled, careful or error-prone, to take out car insurance.

In these three examples, you have made a mistake (or, as in the last example, you are dreading the prospect of making one) but it seems plausible that you may require others to protect you, in whole or in part, against the burden of repair for it, despite the fact that they have not agreed to do so. Sometimes the reason has to do with the fact that it would have been very easy for others to take precautions that would have prevented your mistake from causing harm. This is clearly the case in the contributory negligence example, but it may be true of the employment example too, at least insofar as the case for requiring the employer to take out insurance against workplace accidents relies on the fact that the employer is well-placed to implement safeguards that would reduce the incidence of such accidents. Sometimes the key consideration seems to be that others can utilise or put in place a certain insurance structure that is not otherwise accessible to you at all, or is accessible under unfavourable conditions. This is clearly true in both the employment and the car insurance examples, though each example involves a rather different insurance structure (eg the structure for workplace accidents may allow the employer a right to an indemnity, thereby passing some part of the burden of repair back to you).

Moreover, note that what others ought to do for you differs not only between those examples, but also between different persons in each example. In the garden example, I, your visitor who failed to self-protect, ought to bear a share of the total cost of my injury, under some appropriate standard of apportionment. In the employment and car insurance examples, the burden varies depending on who we have in mind. The employer bears a cluster of different burdens: the burden of finding and paying for an insurance policy for workplace accidents; the burden of having to pass on the cost of that insurance to consumers, or to make cost-equivalent adjustments in the process of production (eg cut salaries), or else have the enterprise itself bear the cost; and the further risk that changing the costs of production may make the enterprise less competitive, either by making the product less attractive to consumers or by making the enterprise less attractive to qualified employees, and so on.[20] In turn, the fact that the employer can and typically will pass on the cost of insurance for workplace negligence to consumers or other persons involved in the production process means that these classes of persons too will bear a burden. For consumers, that burden will be the marginal increase in the cost

---

[20] Simon Deakin has pointed out that, once they take out an insurance policy for workplace accidents, employers are also subject to insurers monitoring their compliance with the applicable standards of care, see S Deakin, 'Tort Law and Workmen's Compensation Legislation: Complementary or Competing Models?' in Arvind and Steele, above n 15, 253 at 254.

of the goods or services produced by the employer that reflects the proportion of the insurance cost that the employer chooses to pass onto consumers; for employees, it will be the marginal equivalent in the form of salary reduction (I discuss the position of each group of persons in more detail in Chapter 7). Finally, in the car insurance example, other drivers are called to bear the burden of having to find and purchase car insurance and of incurring the cost of the premium, while the state bears the burden of setting up and monitoring the implementation of the mandate as well as enforcing sanctions for its violations. Given that variety of possible burdens and burden-bearers, the determination of when you may require others to protect you from the burden of repair must take account of the position of each of those classes of persons.

Note, finally, that the protection that you are receiving in each example improves your position in a different way. In the garden example, the principle of contributory negligence saves you from having to make repair for the whole of the harm that your carelessness has caused; some part will fall on me, the rest will fall on you. In the employment example, the principles of vicarious liability save you from the burden of repair completely, by allocating it to your employer and—through them—to consumers, though they leave you exposed to the possibility of having to provide your employer (or their insurer) with an indemnity. In the insurance example, the relevant compulsory insurance scheme does not allocate the burden of repair to someone else, but makes it more affordable for you to obtain adequate insurance coverage against it. We should therefore expect a principle that justifies why others ought to do these things for you to offer some explanation of the variety in the forms of protection.

B. Easy Variations

There is similar variety in situations where it seems intuitively clear that you would *not* be able to require others to protect you against the burdens of repair for your mistake. In the garden example, suppose that someone walks down the street, sees me moving unwittingly towards the hole in your garden, and estimates that I am likely to get hurt if I fall in. However, the passer-by chooses to refrain from alerting either of us, and I go down. It is settled English law that you may not require the passer-by to share in the burden of repair for my injury, as that person has had nothing to do with the creation of the danger in your garden, and has not undertaken to protect either of us against it. In the employment example, suppose that you work in my restaurant kitchen, take a knife, walk three blocks and stab the guy who stole your watch. Again, it is trite law that you may not require me to feed the cost of repair for that tort into the insurance structure for workplace accidents. The reason here is that you are committing a tort that has very little relation to your employment, or the kind of accidents that the relevant insurance structure is meant to cover. In the car insurance example, suppose that you have decided to paint your car bright yellow and discover that the colour attracts birds that go on to deposit generous amounts of their droppings on your car. Were that particular danger covered under a mandatory insurance scheme, the financial burden of protecting your car against fouling would be much lower for you, but there is no doubt that you may not require other drivers to accept this cost into the risk pool. The reason is that the danger you are running is not a danger related to driving, so the state and other drivers will not, in the main, have sufficient reason to offer you protection against it.

C. Tricky Variations

Finally, consider some variations in which intuitions may be less decisive and the help of some moral principle would be more clearly welcome. In the garden example, suppose that you know both that the hole poses a risk to me and that I am likely to miss it even if you warn me about it in advance, eg say that you know very well from past experience that while for most purposes I function as a normal adult, I find your garden so beautiful and entrancing that I cannot help letting out the carefree and danger-blind three-year-old in me. Here are some aspects of the variation that we might consider significant. The warning you have provided to me as your visitor improves my ability to avoid injury, in that it conveys to me some information that I would otherwise not have about the dangers lurking in your garden. The effect your garden has on my behaviour seems to make me less-well placed to avoid those dangers, ie it makes it more difficult for me to protect myself by heeding your warning and watching my step in the way I would in other situations. The further fact that I am an adult suggests that my becoming infantilised when I find myself in your garden may be more of an akratic reaction than an incapacity (ie it suggests that I find myself unable to take measures I know I should take, rather than that I am oblivious as to the lurking dangers). Still, the fact that you know that your garden has an infantilising effect on me suggests that, by your own lights, the protective value of your warning will be limited in my case. A principled account of how far you may require me to protect you against the burden of repair should explain how those facts bear on the apportionment of that burden, or show why those facts do not have the significance I have intuitively claimed for them.

In the employment example, suppose that you injured another restaurant worker by punching them in the face, following a heated exchange between the two of you earlier in the day. The intentional character of your act cries out as being significant in determining what you may (or, in this case, may not) require of me, as your employer, by way of sharing or shifting the burden of repair for the injury you have caused. However, the precise weight that we should attach to that fact may need to be assessed in the light of further possible aspects of the situation. Perhaps the battery you committed was the result of the pressures of work, or the bad blood between you and your fellow employee from the earlier argument had been apparent to everyone in the restaurant, and I could have re-assigned either of you to a different post, or taken other measures that would have allowed the tension to dissipate. Again, an account of how such facts affect the distribution of the burden of repair between me and you would need to justify their significance, or explain why they lack it. Perhaps employees should not be able to invoke the pressures of work as a ground for requiring their employers to feed the cost of repair for their intentional torts into the insurance structure that employers have access to. Or perhaps the fact that I, as your employer, was well-placed to take measures to prevent the battery from occurring justifies you requiring me to bear part of the burden of repair, but still leaves some part of that burden with you (either directly or by requiring me to feed all of that cost into the insurance structure and allowing me to claim an indemnity from you).

In the insurance example, suppose that we are not concerned with cars but with homes and let it be the case that you lack the resources to cover the cost of losing your home to a mistake you or a member of your family might make, eg carelessly start a fire; that the market rates for home insurance are too high for a person of your means; and that the state could put in place a mandatory home insurance scheme that would make home insurance affordable for you in the same way that mandatory car insurance does for drivers. Here it seems to me that we might attribute significance to whether the insurance structure that might help you here would be one of first- or of third-party insurance (ie whether it would protect you against the cost of self-harm or harm caused by others); to the magnitude of the risk of family homes being destroyed by fire; to whether, absent further subsidy, the post-mandate insurance premium would be affordable for people in a worse financial position than yourself, and so on. Each of those aspects, or any others that an appropriate moral principle would single out as significant, would affect whether our institutions ought to put in place a compulsory home insurance mandate, and whether other people ought to accept the relevant harms into the risk pool.

V. THE PROTECTION PRINCIPLE

I think that we can account for the degree of protection that you may require others to provide you with in the variations of the garden, employment and insurance examples under the following principle:

Protection principle: Others ought to protect you against the burden of repair for the outcomes of your mistakes insofar as they have reason to want you to bear certain burdens in the course of an activity, and, absent such protection, the opportunity to engage in the activity would not be something you have reason to value.

The protection principle is a more or less direct application of the value-of-choice account. Its aim is to describe the conditions under which the supply of protection against the burden of repair for your mistakes in some activity is a condition for imposing on you the original burdens and responsibilities that an activity involves. Those conditions essentially turn on an ex ante judgement about the value for you of the opportunity to engage in the relevant activity. If others had done enough for that opportunity to be valuable for you at the point when we were presented with it, you may not require them to protect you against the burden of repair for your mistakes in the course of that activity. If they had not done enough for you, you may disclaim responsibility for the whole or part of the burden of repair for those mistakes. Note that the fact that others have voluntarily undertaken to provide you with the appropriate degree of protection is sufficient to satisfy the principle, but it is not necessary for that purpose. Since I have already laid out the general argument in favour of the value-of-choice account, here I propose to focus more on the relationship between the availability of such protection and the value for a person of the opportunity to engage in a certain activity.

Sometimes being able to avoid a mistake is not much comfort. Knowing that, human as you are, you are bound to make mistakes *at some point*, you have good reason to try and put yourself in a position that would allow you to avoid the risk of having to bear the burden of repair for them. One option you have is to set up some form of self-protection, eg to set aside some resources in case you need to provide repair for your mistakes. That option seems bad for several reasons, chief of which is that our capacity to repair harms is no match for our capacity to cause them. So in most cases putting yourself in a good position to avoid the burden of repair will involve seeking some form of protection from others.

The typical and familiar form in which others may put you in good position in that regard is through an insurance agreement. The ground of the insurer's responsibility to bear the burden of compensating those you have harmed is, obviously, that the insurer has voluntarily undertaken to give you that option of protecting yourself from the relevant burden. The content and limits of that protection will, accordingly, be those specified in that agreement (subject to any regulatory requirements).

However, sometimes you may reasonably want others to protect you from the burden of repair even when you have no agreement with them to that effect. The three examples I have been discussing are instances of that sort. The protection principle says that the reason why you may require others to provide you with such protection has two aspects. One is that others want to have the opportunity to engage in a certain activity with you (eg to visit your garden, to have you work in their factory, to share the roads with you), and this activity involves certain burdens for you. The other is that the opportunity to engage in that activity is something that you too have reason to value, but only on the condition that those persons give you some protection against the burden of repair for at least some of the mistakes you might make in its course. I will discuss below how these ideas play out in the three examples I have used, but the point can be made in other familiar situations too. Consider contexts in which others are teaching you some skill, during the acquisition of which you are more or less expected to make mistakes. Suppose that during a driving lesson you confuse the brake and the throttle, while your instructor is giving his undivided attention to his Twitter feed, and you end up smashing into the car in front. It seems to me that part of the value for you of the opportunity to learn how to drive lies in being able to rely on your instructor to intervene, so that such mistakes will not lead to harmful consequences. And that will be the case whether or not the instructor has expressly agreed that you may rely on him for that purpose (we might say that the instructor has 'implicitly' agreed to do this for you, but we would still need to justify the implication). More generally, learners can reasonably want the opportunity to rely on their instructor to exercise such care that would prevent typical learner mistakes from exposing others to harm and leaving the learner at risk of having to provide repair for it. Take away that opportunity, and being able to learn to drive becomes a much less attractive proposition for learners.

The conditions under which the opportunity to engage in an activity will be valuable for you will, of course, depend on the activity that we have in mind, and perhaps on the capacities of particular categories of persons who might undertake it (eg learners). In the learner driver example, I have focused on the fact that you can reasonably want the opportunity to learn how to drive, and to rely on your instructor to intervene or implement safeguards so that your mistakes do not cause harm to yourself and others. In other cases, being in a good position might involve something other than receiving the benefit of such safeguards. It may involve having others feed the cost of repair into an insurance structure that you lack easy access to, as in the employment example. Or it may involve having the state make insurance more affordable for you, eg by giving you the benefit of lower premiums through the mandatory expansion of the risk pool, or by subsidising your premium payments in some other way.

Of course, the fact that you could reasonably want others to give you a measure of protection against the burden of repair for your avoidable mistakes does not settle whether others ought to undertake the sacrifice involved in providing you with such protection. A principle that required them to do so might just be too demanding on them. That will be true when the burden of protecting you would entail that the opportunity to engage in the relevant activity is no longer valuable *for them*. For example, when you sign up for driving lessons, you can reasonably want some assurance that when it comes to certain typical and potentially consequential mistakes, you may rely on your instructor to watch your back. However, the precise level of that protection must also be sensitive to the fact that the value for your instructor of the opportunity to provide instruction depends in part on whether he has the opportunity to avoid the risk of bearing the burden of repair for some of your driving mistakes. In particular, it is plausible that the instructor will value the opportunity to prevent your mistakes from causing harm only when he is in a position to anticipate them, and then only when he has practical alternatives to safeguard you and others against harm, and when the cost of implementing adequate safeguards, or of insuring against their failure is not too high for him, and so on (I return to this point in Chapters 5 and 7).[21]

When we have taken account of what both you and others could reasonably want so that the opportunity to engage in the relevant activity remains valuable for each of you, we may end up with a complex distribution of that risk. In the learner driver example, the final picture might look something like this: the instructor bears the risk of having to provide repair for the learner's mistake to the extent that he had been careless in failing to intervene before that mistake caused harm; the learner bears that risk in other cases; but both may insist on having access to affordable insurance coverage with regard to their respective proportion of the burden of repair. Keeping a tab on that complexity matters because the nature of each risk-avoidance option that the learner or the instructor can reasonably want will also dictate *who* may be required to give them that option (be that each other, third parties, or the state) on pain of having to bear the burden of repair in their stead.

Consider now how we might account for our three working examples and their variations in the light of the protection principle.

Garden: The extent to which you may require me, your visitor, to bear part of the burden of repair for my injury depends on the extent to which I have reason to value the opportunity to take easy measures to protect myself against dangers to my health and safety while visiting your garden.[22] In the original

---

[21] In contexts where the cost of mistakes is not too high, instructors may sometimes appeal to the teaching function of leaving learners without protection against the consequences of their mistakes; nothing drives a lesson home like having to pay for one's failure to heed it. For a discussion of situations that fit that description, see C Sunstein, 'Choosing not to Choose', Harvard Public Law Working Paper No.14-07, available at https://papers.ssrn.com/sol3/papers.cfm?abstract_id=2377364.

[22] The piece on contributory negligence to the intuitions of which I have found myself most frequently nodding in agreement is W Malone, 'Some Ruminations on Contributory Negligence' (1981) *Utah LR* 91.

example, it seems clear that the opportunity to visit your garden will be valuable for me only on certain assumptions, namely that you have a fair idea of the state of your own premises, that you would not let me walk into a danger you know about, and that if such a danger is present, you will bring it to my attention. Those assumptions are important because part of what makes the opportunity to visit your garden attractive to me is that I will not have to be on my guard in the same way I would be if I were, say, in a forest or in some other premises that you did not have control over. That is, I value being able to visit your garden partly because I can let my guard down a little. At the same time, even in that setting, I still value the opportunity to exercise a minimal level of care in self-protecting. After all, even my most diligent friends can make mistakes, and things are more likely to go well for me if, in addition to whatever diligence they have shown, I am also able to protect myself against certain obvious and easily avoidable dangers. Insofar as the presence of the hole in your garden is easily and immediately apparent to my own senses, that opportunity will be practically useful to me. It follows that I could not object to a principle that required me to bear part of the burden of repair, insofar as that principle is sensitive to the fact that I was provided with an opportunity that I have reason to value. The same goes for you: part of the reason you value the opportunity to have people over is that you are able to take care of their well-being and safety. However, the value of that opportunity would be reduced for you (ie you would not be so keen to have people over) if you had to make repair for every consequence of your mistakes in that activity, regardless of whether your victims could easily have averted those consequences. That is, part of the value for you of having people visit your garden is that you want to be able to rely on their ability to exercise at least a minimal level of advertence. By that token, you could reasonably object to a principle that imposed the full burden of repair on you, because that principle would not be sensitive to the value for you of the opportunity to rely on your visitors to take such minimal care.[23]

---

[23] James Goudkamp suggests that applying contributory negligence to some intentional torts, such as the tort of trespass to the person, would sometimes produce awkward results: 'Suppose that C knows that D will shortly attack him. Although C can easily incapacitate D with no risk of injury to himself, to D or to anyone else, he omits to do so because he is lazy. D attacks C. If C sues D in battery, C's damages might be cut back owing to his failure to incapacitate D were apportionment [under the doctrine of contributory negligence] available. This result would offend one's sense of justice', J Goudkamp, 'Contributory Negligence and Trespass to the Person' (2011) 127 *LQR* 519, 522. The protection principle accounts for Goudkamp's intuition: in considering his options for avoiding the burden of repair, C can reasonably want to rely on D *not to follow through* with his intent to cause C physical harm. Things would be different when C can foresee that D may not have enough opportunity to change course even if D goes back on his intent to harm, D does indeed go back on that intent, and C fails to get out of the way despite having had ample opportunity to do so.

This also suggests a way of dealing with the variation in which you do provide me with a warning but know that it is not likely to be effective because of the impact that the beauty of your garden has on me. In fact, the protection principle allows us to see that your warning and the garden's effect on me are simply adding a layer to the proper description of the value of the relevant opportunities for each of us.[24] The additional elements to consider would be whether, despite the infantilising impact of your garden on me, things are still more likely to go well for me if I am given the opportunity to watch my step in your garden, and whether you have reason to value the opportunity to have persons of permanently or temporarily diminished capabilities visiting your garden.

Finally, the protection principle shows why, in the first variation of the garden example, you may not require the passer-by to chip in with regard to the burden of repair for my injury. Of course, it would be great for you to be able to rely on persons who did not create and are not threatened by some danger of your making to put you in a good position to avoid the risk of bearing the burden of repair by alerting you. However, the value for you of being able to invite people over does not seem to be contingent on whether you can recruit strangers to look out for your visitors, partly because you cannot know reliably that those strangers will actually be there. If that is so, then you could not object to a principle that failed to give you the benefit of protection that strangers could conceivably provide you with. But even if you had reason to value the opportunity to enlist the help of strangers, it is clear that, for their part, those strangers could reasonably reject as too demanding a principle that required them to be on the look-out for any dangers that you might create towards other people. Note that our intuitions here are sometimes swayed by our ex post knowledge that those persons would have had to do very little to avert the resulting harm (eg they could just shout 'hey!'). The protection principle suggests that this is misleading and that we should focus instead on whether, as a general matter, third parties have reason to value the opportunity to be on their toes to save strangers from dangers created by others. That seems too demanding for several reasons. First, people do not generally value the opportunity to supervise others. Even when they do, the value of that opportunity for them would be diminished if the failure to supervise others carried the burden of having to make repair for others' injuries. Finally, even when a person still has reason to value that opportunity, it may be very hard for that person to assess the likelihood of someone else making a mistake; the magnitude of the mistake's likely consequences; and the seriousness of the

---

[24] *cf* A Slavny, 'Nonreciprocity and the Moral Basis of Liability to Compensate' (2014) 34 *OJLS* 417 at 434.

practical burden that intervening would involve for the intervener. The fact that sometimes that assessment will turn out to have been easy (eg when the mistake is obvious, the threat serious, and the intervention simple and cost-less) does not make it the case that this person has general reason to value the opportunity to make it.

Employment: One option you have for avoiding the risk of bearing the cost of repair is not to make a mistake at work. However, it is not hard to see why you can reasonably want more than that. For a start, *errare humanum est:*[25] no matter how familiar the work may be and how experienced and skilled you are, chances are that one day you will make a mistake. Furthermore, the nature of modern dependent labour, especially industrial work, is such that the stakes of your mistake will often be very high and almost always far in excess of your capacity to make good the resulting harms. Add to this that our societies are structured in a way that makes it certain that most people will take up some form of dependent labour to secure their livelihood. A principle that made you bear the burden of repair for your mistakes in that context, either directly or by allowing your employers and/or their insurers to claim the relevant cost back from you in the form of an indemnity, would therefore lock you into a particularly unfavourable position. When we turn to your employers, the situation looks markedly different. Employers have reason to value the opportunity to pass on the cost of production down the market chain (or up the chain, by reducing production costs), and to charge a premium (their profit) for doing so. A principle that required them to feed the cost of repair for your workplace mistakes into an insurance structure and pass on the cost of that insurance to the consumers of the goods or services that they are producing would still be sensitive to that opportunity. Similarly, consumers could not object to a principle that required them to bear the cost of marginal increases in the cost of those products or services, precisely because that principle would make the imposition of that burden sensitive to an opportunity that consumers have reason to value, namely to be able to have access to commercially produced goods and services (I return to these points in Chapter 7).

The idea that, absent the protection of an insurance structure, employ-ment locks you into a 'bundle' of opportunities that you have no reason to value also explains the difference between the two variations of the employ-ment example. Even assuming that your employment in my restaurant has some bearing on your options for interacting with the person who stole your

---

[25] The full version of Seneca's aphorism goes: *errare humanum est, perseverare autem diabolicum, et tertia non datur,* which I translate as 'to err is human, to persist in error is diabolical, and that is that'.

watch (eg the hard work makes you edgy), the reason you value being able to work for me is completely unrelated to the opportunity to retrieve the watch from the thief. But that may not be true in relation to persons with whom you will be interacting at work. In those circumstances, part of the value for you of being able to work for me may lie in the fact that the system of work I am implementing will have appropriate means of dealing with situations of workplace friction, and therefore make it less likely that things will turn out badly for you if you happen to find yourself in such a situation. For my part, I value the opportunity to create a workplace where such frictions are not typical, and to have in place a process for dealing with them, or for allowing them to dissipate. It follows that I could not object to a principle that made my liability for torts committed in such situations contingent on me having that opportunity.

Car insurance: The main difference between this and the employment example has to do with the nature of the circumstances that lock you into an insufficient range of options for avoiding the risk of bearing the burden of repair for your mistakes. Modern social life makes either owning or renting our own motor vehicle a virtual necessity for most of us.[26] Furthermore, driving in traffic is both unavoidable and inherently risky, therefore the danger that, like any driver, one day you might make a very costly mistake is considerable. Add to this that, even when it is clear that some road accident has been the result of a mistake, it is often very difficult to establish which driver or other road user made that mistake. It is not hard to conclude that driving would be much less valuable for you unless you had affordable options for insuring against the risk that you may make a costly driving mistake. The best way to make insurance affordable for you is for the state to mandate all drivers to obtain car insurance, as this drives premiums down by expanding the size of the risk pool. You could not, therefore, object to a principle that required you to obtain such insurance, or to take on the full burden of repair in case you have failed to do so. Moreover, given that your position is more or less symmetrical to that of other drivers, the argument as to why they should accept the risk of your driving mistakes into the risk pool will be exactly the same for them too. In short, if the value of driving for all of you turns in part on whether you are able to obtain affordable insurance against traffic accidents, then you all could reasonably require the state to implement a car insurance mandate, and none of you could object to being required to obtain such insurance.

---

[26] The prospect of driverless cars becoming the norm in the near future may change this aspect of things by making the need for individual car ownership obsolete. For a useful discussion of the impact of driverless cars on car insurers, see 'Driverless Cars: Insurers Cannot be Asleep at the Wheel' *Bank Underground*, Bank of England staff blog, 19 June 2015, available at: http:// bankunderground.co.uk/2015/06/19/driverless-cars-insurers-cannot-be-asleep-at-the-wheel.

That symmetry obviously does not hold in the variation involving the damage your car sustains because its colour entices birds to use it as a toilet. It does not appear to me to hold in the home insurance variation either. Owning or renting a home is a necessity for all of us, but it is much less of an inherent source of danger for others than owning or renting a car, so the consequences of mistakes in their use are much less likely to have an adverse impact on others. Furthermore, in many of the cases in which the use of your home may have such an impact on other people, that impact will tend to develop over a period of time rather than suddenly. These points matter because they suggest that the option of taking your own measures to deal with the potential cost of repair may be more valuable for you in the case of mistakes involving the use of your home than in the case of mistakes involving driving, eg because having more opportunity to 'stop the rot' early, you will find it easier to spread out any such costs over time, and so on.

It seems to me that the protection principle also points to a way of thinking about whether agents may reasonably require the state to provide them with affordable options for *general* accident insurance coverage, by mandating that everyone insure against certain kinds of injury, either through one public agency (like New Zealand's Accident Compensation Corporation) or through private providers. One difficulty with treating general accident insurance mandates as instances of the protection principle is that the less we focus on particular activities in which our mistakes are likely to cause harm to others, the more diffuse and therefore less pressing our interest becomes in having protection against the risk of bearing the burden of repair. In particular, it seems to me that people are more likely to value having the opportunity of affordable insurance in relation to specific activities that they typically engage in, especially those activities that are central to their projects in modern societies, and then only in relation to risks typically associated with those activities. Of course, this does not rule out mandatory general accident insurance as a valid policy option. But it suggests that it might be difficult for the argument for such a policy to rely on the idea that the protection it entails is something that the community owes to those who will otherwise have to bear the burden of repair for their mistakes.

VI. COMPARING NOTES: OTHER ACCOUNTS OF CONTRIBUTORY NEGLIGENCE

In this section I want to give my discussion of the protection principle some teeth by asking how some of the legal principles that protect you against the burden of repair might be accommodated under wrongfulness-based accounts.

That accommodation will be straightforward if we say that sometimes you have a moral right that others protect you from the burdens of repair for your negligence, or that sometimes others failing to provide you with such protection counts as a wrong against you. That would certainly be a plausible way of cashing out the claims of the protection principle about what 'you may require' others to do for you. In the garden example, we could say that you have a moral right to require me to bear a proportion of the burden of repair for my injury, or that our institutions holding you responsible for the whole of that burden would count as a wrong against you. In the employment example, we could say that you have a moral right to refuse to indemnify your employer for the cost of insurance for workplace mistakes, or that were our institutions to grant your employer such an indemnity, they would be committing a wrong against you—either statement would constitute a strong call for the abolition of employers' indemnities for workplace accidents.[27] Finally, we could say that you have a moral right to require our institutions to put in place a mandatory car insurance scheme that makes insurance affordable for you, or that the failure to put such a scheme in place would count as a wrong against you.[28]

At the same time, it is clear that in all of the above examples, the rights in question will be violated and the wrongs will be committed no earlier than the moment that someone actually *extracts* from you a greater than appropriate portion of the burden of repair. That is, unless the other party has the capacity to extract repair from you without going to court, the rights violation or the wrong in question will be committed at the moment our institutions order you to pay more than you ought to. The obvious implication is that in those cases the rights-violator or wrongdoer will be the state itself, not the other party. If the other party violates a right or commits a wrong at all in those cases, it will be through asking the state to make you pay more than you ought to, but that would not involve the violation of any of the rights or the commission of any of the wrongs described in the previous paragraph.

The reason why this picture looks awkward is that those models see rights and wrongs as the *input* to a deliberation about how our institutions should allocate the burden of repair, not as the *output* of mistaken allocations of that burden. When we say that your failure to alert me to the presence of a hole in your garden justifies imposing on you some or all of the burden of paying

---

[27] Some jurisdictions have done so, see, eg, the Australian Employee's Liability (Indemnification of Employer) Act 1982 (New South Wales) and the Law Reform (Miscellaneous Provisions) Amendment Act 1984 (New Territories).

[28] We could reach a similar conclusion if we followed John Goldberg and Ben Zipursky's view and took tort law to be concerned with *legal* wrongs and *legal* rights, J Goldberg, B Zipursky, 'Torts as Wrongs' (2010) 88 *Texas Law Review* 917. The difference would be that we would need to ask whether you have those rights in virtue of the proper interpretation of the relevant laws (workers' compensation laws; motorists' insurance schemes; the law on contributory negligence and so on).

for my medical costs, we take your duty to compensate me to be normatively derivative of your violation of your duty (and my correlative right) to take care not to cause me physical injury. But that does not seem to be the case in the examples we have been discussing. Your right to require me to pay part of my medical bills because I failed to watch my step in your garden does not seem to be derivative from any right of yours to require me to watch my step. In other words, I do not owe it to *you* to self-protect. This, I think, is a general and major source of difficulty for wrongfulness-based accounts. I will try to illustrate that difficulty by looking at the way advocates of such accounts address questions of contributory negligence. I focus on contributory negligence both because it serves to make the point I have in mind most clearly, and because it falls undeniably within the core of private law. While a model of private law may conceivably claim that questions of insurance, both in the car and the employment examples, fall outside its domain, such a claim seems much less plausible in respect of contributory negligence.

Robert Stevens concludes his discussion of contributory negligence with the example of *Kirkham v Chief Constable of the Greater Manchester Police*, in which Kirkham, who the police knew to be alcoholic and to have suicidal tendencies, committed suicide while in police custody.[29] The police were held to have breached a duty to take care to prevent Kirkham from causing harm to himself whilst in custody. The defence that Kirkham (and his claimant relatives) should bear part of the burden of repair for his death on account of the fact that he had taken his own life was accordingly dismissed. Stevens notes that while it was clear that Kirkham's weak psychological condition absolved him from responsibility for that burden, Kirkman would not have been so absolved if that condition had caused him to kill another person. He explains the difference as follows:

> If … Mr Kirkham had had homicidal tendencies and had been a defendant in an action for killing another, he would not have been able to rely upon the characteristic in order to exculpate himself. The characteristics relevant in determining liability and contributory fault are not the same. The method by which the [defendant's] liability is established, whether it be for the intentional or unintentional infringement of a right, is irrelevant to the defence under the [Law Reform (Contributory Negligence)] Act. In apportioning responsibility under the Act, the courts are concerned with the parties' relative blameworthiness.[30]

---

[29] *Kirkham v Chief Constable of the Greater Manchester Police* [1990] 2 QB 283.

[30] Stevens, above n 8, at 126. The middle sentence of the quotation reads '[t]he method by which the *claimant's* liability is established, whether it be for the intentional or unintentional infringement of a right, is irrelevant to the defence under the Act' (emphasis added), but I am grateful to Rob Stevens for confirming that this is a typo and that the version in the main text is the one he intended.

The claim that the allocation of the burden of repair in cases of contributory negligence must turn on the parties' 'relative blameworthiness' sounds right, at least if we understand 'blameworthiness' to mean 'fault'. It is certainly consistent with the protection principle's emphasis on the value for a person of the opportunity to engage in an activity, here the activity of protecting one's life and health. People normally value the opportunity to be able to look out for themselves. However, it is not hard to see that this opportunity would be much less valuable for persons in Kirkham's situation. In fact, it is clear that Kirkham's medical condition meant that the opportunity to avoid harming *himself* had much less value for him than the opportunity to avoid harming someone else.[31] He would therefore be able to object to a principle that held him liable for self-harming, but perhaps not to a principle that held him liable for harming others. What is less clear is how that claim fits within a model that says that people should be made to bear burdens of repair only when they have violated another person's rights. After all, the only person to have violated any rights or committed a wrong in *Kirkham* was the police.[32]

Perhaps we should say that the burden of having to pay for part of the cost of one's own injury is not a burden of *repair* at all, normatively speaking, but another kind of burden, and reserve the notion of repair for burdens due to the violation of a right or the commission of a wrong.[33] For example, we could say that, to the extent that the claimant was guilty of contributory negligence, the defendant has not committed a wrong *at all* or that any such wrong is 'cancelled out' and, therefore, the proportion of the burden that falls on the claimant simply reflects an instance of a wrong-less loss lying where 'it originally fell'. I have argued that the idea that some losses simply 'lie' somewhere is a poor reflection of how private law principles go about the task of allocating substantive responsibilities.[34] But even if that idea makes sense, it still requires us to appeal to some account that determines how serious the claimant's lack of care must be in order to have the desired effect on the distribution of the burden between the parties (or the division between the burden of repair and the burden of dealing with a wrong-less harm); that is precisely the role that relative fault plays in Stevens's account. The upshot is that, as long as models built on the ideas of rights or wrongs purport to account not only for burdens of repair but also for burdens imposed under doctrines like contributory negligence, they will have to be models of 'rights or wrongs plus whichever idea justifies the burdens due under the doctrine of contributory negligence', with

---

[31] A notable difference is that it is much harder for one to stay away from oneself.

[32] *cf Froom v Butcher* [1975] 3 WLR 379 at 383 *per* Denning LJ: 'negligence depends on a breach of duty, whereas contributory negligence does not'.

[33] *cf* B Zipursky and J Goldberg, 'Unrealized Torts' (2008) 88 *Virginia LR* 1625, 1709–12.

[34] See ch 2(I).

the protection principle being the obvious candidate for that role. Alternatively, if those models purport to account only for burdens of repair, they will have to say either that they offer a partial account of private law, or that contributory negligence falls outside private law's domain.

The following passage on contributory negligence, by Allan Beever, illustrates another aspect of the same problem:

> The claimant owes no duty of care to herself and, in committing contributory negligence, usually does not breach any duty to the defendant. Hence, when the defendant alleges that the claimant was contributorily negligent, he does not allege that the claimant committed a wrong. Rather, he alleges that the claimant's lack of reasonable care undercut's the claimant's case against him, because the claimant's lack of care is as significant as his own in evaluating the relationship between the parties.[35]

A version of that idea appears in the US Third Restatement of Torts, which reads:

> *Plaintiff's negligence same as defendant's negligence*: the distinction between imposing risks on oneself and imposing risks on others is not a good reason to distinguish between the standard employed to evaluate a plaintiff's conduct and a defendant's conduct. It merely is a reason to distinguish between risk to self and risk to others, whether imposed by a plaintiff or defendant. This Section provides merely that plaintiffs and defendants are evaluated symmetrically, whatever distinctions are drawn between risks to self and risk to others.[36]

Beever's emphasis on the relationship between the parties, and the Restatement's emphasis on the difference between risks to others and risks to oneself both sound very plausible. They draw attention to the fact that the opportunity to protect oneself and the opportunity to protect others may have different respective value for a person. At the same time, that fact also seems to me to cut against their more particular suggestion that the claimant's lack of care is 'equally' significant to that of the defendant. Amongst other things, having a right gives people the opportunity to *let their guard down* in certain respects, and makes it the job of the bearers of the corresponding duty to worry about not exposing those people to certain dangers.[37] For example, saying that

---

[35] A Beever, *Rediscovering the Law of Negligence* (Oxford, Hart Publishing, 2007) 342; E Weinrib, *The Idea of Private Law*, Rev edn (Oxford, Oxford University Press, 2012) 169, n 53.

[36] American Law Institute, *Restatement (Third) of Torts: Apportionment of Liability §3* (St Paul, American Law Institute Publishers, 2000), Comment a.

[37] Note that the protection principle relies on an argument about what risk-avoidance options each party could reasonably want, not on the idea that imposing risks on oneself is somehow less deserving of legal censure or disapproval. For that argument, see G Schwartz, 'Contributory and Comparative Negligence: A Reappraisal' (1978) 87 *Yale LJ* 697, 722: 'the conduct that establishes contributory negligence cannot be regarded as egoistical or antisocial; instead it is behavior that, from the actor's or others' perspective, is merely foolish or stupid. This assessment undermines the supposed moral parity between the "fault" of negligence and the "fault" of contributory negligence.'

I have a right to the exclusive possession of my home entails, amongst other things, that I am entitled to worry to a lesser degree about how to shut you out. It is your job to worry about making sure you do not come into my home uninvited. The fact that I have the right in question means that, normatively speaking, it is your problem to stay out, not my problem to keep you out. The protection principle registers this aspect very clearly.

The problem for Beever and the Restatement is that we want to say that, in failing to watch my step in your garden, I have let my guard down *too much*, but this claim can be difficult to express in terms of rights or wrongs. One alternative is to say that, in letting my guard down too much, I have engaged in conduct that 'cancels out' your wrong towards me. As we have seen, that would still require us to appeal to some idea that determines the conditions for such a 'cancelling out', and it is not clear how *that* idea could be couched in terms of rights or wrongs. Another, more radical, alternative is to say that you do, after all, have a moral right to require me to watch my step in your garden, or that my not having watched my step constitutes a moral wrong against you. Such a view may look awkward, and I am not aware of tort theorists that hold it, but it is not crazy. My failure to self-protect is clearly normatively significant and perhaps it is possible to see that failure as disturbing a normative relationship between us. For example, we could say that you and I are engaged in a *joint project* that aims to ensure my safety in your garden; that, in failing to take care of myself, I failed to do my bit in that project; and that this gives you some ground of complaint against me because now our joint project cannot come to fruition.[38] My point is that, unless they sign up to something like the 'joint project' view, models of rights or wrongs are caught in an awkward bind. They must either reject the intuition that having a right entitles me to the opportunity to let my guard down in relation to some dangers; or they must accept that rights and wrongs are involved in the allocation of the burden of repair between us in the manner, and to the extent, that the protection principle describes.

VII. PROTECTION AND THE 'BACKGROUND CONDITIONS' OF CHOICE

There are many reasons why others might be required to protect a person against the burden of repair for that person's own avoidable mistakes. They might be required to protect that person because this works out best for everyone. They might be required to protect them insofar as that is a means to the end of protecting the victims of the mistakes. They might protect that person insofar as that person is, or will become, financially vulnerable once that burden is imposed. The most natural way of thinking about those protections

---

[38] *cf* the 'heretical' view of joint authorship I canvassed in ch 2(III)(B).

sees them as 'lifting' or 'shifting' responsibilities that belong originally to that person, in the pursuit of some worthwhile aim. In this chapter I have been concerned with a very different possibility, namely that some protections that others may be required to provide to a person against the burden of repair for mistakes in some activity are part of the case for requiring that person to bear other substantive responsibilities in relation to that activity in the first place. In particular, I have proposed that, in some situations, the fact that a person had the opportunity to avoid the burden of repair by choosing appropriately will not be enough for others to require that person to bear that burden. The protection principle picks out those situations by focusing on the relationship between the supply of such protection and the value for the person that receives it of the opportunity to engage in the relevant activity. If this is correct, then we have reason to think about protection before we think about avoidability, as the value for a person of the opportunity to avoid some harmful outcome will, in some cases, turn on whether that person has been provided with appropriate protection against the burden of repair for their avoidable mistakes.

Private lawyers have tended to look at things the other way around because they have tended to start from a more conservative conception of what others owe a person in that respect. Arthur Ripstein speaks for a large and diverse constituency when he takes it as a basic principle of tort law that 'people bear the costs that their conduct imposes on others'[39] and that, in allocating burdens of repair, 'tort law cannot take account of need as such'.[40] I have tried to show that these statements are half-truths. The first statement misses that private law sometimes does allow one to require others to protect one against some or all the burden of repair for one's avoidable mistakes in the course of an activity. The second statement misses that the distribution of that burden should be sensitive to the value for the persons involved of the opportunity to engage in that activity. Considerations of need may sometimes matter for that distribution, to the extent that they affect that value. This seems to me consistent with Ripstein's more general claim that we should decide questions about the allocation of the burden of repair by aiming for a 'fair division of risks' between persons, based on everyone's basic interest in liberty and security.[41] Applying that idea

---

[39] A Ripstein, 'Philosophy of Tort Law' in J Coleman and S Shapiro (eds), *Oxford Handbook of Jurisprudence & Philosophy of Law* (Oxford, Oxford University Press, 2004) 661.

[40] Ibid at 664.

[41] A Ripstein, *Equality, Responsibility, and the Law* (Cambridge, Cambridge University Press, 2001) at 50: 'If neither liberty nor security interests are to totally cancel the significance of the other, some balance must be struck between them. Rather than trying to balance those interests *across* persons—supposing, in some way, that one person's gain can make up for another person's loss—the fault system balances them *within* representative persons. By supposing that all have the same interests in both liberty and security, the fault system treats parties as equals, by allowing a like liberty and security to all.'

in the context of driving, Ripstein argues that drivers who expose others to an unreasonable degree of risk, ie a degree of risk that fails to strike a fair balance between a person's interests in liberty and security, may be said to 'own' that extra degree of risk, and to owe a duty to make repair for the consequences in case the risk materialises.[42] To the extent that Ripstein's account implies that a driver 'owns' the risk of having to make repair *simply* by appealing to the fact that this driver has failed to discharge an original burden (by creating unreasonable risks for others), that account is vulnerable to the objections I have raised against wrongfulness-based accounts of the burden of repair. However, I believe that the appeal to a 'fair division of risks' can accommodate the element of protection against the burden of repair. One may aim for a fair division of risks between persons on the basis of their common interest in liberty and security, and still accept that people can reasonably want a measure of security not only against the risk of suffering harm, but also against the risk that they might have to bear the burden of repair in case they cause harm to others. And just as people may sometimes require someone else to 'own' the former risk, they may, at least sometimes, also require someone else to 'own' the latter risk too.

I have also claimed that we should resist the temptation to see every instance of protection as a situation in which a person is being 'bailed out' of their responsibilities. Some situations are like that, but some are not, and the difference between them matters not just for the way we make the case for the provision of protection, but also for how we think about the boundaries of private law and about the design of institutions that administer situations involving burdens of repair. In that regard, it seems to me that one of the advantages of the protection principle is that it can provide a robust criterion for determining the significance of insurance and insurability within private law. In many models of private law, insurance is a 'downstream' matter or an afterthought, a way of managing substantive responsibilities one already owes.[43] The protection principle explains why sometimes providing people with appropriate insurance options is part of the justification for requiring them to bear certain substantive (original) burdens in the first place. The principle defends this suggestion without relying on the ability of mandatory insurance to lower aggregate (or social) cost. Rather, it relies on the ability of insurance to make coverage more affordable for each person who can reasonably want to be able to have it as an option against the risk of having the bear the burden of repair for a mistake. Similarly, the protection principle does not say that giving affordable insurance options to those persons matters in order to ensure

---

[42] Ibid at 53–4.

[43] Se, eg, G Fletcher, 'Fairness and Utility in Tort Theory' (1972) 85 *Harvard LR* 537, 540, 547; J Coleman, *Risks and Wrongs*, Reprint (Oxford, Oxford University Press, 2002) 395ff; E Weinrib, above n 35, 171ff.

that the burden of repair stands in some 'proportion' to the moral gravity of the mistake (which will often involve nothing more than a moment's carelessness).[44] The ground on which those persons may require that adequate insurance options be made available to them is independent of both the degree of their carelessness and the proportion between that carelessness and the extent of the resulting harm (ie the protection may be available both to momentarily and repeatedly careless persons, though the terms may differ depending on what other risk-avoidance options are available). Finally, the protection principle may require the introduction of compulsory insurance in a range of situations, but its argument to that effect is not one of distributive justice or social policy.[45] The principle's primary focus is on whether a person has reason to value the opportunity to engage in an activity under certain terms, not on whether that opportunity would be equally valuable for that person and others.

---

[44] *cf* S Hershovitz, 'Harry Potter and the Trouble with Tort Theory' (2010) 63 *Stanford LR* 67, 113: 'large compensatory damage awards are demanded by justice only because the people who might be subject to them have the opportunity to purchase liability insurance in advance. On this story, in the absence of liability insurance, justice would not require people who are momentarily careless (eg by looking away from the road for a split second) to pay "make whole" damages to someone they injure, because the remedy would be utterly out of proportion to the infraction.' See also J Waldron, 'Moments of Carelessness and Massive Loss' in D Owen (ed), *Philosophical Foundations of Tort Law* (New York, Oxford University Press, 1997) 387, 388.

[45] This seems to me to be the position taken by Merkin and Steele, above n 7, who look at legal developments and observe a pattern of 'increased attention to the financial burden of negligence liability ...', which extends beyond cases where existing risk allocations are a matter of private ordering, to those where they are a matter of social (or legal) policy—such as compulsory or simply routine insurance' (at 250).

5

Avoidability

W E HAVE ALREADY come across some views about why, or how far, avoidability matters for a person's responsibilities. One could say that the fact that a person could have avoided some outcome matters because it shows that this person made a choice, and therefore that the outcome may be ascribed to that person in a morally appropriate sense. Or that this fact matters because it signifies that persons who can avoid outcomes are generally able to act in the world and to produce outcomes that match their assessment of the reasons that apply to them in a situation. Or that it matters because it suggests that the action in question lay within a person's domain of secure competence. The value-of-choice account takes a different view. It says that avoidability matters for a person's responsibilities because, or insofar as, that person has reason to value it as an *opportunity*. Just like the opportunity to enter into enforceable agreements and other voluntary commitments, the opportunity to avoid some outcome or burden makes a difference to what we may require of a person insofar as giving that person that opportunity is likely to make things go better for them (for simplicity, I will leave aside the representative and the symbolic value of having a choice).

This way of thinking about avoidability is both narrower and broader than its rivals. It is narrower because it treats avoidability as significant for substantive responsibility *to the extent* that a person has reason to regard the opportunity to avoid a certain outcome as something that makes it more likely that things will go well for them. This allows that sometimes a person will have had the opportunity to avoid an outcome, or to do otherwise, or to engage in an activity that lies within their domain of secure competence, and still be able to object to a principle that requires them to bear a burden on account of that fact. We could use this idea to explain, for instance, the difference between a case in which a person agrees to pay the fee of a top medical practitioner in order to enjoy the best prospects for surviving a life-threatening disease, and a case in which a person agrees to pay some blackmailers in order to avoid their threats of violence (my examples are modelled on David Hume's). Both persons could avoid suffering life-threatening harm by choosing appropriately, but only the first person may be required to live up to what they agreed to. That is because 'you had a choice in this' is a good argument against the first person, but not against the second, as the second person could object to the background conditions of the choice the blackmailers presented them with. At the same time, the view of avoidability as an opportunity that a person has reason to value is broader than its rivals because it acknowledges that there are limits to how much others have to do to ensure that one is sufficiently well-placed to make the most out of whatever opportunities are available. Like the unlucky person who, despite every reasonable effort, never got word of the warnings in Scanlon's hazardous waste removal example, a person may sometimes be legitimately saddled with certain burdens, even if they never had access to the facts of the situation, or got to make a choice or form some other response in relation to it, as long as they had all the protection that others could be reasonably required to provide them with.

I will develop the 'avoidability as valuable opportunity' view by considering how we might approach two familiar questions of liability for the burden of repair in private law in its light. One question is whether legal liability for the burden of repair ought to be negligence-based or stricter.[1] The other is how far the conditions of liability ought to make special allowance for persons who lack the capacity to meet the relevant standard of conduct.

Accounts of avoidability that focus on a person's general capacity to act in the world, or to do otherwise, or their mastery over an activity, largely underdetermine those questions. Consider cases like *Rylands v Fletcher*.[2] The law could say that Rylands ought to make repair for the flooding of Fletcher's property only if the former failed to take due care in putting up and maintaining the water deposit in his land. Or it could say (as the House of Lords did) that it is enough that Rylands accumulated in his land a dangerous substance, which then escaped and caused harm to Fletcher's property. Both rules would allow Rylands options for avoiding the burden of repair. Under the first rule, he could have avoided liability by not erecting a deposit in his land, or by exercising reasonable care in doing so and in maintaining it, or by taking out insurance in case his failure to take such care caused harm to others, and so on. Under the second rule, he could have avoided liability by not erecting a

---

[1] I am using 'stricter' in the loose sense of 'more demanding than'. The term is sometimes employed to denote liability without negligence, and sometimes to denote liability without fault, ie liability that is not contingent on the breach of a standard of conduct (be that a standard of care, as in 'drive carefully', or not, as in 'do not trespass'). For the first (and less common) use, see G Keating, 'Tort, Rawlsian Fairness and Regime Choice in the Law of Accidents' (2004) 72 *Fordham LR* 1857, 1870–1. For the second use see, eg, R Epstein, 'A Theory of Strict Liability' (1973) 2 *Journal of Legal Studies* 151. For criticisms of Epstein's position, see S Perry, 'The Impossibility of General Strict Liability' (1988) 1 *Canadian Journal of Law & Jurisprudence* 147; A Ripstein, *Equality, Responsibility, and the Law* (Cambridge, Cambridge University Press, 2001) 38–42; R Wright, 'Causation in Tort Law' (1985) 73 *California LR* 1752; E Weinrib, *The Idea of Private Law*, Rev edn (Oxford, Oxford University Press, 2012) 171.

[2] *Rylands v Fletcher* (1868) 34 LJ Ex 154.

deposit in his land, or by insuring against the risk that it might break and cause harm to others. What changes from one rule to the other is the range of burden-avoidance options that the law would afford Rylands: the first rule would give him one more such option, namely that of avoiding the burden of repair by exercising reasonable care. Note that even a much stricter liability rule would still allow a person in Rylands's position to avoid the burden of repair. For instance, under s 209 of the Water Industry Act 1991, a water services provider ('water undertaker') is liable to make repair 'where an escape of water, however caused, from a pipe vested in a water undertaker causes loss or damage' to another person.[3] Supposing that Rylands had been a 'water undertaker' for the purposes of the Act, that stricter rule would allow him a clear option of avoiding liability: he could simply have stayed out of the water business.

We could map out similar options in respect of liability for breach of contract. The law could say that defaulting promisors ought to make repair only when they have failed to make every reasonable effort to perform. Or it could say (as it generally does) that it is enough for the purposes of such liability that promisors fail to perform. Both liability rules would allow promisors to avoid the burden of repair, but each would allow them a different range of options for doing so. Under the latter rule, promisors could avoid that burden by performing, or by not entering into a contract. Under the former rule, promisors have one additional avoidance option, namely to make every reasonable effort to perform.

Mansfield v Weetabix[4] illustrates the same issues in relation to limited capacity. In that case Mr Tarleton, a driver for Weetabix, was unaware, and had no reason to be aware, of the fact that he was suffering from a disease that exposed him to the risk of hypoglycaemic attacks. He suffered such an attack while driving. As his brain was starved of glucose, he lost control of the car and crashed into the Mansfield's property. It later emerged that Tarleton had been involved in two minor road incidents earlier that day, but that he had no reason to suspect that these were due to him suffering a disease or being unfit to drive. The law could say that Tarleton, in his own capacity, and Weetabix, as his employer, ought to make repair for the harm caused by the former insofar as his driving fell below the standard applicable to a person of normal capacities. Or it could say (as the Court of Appeal said it did) that Tarleton

---

[3] *cf Transco v Stockport MBC* [2003] UKHL 61, *per* Lord Hoffmann at [42]: 'This provision is designed to avoid all argument over which insurers should bear the loss. Liability is far stricter than under the rule in *Rylands v Fletcher*. There is no exception for acts of third parties or natural events. The undertaker is liable for an escape "however caused" and must insure accordingly.' The section did not benefit the claimant gas suppliers in *Transco* because s 209(3)(b) of the Act explicitly bars gas suppliers from relying on it.
[4] *Mansfield v Weetabix* [1998] 1 WLR 1263.

and Weetabix ought to make repair only if Tarleton fell below the standard applicable to drivers who have no reason to be aware of the fact that they are incapable of meeting the normal standard. Both rules would allow the defendants to avoid the burden of repair. The first rule would allow Weetabix to avoid that burden either by not employing people to drive its cars, or by taking out insurance against the possibility that one of their driver's capacity might fall below the normal standard. That rule would also allow Tarleton to avoid that burden by not driving, and by taking out insurance of his own. The second rule would give the defendants all these avoidance options, plus another one, namely showing that Tarleton had no reason to suspect that his capacity had fallen short of what was necessary to meet the applicable driving standard.

I will make two working assumptions here. One is that 'you could have stayed out of this line of business' might be a good response to a water undertaker, but 'you could have stayed out of the roads' would not be a good response to Weetabix or to Tarleton. The other is that 'I exercised all reasonable care' and 'I lacked the capacity to meet the reasonable standard of care' are good objections against the imposition of the burden of repair in some situations, but not in others. Accounts that understand avoidability as the ability to do otherwise, or the general capacity to act in the world, or the secure competence in some activity, cannot explain why those assumptions might be justified. The reason for this, I think, is that those accounts have no obvious way of fixing attention to the right moment for assessing avoidability. Even when a person could not have avoided a certain outcome in a given situation, that person may well have been able to avoid *getting into* that situation in the first place. Tarleton could not have avoided the crash while he was driving, but he could have avoided getting behind the wheel. Water undertakers may not have been able to avoid the damage caused by some of their water pipes, but they could have avoided getting into the water business. Assuming, as I have, that the two situations are different, we need some account of why in Tarleton's case we ought to focus on the moment more proximal to the accident, while in the water undertakers' case we ought to focus on the more distal moment of them entering the business.

The 'avoidability as valuable opportunity' view helps in that regard, because it allows us to make our judgements about responsibility sensitive to the difference between avoidance opportunities that are generally valuable for a person (eg not being able to getting into a contract, or a business), and avoidance opportunities that are not (eg not being able to drive). Leaving contract settings to one side for the moment (I turn to them in Chapter 6), in what follows I try to show how we can build on this idea to generate an explanation of why liability may be negligence-based in some situations and stricter in others, and when the law ought to make allowance for a person's limited ability to discharge the reasonable standard of care.

We can expect that explanation to be complex in a couple of ways. First, we can expect it to vary in content depending on who it is addressed to. One reason for this is that private law settings feature a layer of complexity that is not clearly present in examples like Scanlon's hazardous waste removal case. In that case, all citizens are being threatened by a single hazard: the threat of exposure to the dangerous waste. Similarly, the city officials have but a single aim: to take all reasonable measures to protect everyone's health against that hazard. Attaining that aim is, of course, challenging, as it involves weighing the likely consequences of different responses to that hazard, from evacuating the city, to removing the material urgently while warning people about the risks and putting additional non-warning-based protective measures in place. However, it is still the case that all the options on the table are different ways of achieving the same thing or of promoting the same aim. As Ronald Coase famously pointed out, private law settings differ in that they typically involve *clashes* of activities and projects.[5] In *Rylands*, Rylands wants reliable water supply for his crops, Fletcher wants his property to be free from flooding. In *Mansfield*, Mansfield wants to keep his property safe, while Weetabix and its driver want to transport goods. The value-of-choice takes seriously the fact that these cases involve more than one activities or projects, though it does not frame the debate about its significance in terms of social cost. Under that account, a principle that imposes a burden on a person will be justified if the principle is sensitive to the opportunities to choose that this person has reason to value having in the situation. It follows that when each party is engaged in a different activity or project, the opportunities valuable to each one of them may be different. The justification given to each may need to vary accordingly.

The task of justifying private law principles by reference to the 'avoidability as valuable opportunity' view will be further complicated by the degree to which one or more parties in the situation may reasonably require others to offer them some protection against the burden of repair. For example, it is possible that Weetabix and its driver may reasonably require the state to make their car insurance affordable for them by mandating every driver to insure, while Mansfield may not require the state to help him in a similar way with regard to property insurance. Furthermore, as we have seen, the relevant principles of liability will need to be justified both to those who may require others to supply that protection, and to those who will be required to supply it.[6] That complexity will be easily manageable when there is a clear overlap between the two classes of persons, eg drivers both receive the benefit of protection in the form of the lower insurance premiums generated by an insurance mandate, and provide similar protection to others by being required to

---

[5] R Coase, 'The Problem of Social Cost' (1960) 3 *Journal of Law & Economics* 1, 2.
[6] See ch 4(V).

insure themselves under that mandate. In other situations, eg those involving the spreading of the cost of industrial accidents to the consumers of the goods or services that an enterprise is producing, the overlap will be smaller, so the justification of the relevant principles will need to be tailored to those persons' particular position. I will discuss some situations of this sort in Chapters 6 and 7.

Sections I and II discuss how the 'avoidability as valuable opportunity' view would go about justifying a liability rule that would allow 'I exercised reasonable care' as an objection in some typical negligence contexts (my main example will be driving) but not in the context of *Rylands*. Section III does the same with respect to 'I lacked the capacity to meet the standard of reasonable care', and shows how the value-of-choice account would explain the difference between *Mansfield* and cases in which a defendant's lack of capacity does not affect their liabilities. To amplify and sharpen my claims on those fronts, I will try to contrast those explanations with those provided by some other familiar accounts. Section IV considers whether a person may object to liability on grounds such as 'I was trying to rescue the claimant', or 'I acted for the benefit of society', or 'I am generally responsible in my activity'. The recent Social Action, Responsibility, and Heroism (SARAH) Act 2015 requires English courts to take such complaints into account in negligence cases, so I want to discuss the extent to which those complaints would be justified under the view of avoidability I am proposing.

I. EXERCISE OF CARE AS AN OBJECTION TO LIABILITY

People can reasonably want to be able to go to places, and to go there safely. Our current technological capacities do not allow teleportation. Public transport only covers so many possible destinations, and can only run so often. Plus, it can be crowded, and sometimes one does not want to travel with others. Being able to drive one's own car (or other vehicle), and to choose where to go, who with, what time to set off, and what route to take, are all good opportunities for a person to have. Of course, quite a lot in the situation is not up to one to decide. For the most part, one can only drive where there is a road. There are speed limits and other traffic regulations to observe, many of which require one to exercise a certain level of skill and advertence. Under the value-of-choice account I have been defending, those limitations on where and how one may drive, and the penalties or other burdens that a person may be subject to when they violate the traffic code, are justified when having that code in place puts them in a good position to do what they want: to go to places, and to go there safely. That applies also in respect of the burden involved in having to making repair.

As long as drivers have reason to value the opportunity to drive where and when they want to, they cannot object to a principle which makes the imposition of the burden of repair on them contingent on whether they had that opportunity.

As we have seen, this is not the whole story. The value for a person of attaining the benefit of some activity, and the value for that person of avoiding the burden in case they fail in that activity are not always symmetrical.[7] Sometimes a person will want both the opportunity to engage in an activity and the opportunity to avoid the burden of repair in case that activity goes wrong. That will be particularly true when it is likely that the weight of that burden will be crushing, or that a person will not be in a good position to predict with sufficient accuracy the probability of incurring it. It follows that a more precise statement of what one wants from driving is this: to go places, to go safely, and to avoid crushing liability for one's mistakes in the process. Adding this last bit in the value for a person of the opportunity to drive helps explain why sometimes that person may sometimes require others to give them a measure of protection against the burden of repair for accidents that arise from breaches of the traffic code, in the form of making car insurance more affordable by requiring everyone to insure.[8]

Note, in particular, that this account can explain not only why such protection is due to drivers, but also what *form* that protection ought to take, namely the provision of the opportunity to obtain affordable car insurance. Not giving a driver any protection against the burden of repair would make the opportunity of going places in their own car much less valuable for them, especially if that person's income and means lie at the lower part of the distribution spectrum. But having, say, other drivers bear the burden of repair for one's driving mistakes would make the same opportunity less valuable for *them*. By this token, the appropriate form of protection should have value not only for the person who receives it, but also for the person who supplies it. Insurance is a perfect fit for that bill, as its value for both insurers and insured lies in the fact that its provision protects people against future risks. Given that all drivers have reason to value the opportunity to get the benefit of such protection, the imposition of the burden of repair on them must be sensitive to whether they had that opportunity. Making car insurance premiums more affordable for all by requiring everyone to insure is therefore justified, insofar as it improves the terms in which any driver has the opportunity to insure (ie insofar as no other insurance policy would be likely to provide similar protection at lower premiums).

---

[7] See ch 3(I).
[8] See ch 4(V).

I think that this explanation has enough resources to answer Jane Stapleton's objection to making insurability a condition of responsibility. She writes:

> It would seem morally incoherent for the liability insurance factor to have any independent force, for it would mean that there would be cases, for example, in which the fact that tipped the balance in favour of the defendant being held liable would simply be that he had or could have had liability insurance cover, while an equally culpable but uninsured or uninsurable actor would escape. It is not self-evident why the latter party taking an uninsured or uninsurable risk should be so favoured and his victim denied the law's protection on this account.[9]

Stapleton's conclusion is, I think, correct inasmuch as it suggests that whether the victim is entitled to require the tortfeasor to make repair ought to not depend on whether that *particular* tortfeasor was 'insurable'. The 'avoidability as valuable opportunity' account agrees with this conclusion, because it does not focus on the 'individualised' but on the 'generic' reasons people have to want the opportunity to insure, and for that insurance to be affordable for them. The difference matters because in any given setting there may be different explanations as to why a given tortfeasor is uninsurable. Sometimes the reason will be that persons in the tortfeasor's position have no good insurance options, eg the premiums for car or health insurance are well above their means. Sometimes the reason will be more 'individualised', eg when the particular tortfeasor has amassed too many penalty points on their license and insurers will only agree to cover them on payment of a very high premium. While the tortfeasors will be 'uninsurable' in both situations, there is a fairly obvious case for treating them differently, and that the 'avoidability as valuable opportunity' story can account well for that difference.

An important part of that story is that the insurance protection that drivers receive is mandatory rather than optional. As we have seen, the usual way of understanding the significance of mandatory insurance is to treat it as a way of protecting the victims of certain activities against the risk that their injurer will be unable to make full repair. My account asks us to note another aspect of mandatory insurance: its capacity to protect those who may make avoidable mistakes in those activities against the risk of bearing the burden of repair on their own. The account's distinctive claim in that regard is, accordingly, that the imposition of a mandate is justified towards those persons because (or insofar as) it allows them to receive the insurance protection they can reasonably want, at lower rates. In other words, the value-of-choice account justifies restricting drivers' freedom to decide how to protect themselves against the risk of bearing the burden of repair for their driving mistakes, by appealing to the way in which a mandate *improves* drivers' ability to procure such

---

[9] J Stapleton, 'Tort, Insurance and Ideology' (1995) 58 MLR 820, 825–6.

protection for themselves.[10] It follows that when there is no reason to expect that a mandate is likely to bring insurance premiums down, the case for imposing that mandate on those persons will weaken.

The 'avoidability as valuable opportunity' account accords a more limited role to an idea that has been thought to justify a fault-based regime of liability for traffic accidents, namely that, generally speaking, drivers expose each other to the *same* kind of risk and to more or less the same degree. George Fletcher has argued that the reason why liability for traffic accidents is fault-based has to do with the fact that the risk imposition between drivers is *reciprocal* in a way that the risk imposition in *Rylands* is not.[11] Every driver is a risk to every other, but not every neighbour is a risk to every other in the way Rylands was to (claimant, not author) Fletcher. The account I am proposing here agrees that justifying a principle requires us to take account of the risks that each party's activity may entail for them and others, including the risk of liability for the burden of repair. However, it does not attach special significance to the fact that, in a given situation, the parties are exposing each other to risk of the same type and to the same degree.[12] Rather, it takes that fact to *simplify* the task of justifying the relevant principle, in the sense that the justification given to one driver will likely satisfy other drivers too. By the same token, that account is not committed to the conclusion that non-reciprocal risk imposition justifies stricter conditions of liability. This is particularly significant in the light of the fact that some risk imposition in road traffic settings is clearly non-reciprocal, eg between drivers and pedestrians. Whereas a reciprocity test would justify stricter conditions of liability for harm caused to pedestrians,[13] an 'avoidability as valuable opportunity' test would not support such a differentiation. The opportunity that drivers have reason to value, namely to drive with a certain level of skill and advertence, remains the same and carries similar significance, no matter whether that skill is displayed in relation to fellow road users or pedestrians.

---

[10] I think that this answers Arthur Ripstein's objection that taking insurance as a condition of liability would hold those conditions 'hostage' to people's overall patterns of activity, see Ripstein, above n 1, 62: 'Whether a defendant will insure against injuring a certain class of plaintiff depends on the overall likelihood of the defendant causing that type of injury. Those who repeatedly expose others to a similar risk of injury will insure; those who are repeatedly exposed to those risks will insure themselves against injury. Thus, both liberty and security are hostage to the overall patterns of activity of particular plaintiffs and defendants'. The problem Ripstein has in mind does not arise when insurance is mandatory.

[11] G Fletcher, 'Fairness and Utility in Tort Theory' (1972) 85 *Harvard LR* 537. See also C Fried, *An Anatomy of Risk* (Cambridge, Mass, Harvard University Press, 1970) 186ff.

[12] For a similar argument, see A Slavny, 'Nonreciprocity and the Moral Basis of Liability to Compensate' (2014) 34 *OJLS* 417, 432–4.

[13] Fletcher, above n 11, at 570–1, discussing with approval the obiter comments of the Supreme Court of California in *Elmore v American Motors Corp* (1969) 70 Cal.2d 615.

A different conclusion may be warranted in other contexts. Consider *Caparo v Dickman*.[14] The defendant auditors were careless in auditing a company in which the claimants were shareholders. Acting on the strength of the auditors' report, which presented the company in good financial shape, the claimants bought further shares in the company, and suffered significant losses when it emerged that the company was worth much less than the report made out. The auditors argued that while they owed (and had breached) a duty of care towards the company and its organs, they owed no similar duty towards the company's existing shareholders, who would receive copies of the audit in that capacity and whose own investment decisions might be influenced by the audit's results, or to members of the investing public, who would see the summary of the audit in the press and might rely on it in deciding to invest in the company. The House of Lords agreed with the auditors. The 'avoidability as opportunity' account can explain why the court was right to take this differentiated approach. A principle that held the auditors liable should be sensitive to the value for them of having the opportunity to carry out auditing subject to the appropriate standards of care. But it should also be sensitive to the value for auditors of the opportunity to determine the *scope* of their activity, ie the range of persons that they would do business with.[15] The auditors had that opportunity with respect to the company itself, and they acted on that opportunity by agreeing to prepare an audit for it. By contrast, they had no similar opportunity with respect either to the company's individual shareholders, or the investing public. Those two classes of persons received the results of the audit because the law required *the company* to disclose those results to them (in full, for shareholders; in summary, for the public) in the interest of market transparency.[16] Things would have been different if the auditors themselves had had a choice about whether or not to pass the audit report to those classes of persons, and had gone on to exercise that choice in a particular way.

On that ground, it seems to me that Lord Bridge's formulation of the applicable principle with regard to negligent misstatement is not entirely correct. According to that formulation, a defendant owes a duty of care to a plaintiff when

> the defendant knew that his statement would be communicated to the plaintiff, either as an individual or as a member of an identifiable class, specifically in connection with a particular transaction or transactions of a particular kind (eg in a

---

[14] *Caparo Industries plc v Dickman* [1990] 2 AC 605.

[15] Ibid at 627 *per* Lord Bridge: 'It is never sufficient to ask simply whether A owes B a duty of care. It is always necessary to determine the scope of the duty by reference to the kind of damage from which A must take care to save B harmless'.

[16] The law in question was the Companies Act 1985. Lord Bridge discusses the requirements of that Act in relation to shareholders at, ibid, 625–6.

prospectus inviting investment) and that the plaintiff would be very likely to rely on it for the purpose of deciding whether or not to enter upon that transaction or upon a transaction of that kind.[17]

The problem with this formulation is that it fails to distinguish between situations where the defendant can avoid communicating a statement *to the plaintiff*, and situations where the defendant can avoid a statement reaching the plaintiff only by not communicating that statement *to a third party*. While in both situations the defendant may know that the statement will reach the plaintiff, the two situations are clearly distinguishable. Holding defendants liable in the first situation would be making their liability contingent on an opportunity that they have reason to value, namely to choose whether or not to transact with the plaintiffs.[18] That is not the case in the second situation. The defendants' knowledge that a statement is bound to reach the plaintiffs through third parties does not necessarily make it the case that being able to avoid setting that train of events in motion is an opportunity that the defendants have reason to value. Of course, shutting up because one knows that one's listener is bound to disclose some information to others can be valuable in *some* cases, or for some persons. But it is not valuable for a person who has good independent reason to provide their listener with such information, eg when such information takes the form of professional advice or an expert assessment that the listener paid for. Had the House of Lords held the auditors liable to shareholders, or to the investors who relied on the audit, it would have held them responsible for the fact that a class of persons with whom the auditors never had the opportunity *not* to transact happened to place certain value on the auditors carrying out their job with reasonable skill.

II. *RYLANDS v FLETCHER* AND DOING THINGS ON ONE'S OWN TERMS

Mr Rylands wanted the opportunity to build a water deposit in his property. One aspect of the value for him of being able to do so was that this would give him better control over the irrigation of his crops, as he would have less need to rely on the standard water supply system. Another aspect of that value was that, as both the crops and the deposit lay in his own property, he would be able to set up this alternative means of irrigation without interference, ie without others being able to stop him from doing so, or to make him built and operate the deposit in particular ways, and so on. As far as he could tell, his project had nothing to do with them: it would not require them to suffer on his account, or to chip in to cover for the cost of running it. Rylands, we might

---

[17] Ibid at 621.
[18] A classic illustration is *Hedley Byrne Co Ltd v Heller & Partners Ltd* [1964] AC 465.

say, wanted to do things on his own terms. Under the 'avoidability as valuable opportunity' account, this means that he could not complain against a principle that made the imposition on him of the burden of repair for harms caused by his activity contingent on him having had the opportunity to do things on his own terms. The fact that Rylands took all reasonable care in erecting and maintaining the deposit would not change the situation, because it would not make it any less true that Rylands had that opportunity, or diminish its value for him.

Could Rylands require others to give him a measure of protection against the burden of repair? Perhaps he would not find value in ways of protecting him that would involve others supervising his activity, as this would give him less of an opportunity to do things on his own terms. But he would certainly want others to protect him in other ways, eg by being on the lookout in their own properties, in case his activity threatened to cause harm to them, or by taking our insurance against such harm. The problem is that a principle that required others, including Mr Fletcher, to give Rylands the benefit or one or more of those kinds of protection would not be easily justifiable to *them*. People generally do not place value on having to supervise others. Aside from situations involving personal attachments, this is simply too demanding a thing to have to do. People do place value in having the opportunity to keep their property safe from accidental damage, but that is mostly the case in respect of accidents that people are well placed to guard against, eg in respect of a certain degree of noise or smoke pollution, or in respect of certain natural dangers. It is less clear how that would be the case in respect of the danger of a sudden and huge flooding from a neighbouring property. Finally, many people place value in having some insurance against damage to their property, but it is by no means true that home or property insurance is by far the cheapest or most efficient way to deal with the risk that one's property may be damaged, given the likelihood or frequency of such damage and the normal range of the cost of repairing it. Sometimes people may reasonably want to forego property insurance, and to deal with costs of repair as and when they arise.[19]

Unlike the decision of the House of Lords (which affirmed the decision of Blackburn J at first instance), this way of justifying why Rylands ought to bear the burden of repair does not lay direct stress on the fact that building the water deposit was 'extraordinarily dangerous', or that the thing he accumulated in his land was 'likely to do mischief' if it escaped.[20] These factors *do* play a part in the justification of liability, but their significance is tied to the value for Rylands, Fletcher and any other involved parties of having certain

---

[19] See also ch 4(V).

[20] *Rylands*, above n 2, *per* Lord Cairns at 162, quoting with approval the judgment of Blackburn J at 156. See also Ripstein, above n 1, at 70–1.

opportunities. They might suggest, for example, that people do not have general reason to value the opportunity to engage in certain particularly dangerous or foolish activities (as when a person amasses tons of explosives in their land for the fun of it), and so may not, on that basis, make moral demands about the distribution of the burden of repair between themselves and others. Yet the same principle can also lead to some surprising, but in my view reasonable, conclusions. When a person does have general reason to value being able to engage in a dangerous activity, then the more dangerous or risky that activity is, the more likely that a person would value allowing others who have better expertise to protect them against the activity going wrong, by regulating its operation. That will be true even when that activity is taking place in a space from which this person may normally exclude others. This, in turn, would be part of the justification for imposing such regulation on the activity (or, of course, banning it altogether, when there is no generic reason to value that activity). In other words, whether the dangers that an activity involves are typical or extraordinary matters insofar as it affects whether a person has reason to value the opportunity to engage in that activity, and whether the activity is, as a general matter, more likely to go well if it is supervised by that person alone, or if it is suitably regulated. The upshot of that idea is that when the state fails to regulate appropriately a dangerous activity that a person should otherwise be free to engage in (from the lighting of field fires, to the running of a nuclear power plant), the state may be failing to provide that person with the necessary degree of protection against the burden of repair, and may, accordingly, be required to shoulder part of that burden.[21] The conclusion is surprising because it is natural to think that the more dangerous the activity, especially when the dangers it involves are non-reciprocal, the stronger the case for imposing the burden of repair on the person who engages in it. But this holds true only on the assumption that this person is not entitled to protection against the burden of repair, or that the dangerous character of the activity itself precludes that person who carries it out from requiring others to provide them with such protection. That assumption will be clearly warranted in some cases, but not in all.

Similar considerations explain the significance of whether Rylands could have *foreseen* that the substance in his property might escape and cause harm to others. The significance of foreseeability in this context was addressed in the case of *Cambridge Water v Eastern Counties Leather*.[22] The defendant's tannery used

---

[21] This would be of particular significance in the context of so-called environmental torts, though I cannot explore this issue here From a vast literature, see T Brennan, 'Environmental Torts' (1993) 46 *Vanderbilt LR* 1; M Latham, V Schwartz and E Appel, 'The Intersection of Tort and Environmental Law: Where the Twains Should Meet and Depart' (2011) 80 *Fordham LR* 737; P Strand, 'The Inapplicability of Traditional Tort Analysis to Environmental Risks: The Example of Toxic Waste Pollution Victim Compensation' (1983) 35 *Stanford LR* 575.

[22] *Cambridge Water Co Ltd v Eastern Counties Leather plc* [1994] 2 AC 264.

certain solvents in processing leather. Those solvents were stored in barrels in the defendant's factory. Over a period of time, the solvents seeped through the barrels and the concrete floor, and eventually contaminated the borehole owned by the claimant, who had to cease using it. The House of Lords held that, properly interpreted, the principle in *Rylands* requires that a defendant be able to foresee that their activity may cause a certain type of harm to others.[23] This seems hard to justify. Requiring foreseeability in *Rylands* and *Cambridge Water* entails that the burden of repair for unforeseeable harms in such situations will lie with the claimants, so that principle ought to be justified to them. However, it is difficult to see how that principle would pass the test of avoidability under the 'avoidability as valuable opportunity' account, for the reasons discussed in relation to *Rylands* itself, namely that people normally place limited value in being able to supervise strangers; that they tend to value self-protection only in relation to activities they can easily guard against; and that they sometimes find value in protecting their property in ways other than taking out property insurance. By contrast, a principle that required Rylands and Eastern Counties Leather plc, respectively, to bear the burden of repair even for unforeseeable harms would *still* make such responsibility sensitive to whether those persons had an opportunity that was valuable to them, namely to erect a water deposit or to run a tanning factory, subject to the necessary regulatory controls. The same would obviously be true of even stricter liability rules, like those applicable to water undertakers in s 209 of the Water Industry Act 1991.

Gregory Keating agrees that the creation of an 'extraordinary' risk should not be a condition of liability in cases like *Rylands*. However, he has argued that we should not see the relevant liability rule as special to activities that one gets to undertake under one's own terms, but as an instance of general principle of 'enterprise liability'. Under that principle, it is fair for persons who benefit from imposing even ordinary risks on others to bear the costs of any accidents that result when those risks materialise.[24] My account agrees with several aspects of this idea. For a start, it too is favourably disposed to the general claim that the burdens and responsibilities that people may be required to bear in the context of an activity are connected to the value for them of engaging in that activity. A further common feature of the two accounts is that they treat the protection that people receive under various insurance schemes as part of the justification for imposing certain burdens on them under private law.[25] Finally, both accounts take the justification for imposing the burden of

---

[23] Ibid *per* Lord Goff at 305–6.

[24] G Keating, above n 1. See also J Murphy, 'The Merits of Rylands v Fletcher' (2004) 24 *OJLS* 643.

[25] Ibid at 1860: 'Identifying fairness with the fair distribution of harm ... leads to seeing a wide variety of administrative schemes, including workers' compensation, no-fault automobile insurance, industry-wide liability for black lung disease, and even the society-wide liability of the New Zealand Accident Compensation scheme, as continuous with the tort law of accidents'.

repair to be a question separate from the justification of the relevant original burden, and allow that the demandingness of the burden of repair may itself be a parameter of deciding whether one may require others to provide one with some measure of protection against it.[26] At the same time, it seems to me that in certain situations the 'enterprise liability' account makes the conditions of liability far too strict. That is particularly true in situations where the opportunity to take care is part of what makes a risky activity valuable for a person. Driving is, again, an obvious example. Given our technological capacities, the best way for people to go places with their own vehicles in safety is to observe certain traffic rules and to exercise a level of skill and advertence on the road. It follows that the value of driving for people lies partly in having the opportunity to exercise the appropriate level of skill and advertence. This suggests that a principle that imposed the burden of repair on drivers *simply* because their activity involves risks for others—as Keating's enterprise liability principle would recommend—could not be justified to drivers, inasmuch as it would fail to register the conditions under which drivers have reason to value the opportunity to undertake that activity.

Keating accepts this conclusion, but argues that the real reason why liability for traffic accidents ought to be care-based rather than enterprise liability-based is down to certain *epistemic* considerations. He explains that reason as follows:

> In some circumstances, it is impossible for the common law of torts to attribute responsibility for an accident to one of the parties to it without employing some criterion of fault. Highway accidents are the canonical case. In the absence of norms—usually statutes—specifying duties of precaution, rights of way, and so on, it is often impossible to attribute responsibility for accidental injury. In the absence of crosswalks, we may not be able to say if a pedestrian or a driver was responsible for an accident between the two. In the absence of rules ordering priorities among vehicles at four-way intersections, we may not be able to say whose activity is responsible for an accident between two cars at such an intersection.[27]

Keating may be right that the lack of such knowledge makes it difficult to determine which results are linked with which risks, eg to tell whether a traffic accident occurred because a driver was careless, or because of some other event that is in no way specific to driving. However, it seems to me that if that epistemic problem has the dimensions and significance Keating attaches to it, it is bound to appear in any setting, and in relation to any liability rule, be that a rule about damage from water deposits, harm occurring in the

---

[26] Ibid at 1861. Keating's claim in that regard is that 'irrespective of the initial distribution of risk, it is fairer to distribute the costs of accidents across those who benefit from the imposition of the relevant risks than it is to leave those costs concentrated on random victims'.

[27] Ibid at 1911.

provision of medical services, and so on. There too, it will sometimes be difficult to tell whether the damage was the result of the risk that the relevant activity exposes people to, or whether it was due to some external factor. If that is correct, epistemic difficulties do not provide us with a compelling criterion for preferring one liability rule rather than another, so Keating must seek a different explanation of why traffic accidents are an exception to the enterprise liability principle.

III. LIMITED CAPACITIES AND THE STANDARD OF CARE

In *Mansfield*, the court accepted on the facts that Mr Tarleton was generally a careful and conscientious driver, and that he would not have continued to drive if he had appreciated that his ability had been impaired. It was also established that, although Tarleton had not lost consciousness during the events (there were indications that he tried to brake just before the collision), he would not have appreciated the fact of his impairment. That was due to one of the peculiarities of the condition, which, for all its adverse effects on his capacity to drive, did not give rise to any physical symptoms or other signals that would have allowed him to realise his progressive incapacitation.[28]

The claimants argued that Tarleton's limited capacity at the time of the accident could not excuse him from the normal standard of care, unless it could be established that he had no control over his actions. The standard of care in tort, they pointed out, is 'objective' rather than 'subjective'.[29] Given that Tarleton did not lose consciousness but only suffered a gradual diminution in his driving ability, the claimants argued that he should have been held to the standard of care applicable to all drivers. The fact that he had been doing his best under the circumstances should not, in the claimants view, change this assessment, as long as Tarleton's best was not as good as people are generally entitled to expect of drivers. The Court of Appeal disagreed. Leggatt LJ held:

> There is no reason in principle why a driver should not escape liability where the disabling event is not sudden, but gradual, provided that the driver is unaware of it. A person with Mr Tarleton's very rare condition commonly does not appreciate that his ability is impaired, and he was no exception ... Of course, if he had known that it was, he would have been negligent in continuing to drive despite his knowledge of his disability.[30]

---

[28] *Mansfield*, above n 4, at 1266 *per* Leggatt LJ.

[29] The classic statement of this 'objective' principle is *Vaughan v Menlove* (1837) 132 ER 490.

[30] *Mansfield*, above n 4 at 1267 per Leggatt LJ. Compare this with *Roberts v Ramsbottom* [1980] 1 WLR 823 and *Waugh v James K Allan Ltd* [1964] 2 Lloyd's Rep 1, where the defendants were held to have been aware of their limited capacities.

On that basis, he concluded:

> In my judgment, the standard of care that Mr Tarleton was obliged to show in these circumstances was that which is to be expected of a reasonably competent driver unaware that he is or may be suffering from a condition that impairs his ability to drive. To apply an objective standard in a way that did not take account of Mr Tarleton's condition would be to impose strict liability. But that is not the law.[31]

Consider how the 'avoidability as valuable opportunity' account would go about justifying this result. Note, at the outset, that the court discussed the position of Tarleton and the claimant only. It did not examine as a separate question whether Weetabix, as Tarleton's employer, ought to bear the burden of repair. The reason for this is familiar. Under common law principles of vicarious liability, it is a requirement for holding an employer liable that the employee have committed a tort (which, in the court's view, Tarleton had not). However, whether that requirement is justified should itself be open to question; perhaps employers ought to bear the burden of repair even when the employee's conduct does not amount to a tort (I take up that issue in Chapter 7).[32] For present purposes, I will assume that the case concerns only the claimant and the defendant driver.

Suppose that the court had accepted the claimants' contention that the fact that a driver could not have met the standard of reasonable care should not make a difference to that driver's responsibilities. It seems to me that the account I have proposed would allow Tarleton to object to such a principle, on the ground that this principle would fail to make his liability sensitive to the value for him of the opportunities he had in the situation. For a start, it will not be any good to tell Tarleton that he could have avoided liability by not driving in the first place. People can reasonably want the opportunity to be able to drive their own vehicle, so that they can go places, and go safely. However, people normally value that opportunity on the assumption that they possess the necessary skill and capacity to engage in it, and to observe the relevant driving standards. They do not, as a general matter, find value in sitting behind the wheel unless they believe that they are fit to drive. It follows that holding a person liable for the burden of repair when that person's belief that they had the capacity to engage in that activity was mistaken would not be sensitive to the conditions under which the opportunity to drive is valuable for that person. And that will sometimes be true even when that person has maintained a certain degree of consciousness in the process. This person's complaint is not 'I was not acting', but 'I had no way of realising I had lost competence'.

---

[31] Ibid at 1268. Also *per* Aldous LJ at 1268–9: '[Tarleton] did not know and could not reasonably have known if his infirmity which was the cause of the accident. Therefore he was not at fault. His actions did not fall below the standard of care required'.

[32] See ch 7(V)(A)–(B).

This story about the significance of limited capacity seems to me to explain the emphasis that Leggatt LJ laid on what Tarleton *could have known* about his capacity. Irrespective of how much one actually knows about one's capacity to engage in an activity in a given situation, one may not object to a principle that makes one's liability contingent on whether one *had the opportunity to find out* if one is capable of engaging in that activity.[33] Obviously the same applies in respect of persons who incapacitate themselves, those who are reckless, those who suffer momentary lapses of concentration, or those who are learning a skill.[34] In all these cases, a principle that makes those persons bear the burden of repair is justified towards them, insofar as they had the opportunity to remain competent or vigilant, subject to any protection that those persons may require from others against the burden of repair (including regulation about licensing, learner insurance and so on). Things may be different in situations where the opportunity to find out whether one is competent in an activity has less value for a person, say, because this person suffers from a disposition that, while not completely robbing them of consciousness, makes it less likely that this person will form an accurate view of their own abilities. This is why Tarleton was held not to liable to make repair in *Mansfield*. His condition deprived him of an opportunity that he had reason to want to have available to him, namely to be able to assess his driving ability with reasonable accuracy. Holding him responsible to make repair would not have been sensitive to the value for him of having that opportunity.

It seems to me that the same reason justifies the special allowance that the law makes with regard to the standard of care in respect of the actions of children. The reason for treating children differently does not, as has been suggested, turn on the fact that children are less worthy of respect, or that treating them differently is generally OK.[35] It is, rather, that children are much more likely than adults to form an overoptimistic view of how things will go, partly because they are less likely to form a correct view of their own skills

---

[33] This seems to me to explain why the court referred to the 'standard of a reasonably competent driver unaware of the impairment to his ability to drive'. This is not the same as a standard of a 'careful unconscious driver', as Robert Stevens has suggested, *Torts and Rights* (Oxford, Oxford University Press, 2007) 110. Stevens is right that an unconscious driver is not subject to any meaningful standard of driving. But the driver that the court describes *is* subject to such a standard, though only to the extent that his limited abilities allow him to discharge it. As I explain in the text, I think that the position is very similar to that of children, and can be adequately accounted for under the same principles.

[34] A locus classicus of the last type of situation is *Nettleship v Weston* [1971] 2 QB 691. I discuss *Nettleship* and the protection that learners may be entitled to in ch 7(III)(C).

[35] For this view, see Stevens, above n 33, at 111, arguing that 'a better explanation for the exceptional treatment of children is that members of society are deserving of equal respect, and that part of that respect is that all adults should be treated in the same way ... Infantilizing children is acceptable and so we expect less of them.'

and abilities, and partly because they have a less developed sense of danger.[36] This suggests that a principle that failed to distinguish the position of children from that of adults would fail to register that an opportunity that is generally valuable for adults, namely to be able to assess their own skills with reasonable accuracy, can be of significantly lesser value to children.

The 'avoidability as valuable opportunity' story about *Mansfield* reaches a conclusion similar to the one Joseph Raz reaches on the basis of his Rational Functioning Principle for negligence. That principle says that one is responsible for outcomes that one intended, and for outcomes that result for the failure, due to the malfunction of one's powers of rational agency, to complete as intended an action within the domain of one's secure competence.[37] Raz's principle might seem to suggest that Tarleton is responsible for the accident he caused, inasmuch as that accident was the result of a malfunction in his decision-making ability. However, that is not so: in Raz's view, there is an important difference between a person who lacks (temporarily or permanently) the ability to form a certain decision, and a person who possesses that ability but fails to use it successfully on a certain occasion. Raz explains the difference by means of the following example. Suppose that a parent fails to check up on their baby in a certain situation, and the baby suffers some harm as a result. Under the Rational Functioning Principle, the parent will be responsible if they intended that harm, or simply forgot about the baby (that is the sense in which their powers of rational agency will have malfunctioned). But what if the parent is merely ignorant of their duty to check on the baby? Would they be responsible then? Raz says that the answer will depend

> on whether [the parent] not being aware of the duty is due to a malfunction of the parent's powers of rational agency. If the parent has normal competence and he lives in a society in which such a duty is widely understood, then he ... will be responsible for the ignorance (which is due to a malfunction of his rational powers) and derivatively responsible for the omission which arises out of that malfunction. If, however, the parent is disabled (has limited mental powers) then he will not be responsible, for the omission will not be due to a malfunction of *his* powers.[38]

Both points are, I think, correct. Holding the ignorant parent responsible would be justified, and for the reasons Raz gives, insofar as those reasons tie the parent's responsibilities to an account of whether the parent had the

---

[36] See, eg, *Yachuk v Oliver Blais Co Ltd* [1949] AC 386; *Gough v Thorne* [1966] 1 WLR 1387; *Mullin v Richards* [1998] 1 All ER 920. In these cases, courts accepted that the standard of care needs to be adjusted to what could reasonably be expected of a child of a certain age. *Mullin* is particularly on point, as the question of limited capacity was raised in respect of the child-defendant's liability rather than a child-claimant's contributory negligence, as in *Yachuk* and *Gough*. I touched upon the value for children of having a choice in ch 3(I).

[37] J Raz, 'Responsibility and the Negligence Standard' 30 *OJLS* (2010) 1, 16.

[38] Ibid at 18, n 35 (emphasis in original).

opportunity to find out about the duty to check on their baby in a certain situation, and that opportunity was something that the parent had reason to value. On the other hand, it seems to me that Raz's claim about the disabled parent would be correct not only in respect of the parent who failed to find out about the duty, but also in respect of a parent who failed to discharge that duty on a certain occasion due to a medical condition like Tarleton's.

The upshot of this way of justifying *Mansfield* is that the claim that the standard of care in negligence is 'objective' is an unhelpful half-truth. It is certainly correct to the extent that it suggests that the determination of that standard cannot be sensitive to every particular characteristic of every possible defendant. The 'avoidability as opportunity' account agrees, insofar as it only allows persons to object to principles of responsibility on the basis of 'generic' rather than 'individualised' reasons, but the point is clearly not special to that account.[39] Any theory about what people owe to each other will need to rely on 'objective' standards inasmuch as it must set certain limits to the degree of attention it will pay to each person's individual situation. As we have seen, however, this point is perfectly consistent with adjusting those generic standards with regard to certain classes of persons, and with regard to certain activities. *Mansfield* and the well-established case-law with regard to children illustrate that the law is sufficiently sensitive to this.

Arthur Ripstein disagrees. In discussing *Vaughan v Menlove*, where the court rejected the defendant's argument that he should escape liability because he was not intelligent enough to understand that his actions would start a fire, Ripstein says:

> The only way one can be exempt from the need to bear the costs of one's activities is not to be an agent at all. Had the court relieved Menlove of responsibility, and treated the bad luck as Vaughan's, they would have been treating Menlove himself as a mere natural thing rather than as an agent.[40]

Applied to *Mansfield*, this claim seems to me too strong both in its metaphor and its substance. The court in *Mansfield* may have relieved Mr Tarleton of responsibility for the burden of repair, but it clearly did not treat him 'as a mere natural thing rather than as an agent'. The court simply treated him as an agent who lacked a certain opportunity at a certain time, and it decided that this fact mattered in the assessment of that agent's responsibilities to others. Of course, one could sensibly say that, in the view of the court, our practical conclusion as to who ought to bear the burden of repair

---

[39] See ch 3(I).

[40] Ripstein, above n 1, at 85. As Ripstein notes (at 86) the facts of *Vaughan* leave open whether Menlove was unable to foresee the risk his actions posed, or whether he was 'taking a chance'. That said, the court has been interpreted as having held that Menlove would not have escaped liability even if the former were the case.

in *Mansfield* is the same that it would have been if the harm had been caused by a natural event. But that does not justify the claim that, in reaching that conclusion, we are treating *Tarleton* as a natural thing. It only justifies the weaker, and more sensible claim, that we are treating the *consequences* of Tarleton's actions as the consequences of a natural event (and therefore that we may justify in a similar fashion to the claimant why they ought to bear the burden of repair). That issue aside, the substantive claim that persons whose abilities do not allow them to live up to the normal standard of conduct are to bear the burden of repair *because* they engage in the activity that the relevant standards regulate seems much too sweeping.[41] Sometimes persons engage in activity without realising that carrying it out well requires skills and competence that exceed their abilities, or in the reasonable belief that they possess such skills and competence. *Mansfield* and the 'avoidability as valuable opportunity' account suggest that we should adopt a discriminating attitude to those cases. Instead of taking the fact that those persons engaged in the activity as settling whether others may hold them to the normal standard of care, we should ask whether those persons had the opportunity to assess their own level of competence in the activity with reasonable accuracy. And this involves no more argument than we already make in justifying similar allowances in respect of children and persons of limited mental capacity.[42]

IV. NEGLIGENCE LIABILITY AND THE UK SARAH ACT 2015

Suppose that a defendant claims that they ought to be protected against the burden of repair for their negligence because they 'were acting heroically by intervening in an emergency to assist an individual in danger', or because they were 'acting for the benefit of society or any of its members', or because they 'demonstrated a predominantly responsible approach towards protecting the safety or other interests of others' in carrying out the activity in the course of which they were negligent. Are these good complaints? UK

---

[41] Ibid at 86: 'Menlove cannot both claim incapacity in a particular case, yet also insist on the liberty to engage in risky activities. Insofar as he escapes responsibility, his liberty can be constrained for the safety of others'. *cf* Weinrib, above n 1 at 180: 'In pleading that he is too stupid to have taken account of the external effects of his action, the defendant is claiming an entitlement to realize his projects in the world while retaining the exclusively internal standpoint applicable to projects as mere possibilities'.

[42] At another juncture, Ripstein agrees with the application of differentiated standards for children in respect of contributory negligence, ibid at 112, n 27. While he considers the point confined to that context, cases like *Mullin v Richards*, above n 36, and the fact that parents are generally not held responsible for their children's carelessness, suggest that this is be the case.

Parliament thinks so, and has recently passed legislation that requires courts to 'have regard' to them in deciding whether a defendant in a negligence suit ought to bear the burden of repair. The quoted phrases are taken from sections 4, 2 and 3, respectively, of the Social Action, Responsibility, and Heroism (SARAH) Act 2015 (I have listed the complaints in what seems to me as their natural order). The SARAH Act does not lay down a specific way in which courts must 'have regard' to the three circumstances that it describes. Presumably, courts could discharge that requirement in the context of a decision as to whether a duty of care is owed, or in the context of a decision as to the appropriate standard of care. In this section I want to consider whether the 'avoidability as valuable opportunity' account would allow a person to complain on any of those three grounds against bearing the burden of repair, assuming (as the Act does) that this person already had valuable opportunities to avoid that burden by choosing appropriately. Although I will argue that none of those complaints should be allowed, I believe that giving a precise account of where the SARAH Act goes wrong can help us reach useful practical conclusions about how courts should respond to the requirement to 'have regard' to those complaints.

The government based the case in favour of the Act on three arguments. The first was that there was evidence to suggest that people are deterred from volunteering in emergencies due to the fear of the risk of liability.[43] In its view, the Act provides reassurance that if something goes wrong when people are acting for the benefit of society or intervening to help someone in an emergency, 'the courts will take into account the context of their actions in the event they are sued'.[44] The second argument was that giving those persons that protection would 'help to support the Government's broader aims of encouraging and enabling people to volunteer and to play a more active role in civil society'.[45] Finally, it was argued that the Act would 'reassure people, including employers, that if they demonstrate a [predominantly] responsible approach towards the safety of others during a particular activity, the courts will take this into account'.[46]

---

[43] See the Bill's *Explanatory Notes*, HL Bill 47-EN, 21 October 2014, available at http://www.publications.parliament.uk/pa/bills/lbill/2014-2015/0047/en/15047en.pdf which states (at [6]) that a 2006–7 survey of 'just under 300 respondents' who did not currently volunteer found that 47% cited the risk of liability as a reason for not doing do.

[44] UK Government, *Fact Sheet—Social Action, Responsibility and Heroism Bill*, Introduction at [1], see https://www.gov.uk/government/uploads/system/uploads/attachment_data/file/318839/sarah-bill-fact-sheet.pdf.

[45] Ibid at [2].

[46] Ibid at [3]. Note that the phrase in the original Bill was 'a generally responsible approach'. This was amended in the Act, which requires 'a predominantly responsible approach'.

I consider each of the three complaints, and the government's arguments for investing those complaints with legal force in the SARAH Act, in turn.

A. Assisting a Person in an Emergency

People may reasonably want the opportunity to rescue others from external dangers (ie dangers that those persons have not created or are otherwise responsible for). This is not just a nice thing to be able to do for someone, or a chance to become a hero by going over the call of legal duty. Sometimes having that opportunity will be central to discharging what one may reasonably regard as one's moral duty to others, eg to effect an easy rescue from a grave danger. It therefore makes sense that a person would want any principle of liability for cases where something goes wrong in the course of a rescue attempt to be sensitive to the value for that person of the opportunity to undertake such an attempt. Things look similar from the point of view of the person exposed to the external danger. That person has reason to value the opportunity to be rescued by others, and may therefore not object to a principle that is sufficiently sensitive to the value of having that opportunity. The case for the SARAH Act suggests that the law of negligence, as it stood before the Act came into force, allocated the burden of repair for rescue attempts that went wrong in a way that did not pass those tests of justification.

This suggestion seems to me demonstrably false. For a start, both would-be rescuers and persons in danger have reason to value the opportunity of a rescue only to the extent that such a rescue is carried out in certain ways, and according to certain basic standards. Sometimes a botched rescue attempt will not simply be 'not as good' as a more careful one; it will be disastrous for both rescuer and victim. That is because the value of the opportunity to rescue and to be rescued does not turn merely on the intentions or on the attitude with which the would-be rescuer engages in the task. While a person's *willingness* to undertake a rescue attempt may depend on those factors, the *effectiveness* of a rescue attempt is clearly independent of them. But the reason both parties place value on the opportunity of a rescue is precisely the prospect that such a rescue will be effective, and the exercise of a certain level of care makes it much more likely that the desired effect will come about. It follows that would-be rescuers could not reasonably object to a principle that required them to bear the burden of repair on the condition that they had the opportunity to exercise that level of care. 'I was acting with the aim of rescuing that person' is therefore not a good objection to the imposition of the burden of repair for one's negligence while attempting a rescue. It may, of course, be a good objection in other contexts, eg in a criminal trial or in the course of disciplinary proceedings, inasmuch as the relevant principles are justified in attributing significance to the intentions or other attitudes with which a person has acted.

Note, moreover, that this explanation allows the relevant standard of care to depend (as it does under the common law) on whether rescue is undertaken by a professional rescuer or a layperson.[47] If the value of the opportunity to rescue and to be rescued turns on the prospects of such a rescue being effective, this value must be judged according to what a person in the rescuer's position could reasonably believe about those prospects.

The same explanation shows why we should not attach any independent significance to the (let us assume, true) fact that society ought to encourage people to rescue others, or to the fact that encouraging people to do so is official government policy. These facts make a case in favour of cultivating in people a willingness to volunteer to rescue. Neither of them does anything to improve or otherwise bear on the effectiveness of such a rescue. As the value of the opportunity to undertake a rescue, for both rescuers and victims, turns on the latter consideration, neither fact bears on the justification of the relevant principles of liability.

At the same time, this line of thought seems to me to point towards an alternative policy that could pursue the government's aim to foster a culture of volunteering in the community, without prejudice to the interests of the victims of careless rescue attempts. In particular, it suggests that if the government is serious about promoting volunteering, it should put its money where its mouth is and require *taxpayers* to bear some part of the burden of repair for the consequences of careless rescue attempts. Such a scheme would pursue the aim by protecting would-be rescuers from some part of the burden of repair for any carelessness they display in effecting a rescue. And it would do this without depriving the victims of that carelessness of an opportunity they have reason to value, namely to be able to require anyone who undertakes their rescue voluntarily to exercise a basic level of care and advertence in doing so. With that in mind, one may conjecture whether English courts would be willing to act on the Act's injunction to them to 'have regard' to the defendant's willingness to rescue, heroically or not, by sending part of the claimant's bill to the Treasury. Measured against the alternative of letting government pursue its objectives at the expense of the victims of careless rescuers, that possibility should be welcomed. The fact that seeing it materialise might perhaps lead to a more informed debate about how much our community is willing to do to promote volunteer rescue operations would be an added bonus.

B. Acting for the Benefit of Society

The case for treating this complaint as a valid objection to liability for negligence is even weaker. Any principle that shields defendants from such

---

[47] See, eg, *Phillips v William Whiteley Ltd* [1938] 1 All ER 566; *Wells v Cooper* [1958] 2 QB 265.

liability imposes a corresponding burden on claimants. It says that the fact that a defendant is acting 'for the benefit of society or any one of its members' is a reason for claimants to bear a greater part of the burden of dealing with their misfortune than they would otherwise have to bear. That principle would therefore need to be justified to them.

It is not clear how such a principle would clear that hurdle. People sometimes value the opportunity to undertake burdens for the benefit of others, and, in certain cases, for the 'greater good' or for society as a whole. But people do not, as a general matter, value having *another person* decide when they should act on that opportunity. One reason for this is, of course, instrumental. People's lives will go better if they are able to judge for themselves whether it is worth worsening their position for the benefit of society or others, and what counts as a sufficient 'benefit' in that respect. But that reason can carry both representative and symbolic connotations too.[48] Sometimes the reason why people want to be able to take on burdens for the benefit of others is to signify—to themselves, to others, or to both—that, in doing so, they are undertaking a *sacrifice*. Having someone else decide the matter would therefore deprive that act of its representative value. Similarly, allowing someone else to decide that a person ought to bear some burden for the benefit of society, or of another, risks conveying the impression that the former person is less worthy of protection, or that their interests are expendable. It may therefore diminish the symbolic value for that person of the opportunity to decide for themselves whether to take on the relevant burdens. If this is correct, then a principle that asked claimants to bear a greater part of the burden of repair than they would otherwise be required to, on the ground that the defendant was acting for the benefit of society or any one of its members, would not be sensitive to a host of opportunities that claimants could reasonably want to have available to them.

C. Taking a Predominantly Responsible Approach to an Activity

This provision too would need to be justified towards the persons that it imposes burdens on, namely claimants. One difficulty in finding any such justification is that this complaint seems, by analogy, much weaker than the other two. If we should not allow defendants to escape liability for their negligence on the ground that they were engaged in rescuing the claimant, or that they were acting for the benefit of society or any one of its members, it would be extraordinary if we should allow them to escape liability on the ground that

---

[48] For the distinction between the 'instrumental', 'representative', and 'symbolic' value of choice, see ch 3(I).

they have been predominantly successful in taking care. The former two complaints are based on the claim that the defendant was *helping*, or was trying to help, others. The present one is based on the claim that the defendant has been overall successful in *not harming* others. If the defendant should not be allowed to rely on the former two arguments, it makes sense that they should not be allowed to rely on the latter either.

The 'avoidability as valuable opportunity' account gives us clear reason for the same conclusion without appeal to relative analogies. The principle proposed in s 3 of the SARAH Act 2015 could not be justified to the claimants in a negligence action, because it does not make the imposition of a greater than normal part of the burden of repair on those persons contingent on an opportunity that they would value having in the situation. In that regard, one should note that s 3 speaks of the defendant having taken a 'predominantly responsible' attitude not to the *act* or *omission* which constitutes the negligence, but to the *activity* in the course of which the negligence occurred. This matters, because it broadens the frame of assessment for the allocation of the burden of repair. As it stands, s 3 allows a defendant to say that, apart from looking into their conduct in the circumstances of the negligence, courts *also* ought to 'have regard' to how that defendant has been going about their business generally.[49] Accordingly, justifying this provision involves asking whether this broadening of the frame for deciding who ought to bear the burden of repair could be justified to claimants.

I think that the answer is clearly 'no'. The obvious problem is that s 3 does not tie the possibility that claimants may be required to bear a higher than normal part of the burden of repair to whether they had any opportunity to *become familiar* with the defendant's record of safety. When claimants have not been given that opportunity, making the burdens that they have to bear depend on the character of the defendant's record would be obviously unjustified. However, it seems to me that the same conclusion will hold *even when* claimants are aware of the fact that the defendant has in the past taken a 'predominantly responsible' approach towards the safety and interests of others in the course of the activity in which the negligence occurred. The problem here

---

[49] *cf* the speech, and the amendment proposed, by Lord Pannick in the House of Lords debate, 6 January 2015, Cmn 261–62: 'We all agree, including the Minister, that it is not the intention of this clause that, when a doctor is sued for negligence for cutting off my right leg because I had a pain in my left leg, it should then be open to the doctor to plead in his or her defence, "I have been treating legs for 40 years and have never before made such a mistake". What the claimant is concerned about, and what the court must address, is what happened on the specific occasion when that claimant was treated. The problem is that the word "activity" in the first line of Clause 3 suggests the contrary. The word "activity" might suggest the general practice of medicine performed by the defendant. I suggest that the words "act or omission" are much more appropriate than the broader term "activity".' Lord Pannick's proposed amendment was defeated in the Lords.

lies in the particular way in which the Act connects the defendant's history to the value for claimants of the opportunity to become familiar with that history. In some cases, the two will, in fact, be related. Suppose that a claimant knows that a defendant has a *history of carelessness* in certain situations. Awareness of this fact may sometimes heighten the claimant's sense of danger, and therefore put them in a better position to protect themselves against suffering harm from the defendant's conduct. Assuming that the cost of self-protection is very low, a principle that required the claimant to bear part of the burden of repair for the defendant's carelessness might in some cases be justified towards the claimant. That, in fact, is one of the typical settings of contributory negligence.[50] The problem with s 3 of the SARAH Act is that it attempts to use the same idea in respect of defendants who have a *history of care*. This is a mistake. Knowing of one's history of carelessness puts people on their toes, and therefore places them in a better position to protect themselves. Knowing of one's history of care does not (if anything, the fact that one has had a good record in that regard may even lull people into a false sense of security). A defendant who has taken a 'predominantly responsible' attitude towards the safety and other interests of others is in no way exceptional, so knowledge of the fact that the defendant has taken such an attitude does nothing to improve a claimant's ability to better protect themselves. The Act is therefore wrong to allow the defendant to invoke that fact to escape part of the burden of repair for their negligence.

I conclude that none of the complaints that the SARAH Act invests with legal force has independent moral merit. One should not be able to limit one's negligence liabilities by appealing to the fact that one was acting heroically in rescue of others; or for the benefit of society or any one of its members; or that one had taken a predominantly responsible attitude towards the safety and other interests of others in the course of one's activity.

That conclusion may sound obvious, and the target I have chosen may look too feeble. My anecdotal impression of informed opinion amongst private lawyers is that the SARAH Act is, at best, superfluous and, at worst, a hindrance to the application of perfectly justified principles of the law of negligence. However, I believe that neither criticism goes to the heart of the problem. The various sponsors of the Act would reject the description of it as a hindrance to the law. They would argue, and have actually argued, that the purpose of the Act is to bring the law in line with our intuitions about what people should take responsibility for. In fact, one of the most striking aspects of the SARAH Act is that both the Act and the arguments in its favour are expressly couched in the language of responsibility. The government has claimed that

---

[50] See ch 4(III)–(V).

the Act 'will encourage responsible employers to stand up to speculative and opportunistic claims'; that it will 'make sure the court will give consideration to the fact that people may have taken care when organising an activity but, in spite of their best efforts, an accident has happened'; and that 'it restores a balance to counter the health and safety culture, and provides valuable reassurance to people that courts will take full account of the context of their actions if someone is sued after acting in a socially beneficial way'.[51] In making the case for the SARAH Act in the press, the then Justice Minister said:

> We are a bit of a society that is a bit too inclined to blame someone else ... [We must do something for] the kind of situations which happen all too often and very seldom get to court—where somebody has an accident at work, it's entirely their own fault, they have got a perfectly responsible employer who has the normal health and safety procedures in place but that person does something dumb, hurts themselves and sues the employer anyway.[52]

These claims may be spurious. The overall narrative that feeds them, about the ostensible need to counteract a 'compensation culture', may be far too sweeping and morally suspect. However, they are claims about what things people should take responsibility for, and they owe much of their appeal to the fact that they are framed in that way. It is therefore important to fight and defeat them on that terrain. The danger in saying that the law already takes adequate account of those claims is that we might end up endorsing their mistaken view of responsibility by implication.

V. CONCLUSION

In this chapter I have tried to add more texture and practical bite to the value-of-choice account I developed in Chapters 3 and 4. I have claimed that this account does a good job of explaining the significance of avoidability for a person's substantive responsibilities. In particular, I have argued that avoidability matters as an *opportunity* one has reason to value, rather than an indicator of a person's ability to do otherwise, one's general capacity to act in the world, or competence over certain activities. I have supported this 'avoidability as

---

[51] Ministry of Justice, 'Courts to recognise good intentions of volunteers and small businesses', *Press Release*, 12 February 2015, available at https://www.gov.uk/government/news/courts-to-recognise-good-intentions-of-volunteers-and-small-businesses. It is notable that, while the government trumpeted the protection of volunteer organisations and small businesses as its key concern, it chose to give exactly the same protection to big businesses.

[52] 'Chris Grayling vows to slay "health & safety culture"', Daily Telegraph, 19 July 2014, available at http://www.telegraph.co.uk/news/politics/conservative/10978488/Chris-Grayling-vows-to-slay-health-and-safety-culture.html.

valuable opportunity' view by showing how it can help us explain why liability for the burden of repair may be negligence-based in some contexts and stricter in others, and how far the law of negligence ought to make allowance for a defendant's limited ability to discharge the standard of reasonable care. Finally, I have applied it in assessing the (as it turns out, scant) merits of the recent Social Action, Heroism, and Responsibility Act 2015. As it went, my discussion compared 'avoidability as opportunity' with some well-known rivals. I have concluded that this account matches the conclusions of some of those rivals, and that is resists those of several others.

The next two chapters continue with the task of working out the practical implications of the value-of-choice account for the justification of private law principles. Chapter 6 deals with contracts, and the ways in which a person's position in the social structure affects the value that certain transactional opportunities have for that person. Chapter 7 deals with the principles of vicarious liability as an instance of protection against the consequences of one's mistakes.

6

Contracts and the Social Structure

NOBODY FORCES YOU into a contract. Even when the law mandates that you conclude an enforceable agreement with another person—usually, to sign up for some form of insurance in relation to a certain activity, like driving or owning an airline business—you still have options. Sometimes you can avoid the mandate altogether by avoiding the activity, eg you can choose not to drive a car and therefore avoid the need to obtain car insurance, and at the very least you get to choose who to enter into that contract with. But these are exceptional situations anyway, as most of the time you are free to enter or not to enter into contracts or other voluntary commitments as and when you see fit. Moreover when you are minded to enter into a contract, you have the opportunity to decide not to go through with the deal if one or more of the terms that the other party proposes are not to your liking. You can, of course, try to get the other party to make that term more palatable to you by offering them something in return, and so on. If you find yourselves unable to reach a deal, you are both still free to look for alternative terms and contractual partners. If your negotiation bears fruit, and you choose to make a deal, then neither of you can object to having that deal enforced by the law and its institutions. I will call this the 'classical' story about contracts and their enforceability.

The classical story owes much of its appeal to the way it brings into focus the cluster of opportunities that contracting, understood as the making of legally enforceable agreements (and other voluntary undertakings, but I will let this lie), provides a person with. Chief amongst those opportunities, arranged in the order in which they appear when things go well, seem to me to be:

— the opportunity to not to seek a deal;
— the opportunity to negotiate a deal;
— the opportunity to weigh one's options; and
— the opportunity to say yes or no to the deal on the table.

Having these four opportunities is, generally speaking, a good thing because things are more likely to go well for a person if they have them. That remains true even if a person does not find value in all of those opportunities in every context. Not many of us care to negotiate at the supermarket checkout but we do value that opportunity when it comes to purchasing a home, or a car, and so on.

Following Hart and Scanlon, I have argued that the fact that a principle provides a person with such opportunities is a central part of the explanation of why that person ought to bear the practical burdens that this principle involves.[1] By that token, the classical story about contracting and the four opportunities I have listed is not just a story about why the institution in question is useful for people, but also about why people who enter into contracts may not object to having the coercive force of the state used against them when they fail to perform their part of a deal.

At the same time, the value-of-choice account gives us a clue about why the classical story paints with too broad a brush. We are all familiar with situations in which those four opportunities may not be very valuable for you. If the contract in question is for a job and you are unemployed, the opportunity to say no to an otherwise poor offer loses much of its appeal. The opportunity to say something like 'no to consumerism!' seems to me to fall in the same basket. Giving up on consumer purchases sounds cool, but good luck with going ahead with it. The opportunity to negotiate is something you often do not have at all, eg in relation to health and safety standards at your workplace, or to standard form consumer contracts. In other situations, you may have all the relevant options and information at your disposal and still be likely to make the wrong choice because your judgement is adversely affected by a rational bias, eg you choose to buy property insurance because you have recently been the victim of a burglary, and therefore tend to overestimate the probability of suffering again in the future. The limitations in the value of those opportunities for you can have a knock-on effect on the value of the last opportunity on the list, the opportunity to say yes or no to the deal on the table. If you said yes because the person offering the job held all the bargaining chips; because the sign-up page for the broadband service did not allow you to object to a particularly onerous 'lock in' term; or because your judgement on whether to get insurance was overly influenced by an 'availability' heuristic, it may be less likely that your decision will make things go better for you. The same goes for the opportunity to say no: if on reflection you decide to refuse to deal on the more or less similar terms that every broadband provider is offering, saying no will just leave you without a broadband connection. You recognise these examples because, like all of us, you can experience them every day in consumer, employment or insurance transactions. They tell us that, in certain contexts, the opportunities that the classical story points to will have limited value for you not just occasionally, but *typically*.

---

[1] See introduction, and ch 3(II).

It is this last point that makes the difference. After all, the classical story acknowledges that sometimes you will be in a position of need and unable to refuse the deal you are offered; that negotiating will sometimes be hard and sometimes unappealing; that sometimes you will know less than the other party, or just be worse than them at choosing, and so on. What it says is that, these occasions notwithstanding, the four opportunities are still things you have general reason to value. The alternative story I have in mind points out that, in relation to certain transactions, 'sometimes' and 'occasionally' become 'nearly always' and 'typically'. The reason is that when it comes to such transactions, the limited value of the four opportunities for you is not due to your personal situation, but to what I will call your *structural position*. These opportunities are less valuable for you in certain contexts, not so much because you are out of pocket, or less savvy, or less patient, or less good than others at negotiating, but because you enter those transactions as a job-seeker, as an employee, or as a consumer. These are situations familiar and common enough in our societies to constitute instantly recognisable types, with different persons occupying different transactional roles in them, and with the transactional opportunities available to each of those persons largely determined by their structural position (rich consumers, if you will, are still consumers; the only difference is that they can buy more and pricier stuff).[2] Even when the cause of an opportunity having little value for you is not structural in nature, eg it is due to certain rational biases that can exercise an adverse effect on people's judgement whatever their structural position, the fact that you occupy a weak structural position may leave you more exposed to the influence of that cause, or allow structurally stronger parties to use this to their advantage.[3] I will call the story that draws attention to the fact that the four opportunities may sometimes have limited value for persons occupying a particular structural position the 'structural' story.

My aim in this chapter is to use the contrast between the two stories to explain how the value-of-choice account would justify certain basic aspects of contract law. I begin by setting out and criticising two principles that TM Scanlon has proposed for the enforceability of voluntary undertakings. These principles seem to me to owe their plausibility to the assumption that the classical case for contracting is basically correct. I try to illustrate the limitations of that assumption by showing why Scanlon's principles would be rejected by persons occupying certain structural positions, and how those principles could

---

[2] My description draws on AJ Julius, 'Basic Structure and the Value of Equality' (2003) 31 *Philosophy & Public Affairs* 321.

[3] See generally O Bar-Gill, *Seduction by Contract: Law, Economics, and Psychology in Consumer Markets* (Oxford, Oxford University Press, 2012); MJ Radin, *Boilerplate: the Fine Print, Vanishing Rights and the Rule of Law* (Princeton NJ, Princeton University Press, 2012).

be revised on grounds that Scanlon's own value-of-choice account would recognise. Part of that argument will be that appropriate principles of enforceability ought to give the state more than the binary power to enforce or to
refuse to enforce a given voluntary undertaking. Sometimes those principles
ought to allow the state to protect structurally weaker parties by enforcing
the undertakings those parties have entered into under different terms (or by
'implying' certain terms in those undertakings). This protective regulatory
power is justified by the very idea that motivates the classical story, namely that
contracting provides people with certain opportunities they have reason to
value. The only difference is that sometimes making that institution valuable
for people requires protecting them in ways other than simply enforcing or
refusing to enforce the transactions they enter into. The point will be familiar
to anyone versed in consumer, labour or insurance law. The value-of-choice
account shows why the justification for giving the state the necessary regulatory powers is not incidental to the types of transactions those bodies of law
are concerned with, but general to contract law as a whole.

In earlier work,[4] I claimed that this argument is consistent with the view,
usually dismissed as implausible, that the moral aim of contract law is to do
social justice.[5] I now believe that this claim is largely unnecessary. Instead of
saying that contract law does social justice, and then adding that social justice
requires the imposition of certain limits to bargaining power and the regulation of the content of certain types of contracts, it is better to say directly that
contract law principles are justified to the extent that they do those things.
What matters is the case for imposing limits on bargaining power, and for
allowing the state to regulate the content of certain types of agreements and
to enforce them under alternate terms. That case, I believe, can be made sufficiently clearly by reference to the value for persons of having the opportunities
that the institution of contracting comes with. If that is correct, we can afford

---

[4] E Voyiakis, 'Contract Law and Reasons of Social Justice' 25 *Canadian Journal of Law &
Jurisprudence* (2012) 393.
[5] The *locus classicus* for it is A Kronman, 'Contract Law and Distributive Justice' (1980) 89
Yale LJ 472. See also A Bagchi, 'Distributive Justice and Contract' in G Klass, G Letsas and
P Saprai, *Philosophical Foundations of Contract Law* (Oxford, Oxford University Press, 2014) 193.
For criticisms of Kronman's account see, P Benson, 'Abstract Right and the Possibility of a Non-
Distributive Conception of Contract: Hegel and Contemporary Contract Theory' (1989)
10 *Cardozo LR* 1077, 1121ff; W Lucy, 'Contract as a Mechanism of Distributive Justice' (1989)
9 *OJLS* 132; M Trebilcock, *The Limits of Freedom of Contract* (Cambridge, Mass, Harvard Uni-
versity Press, 1993) 82–91; T Dare, 'Kronman on Contract: A Study in the Relation Between
Substance and Procedure in Normative and Legal Theory' (1994) 7 *Canadian Journal of Law &
Jurisprudence* 331; M Kramer and N Simmonds, 'Getting the Rabbit Out of the Hat: A Critique
of Anthony Kronman's Theory of Contracts' (1996) 55 *Cambridge LJ* 358; S Smith, *Contract
Theory* (Oxford, Oxford University Press, 2004) 137–8; M Hevia, 'Kronman on Contract Law
and Distributive Justice' (2007) 23 *Journal of Contract Law* 105.

to let the question of whether modelling contract law along those lines would also do social justice to take care of itself.

I. THE CLASSICAL STORY AND ITS LIMITATIONS: SCANLON'S EL AND EF PRINCIPLES

TM Scanlon has put forward two principles that he believes we ought to take as the moral measure of laws on the enforceability of voluntary undertakings.[6] In contrast to his work on promises and social practices,[7] his principles on enforceability do not appear to have been discussed much in philosophical and legal literature.[8] I will take them as my main focus in this section for two reasons. The first is that Scanlon's principles seem to me a particularly clear version of what I have called the classical story, ie the story which justifies the enforceability of contracts by reference to the four opportunities I have listed, and regards occasions where opportunities have limited value for some persons as having only peripheral significance. Secondly, Scanlon justifies his proposed principles of enforceability on the basis of the value-of-choice account. As I think that the value-of-choice account supports quite a different conclusion from Scanlon's, I hope to use my argument as to why his two principles are rejectable to illustrate the justificatory resources of the account itself.

The first principle Scanlon proposes is the EL (Enforcement of Loss Prevention) principle:

> EL: If one has intentionally or negligently led another to form expectations about one is going to do, and has neither warned this person or performed as expected, and the person has suffered significant loss as a result of relying on the expected performance, then the coercive power of the state may be used to force him or her to compensate the other person for this loss, provided that a law authorizing this is established and applied in a system of law that is tolerably fair and efficient.[9]

EL justifies the use of enforcement to make one compensate those who have incurred loss in reliance upon expectations one has led them to form. It does

---

[6] TM Scanlon, 'Promises and Contracts' in *The Difficulty of Tolerance: Essays in Political Philosophy* (Cambridge, Cambridge University Press, 2003) 234. The essay appeared originally in P Benson (ed), *The Theory of Contract Law* (New York, Cambridge University Press, 2001) 86. My citations refer to the former volume.

[7] TM Scanlon, 'Promises and Practices' (1990) 19 *Philosophy & Public Affairs* 199 and *What We Owe To Each Other* (Cambridge, Mass, Belknap Press of Harvard University Press, 1998) ch 7; N Kolodny and RJ Wallace, 'Promises and Practices Revisited' (2003) 31 *Philosophy & Public Affairs* 119.

[8] I have come across only one short exposition of Scanlon's two principles, in W Lucy, *Philosophy of Private Law* (Oxford, Oxford University Press, 2007) 242–4, where discussion focuses not on the substantive merits of those principles, but on the relationship between Scanlon's contractualism and general theories about the legal enforcement of morality.

[9] Scanlon, above n 6, at 250.

not justify more intrusive measures, such as actually forcing one to perform or to pay compensation to the equivalent of performance. However, Scanlon thinks that such measures are justified in certain cases and proposes a second principle to describe them. That is the EF (Enforcement of Fidelity) principle:

> EF: It is permissible legally to enforce remedies for breach of contract that go beyond compensation for reliance losses, provided that these remedies are not excessive and that they apply only in cases in which the following conditions hold: (1) A, the party against whom the remedy is enforced, has, in the absence of objectionable constraint and with the adequate understanding (or the ability to acquire such understanding) of his or her situation, intentionally led B to expect that A would do X unless B consented to A's not doing so; (2) A had reason to believe that B wanted to be assured of this; (3) A acted with the aim of providing this assurance, by indicating to B that he or she was undertaking a legal obligation to do X; (4) B indicated that he or she understood A to have undertaken such an obligation; (5) A and B knew, or could easily determine, what kind of remedy B would be legally entitled to if A breached this obligation; and (6) A failed to do X without being released from this obligation by B, and without special justification for doing so.[10]

In line with the value-of-choice account, Scanlon does not build the case for EL and EF on the fact that failing to live up on one's representations, or causing others to suffer loss by disappointing expectations one has led others to form, or going back on the assurances one has given to others, would be wrongful.[11] His account of the two enforcement principles is meant to be 'self-standing' (or—in the language I used in Chapter 1—'direct') in the sense that it proceeds in the same way one would proceed to account for the original obligations generated by undertaking between A and B.[12] In particular, Scanlon asks us to approach the question of enforceability by considering whether EL and EF are sufficiently sensitive to the value for A and B of being able to give and receive the enforceable commitments that the principle describes, no matter whether those commitments could be described as promises or some other form of undertaking, and whether the failure to keep those commitments would count as a wrong.

The EL principle responds to the general value for people of the opportunity to be able to rely on expectations that others have led them to form, secure in the knowledge that they will not thereby be risking uncompensated

---

[10] Ibid at 256.

[11] For such accounts, see C Fried, *Contract as Promise* (Cambridge, Mass, Harvard University Press, 1981); S Shiffrin, 'The Divergence of Contract and Promise' (2007) 120 *Harvard LR* 709; J Raz, 'Promises in Morality and Law' (1982) 95 *Harvard LR* 916, 933.

[12] Lucy, above n 8, at 242–3. Scanlon defends the relevant *Loss Prevention* (L) and *Fidelity* (F) principles in *What We Owe To Each Other*, ch 7 and summarises the argument for them in 'Promises and Contracts', above n 6, at 237–46.

significant losses.[13] That principle could not be rejected as too burdensome by those who could potentially be subject to enforcement measures, Scanlon argues, because EL itself provides them with two valuable opportunities to escape those measures, by giving early warning of their change of mind or by willingly compensating for the other party's loss.[14] Similarly, Scanlon finds support for EF in the fact that people do not want just to be able to shift the cost of their reliance; they also have reason to value the opportunity to give and to receive *assurances* that certain things will happen. Since 'both promisors and promisees have good reason to want to be able to make legally binding agreements that are enforced in a way that provides this kind of assurance … there is good prima facie reason to permit the state to do this'.[15] While EF gives strong protection to people who seek assurances, it may not be rejected by those who provide them, because it affords the latter ample opportunity to avoid unexpected or excessive liabilities, as long as they do not hold themselves out as offering the assurances that EF describes.[16]

I think that, as they stand, both principles are reasonably rejectable, and for reasons that flow from the value-of-choice account itself. Since my argument will be quite general in character, I propose to train it against the more refined requirements of the EF principle, hoping that its extensibility to EL will become obvious on the way. Using the opportunity to negotiate one's wages as an example, I will suggest that EF would be rejected by persons in a certain structural position, because that principle fails to make the responsibilities that those persons incur under the principle sensitive to whether they have reason to value the opportunities available to them when they transact from that position. The sharper end of that problem is that EF fails to justify what is clearly the most appropriate institutional response to the fact that the certain opportunity is not valuable for a person in a certain structural position.

Consider the following example:

Minimum wage: Worker is skilled but unemployed. Boss offers Worker a job for a salary of £100 a month. Worker accepts the offer. At the end of the month, someone informs Worker that the statutory monthly minimum wage is £200. Worker asks Boss for the difference, but Boss declines to pay.

---

[13] Scanlon, above n 6, at 250–1.

[14] In discussing whether his principles are too burdensome, Scanlon distinguishes between the potential costs of complying with his principles ('compliance costs') and the potential costs of the principles being misapplied by state institutions ('error costs'), ibid at 251–2 and 258. For simplicity, my summary of Scanlon's argument omits reference to error costs, assuming that they would not be extensive in any system with reasonably fair and efficient institutions.

[15] Ibid at 258–9.

[16] Ibid.

Suppose that Boss invokes the EF principle and says that Worker should accept the wage they agreed. Does EF allow Worker to object to this arrangement, and, by implication, does it block Boss from claiming against Worker for any loss that Boss might incur if Worker refused to work for less than the minimum wage? And does EF allow Worker to continue to work for Boss and still claim the difference between the agreed and the minimum wage? I will claim that the answer is yes to the first question, and no to the second. In making out this claim, I will take it as a given that enforcing the minimum wage against the employer is legitimate and that enforcing the contract between the parties under the original terms is not. This assumes that, in principle, minimum wage laws reflect justifiable policies that may be legitimately enforced in the place of the parties' original arrangements. Accordingly, I will make no effort to sell the rest of the argument to those that deny this assumption, eg to a certain hard-core brand of libertarian. The question I will take up is whether EF can account for the legitimacy of refusing to enforce the original deal and of enforcing the minimum wage in its stead, or, if EF cannot do the trick, whether that is good reason to reject it as a principle for the enforceability of voluntary undertakings.

On a plain reading of EF, there are three ways in which the enforcement of the minimum wage against Boss might turn out to be justified.[17] I will consider them in what seems to me their more natural order. First, one might look at condition (5) of EF and say that both parties were able to determine easily that the remedy Worker would be entitled to in case Boss breached their agreement would be the minimum wage. Secondly, one could look at condition (1) of EF and argue that Worker's choice to enter into the transaction under the agreed wage was 'objectionably constrained'. Thirdly, one might look at condition (6) of EF and say that even if the requirements of EF are met, there is some 'special justification' for enforcing the minimum wage rather than the agreed one.

The first argument trades on the idea that the existence of minimum wage laws puts the parties on fair notice of how the state will use its enforcement powers in the context of their transaction, and that this could justify enforcing the minimum wage on Boss. The problem is that condition (5) requires that the parties should have been able to determine easily what remedy the law gives *in the event of breach* of the agreed undertaking and, in my example,

---

[17] There is a fourth one. Anthony Kronman has argued that distributive considerations may affect the legitimacy of enforcing a voluntary undertaking by giving a particular content to the intentions of the parties, Kronman, above n 5. Although I am broadly sympathetic to the gist of Kronman's thesis, I think that the reference to the parties' intentions does little real justificatory work. An appeal to what the parties must be taken to have intended is not an appeal to the parties' intentions but to whatever principle justifies our inference about their intentions.

there is no such breach. We cannot get around the problem by taking the highlighted part out of condition (5). The idea that the parties are easily able to determine in advance and what legal remedy is available presupposes that parties should be able to point to some action or event, the occurrence of which they understand as triggering the remedy. But condition (5) seems built in a way such that the action or event in question must be, if not a breach, then at least something *other* than the performance of the agreed undertaking. In my example, both Worker and Boss have done exactly what they agreed to do.

The second argument says that Boss cannot insist on the enforcement of the agreed terms because Worker entered into the contract under what condition (1) of EF terms 'objectionable constraints'. This is clearly a more promising idea. For a start, the 'no objectionable constraints' proviso is sufficiently wide to cover even situations where the constraints are not the result of wrongful conduct by the other part (eg some form of duress). Recall that, under the value-of-choice account, the case for EF as a whole does not turn on the potential wrongfulness of the parties' conduct towards each other. We should therefore expect that the test of whether a constraint on a person's transactional decisions is 'objectionable' under clause (1) of EF turns not on whether that person's options have been 'wrongfully constrained' by the other party, but on whether that person lacks reason to value the constrained opportunity that they are presented with in the situation. The particular source or cause of that constraint—be it that person's own abilities and disposition, some action by other party, or some feature of the social structure—matters only inasmuch as it affects whether this person lacks such reason.[18] Let us suppose, then, that at least some persons in Worker's position will agree to work for less than the minimum wage because the alternative of unemployment will be even worse.[19] While those persons will value the opportunity to

---

[18] See my discussion in ch 5, introduction, of David Hume's examples involving a person who agrees to pay a doctor for a life-saving operation and a person who agrees to pay a blackmailer to avoid suffering harm.

[19] How much worse? For my purposes, 'worse' means worse enough to give Worker a clear incentive to seek employment rather than rely on eligibility for welfare. On this point, see D Zimmerman, 'Coercive Wage Offers' (1981) 10 *Philosophy & Public Affairs* 121, 139: 'Under early market-capitalism, especially where there was a "reserve army of the unemployed", a worker had to choose between taking a miserable job, often in a sweatshop or mill of the worst sort, and living on the margin of urban society, perhaps literally starving. I presume that the recipient of a wage proposal under these conditions would count himself lucky. Under advanced welfare-capitalism, by contrast, the choice is typically between accepting a contract which provides a considerably better paid job, under considerably better working conditions, with some job security and some fringe benefits, and going on welfare, which for most workers would be much worse financially and emotionally. I presume that these workers too would want to move from the pre-proposal to the proposal situation.' Zimmerman also reminds us that if Worker is a migrant, there is a higher chance that he will not be in a union and will live on the margins in relative poverty.

go into employment, they will not value the opportunity to negotiate their salary, because negotiation is likely to make things worse rather than better for them. It follows that a principle that required Worker to accept only £100 in payment *on the ground that this is what the parties negotiated* would make Worker's responsibilities turn on an opportunity that Worker had little reason to value in the situation. So condition (1) seems to allow Worker to object to having to work for less than the minimum wage, and does so regardless of what we make of Boss's conduct in the situation.

The problem with this story is that the appeal to (1) does not explain how the presence of 'objectionable constraints' on Worker's choice to enter into the employment contract can make it the case that Worker is entitled to the minimum wage. That is, it is unclear how the 'objectionable constraint' in question could be made to achieve the effect of not only blocking enforcement of the agreed terms against Worker, but *also* of legitimating enforcement of the employment agreement against Boss under a modified set of terms. If anything, Boss was not facing any relevant decision-making constraint, nor did Boss intentionally lead Worker to expect the minimum wage.

That is a big problem because the enforcement of the minimum wage in the place of the agreed one is a central aspect of the policy in question. If EF cannot explain why Worker is entitled *both* to remain employed under the agreement *and* to receive the minimum wage instead of the agreed one, it will have trouble accounting for the many other cases where the law intervenes to provide weaker parties with more transactional options and alternatives than they would otherwise have been able to bargain for. These include legal regulations on health and safety, working conditions and dismissal in the context of employment contracts, regulations on the exclusion of liability, the right of termination and the interpretation of consumer contracts (including contracts of insurance) and so on.

More specifically, the argument for the law's intervention in favour of employees, consumers or insurance holders seems to me to turn on four aspects of the transactions in question. First, the inequality of bargaining power between parties to employment, consumer or insurance transactions is a feature of the economic structure of our societies, not simply a feature of the parties' personal situation. Secondly, this inequality reduces the value for parties in a weaker structural position of the opportunity to negotiate. Thirdly, the diminished value of the opportunity to negotiate is partly due to the fact that the opportunity not to seek a deal in the first place, or to say no to an offer is *also* considerably less valuable for that weaker party, ie that the respective value for employees and consumers of the opportunity to refuse work or the purchase of basic consumer goods is smaller than the value for the employers of the opportunity to turn potential employees away, or the value for businesses of the opportunity to turn away customers. Fourthly, responding to the limited value of those opportunities for persons in a weaker structural position may require measures that keep the concluded undertaking 'alive' and modify its terms, instead of rendering it flatly unenforceable. The point is that if we refused to enforce employment, consumer or insurance contracts entered into under the influence of 'objectionable constraints', we would not be protecting the value for employees, consumers or insurance holders of the opportunity to negotiate, or to say no. We would be reducing that value *even further* and, in so doing, we would be misunderstanding what is objectionable in the character of the constraints that those classes of agents face. Those agents do not value just the freedom to negotiate on equal terms or to resist the enforcement of a bad deal. They also value—often, very much indeed—the opportunity to enter into an enforceable deal while being protected against the force of certain terms that they could not hope to get rid of through the bargaining process. The problem with the appeal to condition (1) of EF is that it has no obvious way of giving them that kind of protection.

The third way of accommodating my example within EF says that enforcing the minimum wage in the place of the agreed one against Boss may be justified but that, in the grander scheme of things, the reasons to put the state's enforcement powers to such use play only a peripheral role in the justification of enforcing voluntary undertakings, a role adequately accommodated under the 'special justification' rider in condition (6) of EF.

I think that this too fails for reasons similar to those that spoke against the second argument. For a start, it will not do to say that a garden-variety voluntary undertaking does not, as a general matter, require the state to undertake the protective action described in the previous paragraphs. Employment, consumer and insurance agreements *are* the garden-variety case. They constitute the bulk of voluntary transactions in our societies, so one would expect any principle of enforcement to treat them as part of its core subject-matter. That aside, the special justification rider in (6) is meant to leave open the possibility that enforcement may be legitimately refused even when all the other conditions of EF are met. This may accommodate the fact that Boss cannot force Worker to work for the agreed wage, but it does not accommodate the further fact that Worker can force Boss to pay at least the minimum wage for as long as their agreement runs. This fact also makes it hard to suggest a suitable formulation for the rider, because any such reformulation would go contrary to the general direction of EF. As it stands, the special justification rider in (6) cautions *against* thinking that the satisfaction of conditions (1)–(5) is always sufficient for one party to have the undertaking enforced against the other, should that other party fail to do as agreed. But whereas (6) suggests that legitimate enforcement may be available in fewer instances than (1)–(5) allow, the examples I have been discussing suggest that it may be available in more. Neither Worker nor Boss had the requisite intentions or provided the requisite assurances in respect of the minimum wage, but Worker is nevertheless entitled to have it enforced against Boss.

To sum up: EL and EF are 'classical' principles in the sense they assume, first, that parties to voluntary transactions enjoy and have reason to value the four opportunities and, secondly, that when it comes to voluntary undertakings the state has basically two options, namely to take what the parties have agreed as a basis for enforcement, or to withhold enforcement in case no undertaking was concluded, or the concluded undertaking is tainted by the fact that the agent who gave it did so under the influence of objectionable constraints. I have argued that the first assumption does not always hold, and so the second assumption turns out to be much too limiting. Sometimes the most appropriate institutional response to the fact that the choice of a party to enter into an undertaking has been objectionably constrained is not to refuse to enforce that undertaking, but to enforce it under terms different than those agreed. This thought is not only consistent with Scanlon's value-of-choice account, it is entailed by that account. The problem with EL and EF is precisely that they fail to register an important way in which our institutions can make principles for the enforcement of voluntary undertaking sensitive to opportunities that persons in Worker's structural position have reason to value, namely by protecting those persons against the force of certain clauses or of certain agreements that those persons are structurally unable to get rid of through appropriate contract negotiation.

II. A STRUCTURE-SENSITIVE ALTERNATIVE: THE EFS PRINCIPLE

EF assumes that the parties who enter into a voluntary undertaking enjoy the four opportunities I highlighted at the start (not to seek a deal; to negotiate; to weigh one's options; to say yes or no to the deal on the table), and that those four opportunities are valuable to them. Other ways of thinking about contracting share that assumption, with the economists' favourite, the 'complete contingent contract', being perhaps the clearest general illustration. Needless to say, this assumption sometimes does hold true. When two businesspersons negotiate at arm's length and strike a deal that each estimates is beneficial to them, we can reasonably suppose that they both had the four opportunities and that those opportunities were valuable to each of them. Equally, however, there is no doubt that the same does not hold true in respect of several perfectly familiar types of transaction, namely types in which the value of those four opportunities for one party is limited because of that party's structural position. Under the value-of-choice account that drives EF, that party could reasonably reject that principle.

The structural nature of that limitation in question matters because it shows that the problem is not occasional or person-specific, but typical and general. In the language of the value-of-choice account, the fact that a party's position is structurally compromised has the effect of limiting the *generic* value of the four opportunities for that party in the context of the relevant type of transaction. This cuts in two ways. First, it serves as the ground on which that party could reasonably object to bearing certain responsibilities under the transaction. Secondly, it sometimes allows that party to require the state not to refuse to enforce the transaction, but to protect that party by taking the more affirmative step of enforcing the transaction under modified terms. EF could account for the first point, but not the second. Could we modify or supplement EF to deal with this problem?

Maybe, but only as long as we do not expect too much of such a supplement by way of practical detail. The reason is that the problem of the limited value of certain opportunities for parties in a weaker structural position will manifest itself in many different ways, and ground different complaints. Sometimes structurally weaker parties will want the bargaining power to negotiate better wages (eg when the law places a ceiling to worker remuneration). Sometimes they will want something else, namely not to have to worry about negotiating below a certain threshold, ie to be assured that certain onerous terms that the business is likely to succeed in including in the contract (eg wages below the minimum) will not be enforceable against them. Sometimes they will want the opportunity to revise their decision to say yes, if they have good general reason to think that this decision was adversely affected by certain rational biases, and so on. This variety suggests that we cannot hope to make EF watertight by adding, say, an 'equality of structural bargaining power' or an 'unbiased decision' clause to it, for the problem that weaker parties face is not inequality of structural bargaining power, or exposure to rational biases *per se*. It is that, in the context of certain transactions, those things are generally likely to reduce the value for those parties of having the four opportunities that make contracting a useful institution.

With that in mind, I propose that we qualify EF with the aid of the following proviso:

> However, neither party may object to the enforcement of a remedy when that party had an opportunity to affect the content of the obligation to which the remedy relates, and that opportunity was something that this party had reason to value.

Modified in this way, the principle, which I will rename 'EFS' for 'Enforcement of Fidelity in a given Structure',[20] will read as follows:

> EFS: It is permissible legally to enforce remedies for breach of contract that go beyond compensation for reliance losses, provided that these remedies are not excessive and that they apply only in cases in which the following conditions hold: (1) A, the party against whom the remedy is enforced, has, in the absence of objectionable constraint and with the adequate understanding (or the ability to acquire such understanding) of his or her situation, intentionally led B to expect that A would do X unless B consented to A's not doing so; (2) A had reason to believe that B wanted to be assured of this; (3) A acted with the aim of providing this assurance, by indicating to B that he or she was undertaking a legal obligation to do X; (4) B indicated that he or she understood A to have undertaken such an obligation; (5) A and B knew, or could easily determine, what kind of remedy B would be legally entitled to if A breached this obligation; and (6) A failed to do X without being released from this obligation by B, and without special justification for doing so. However, neither party may object to the enforcement of a remedy when (7) that party had an opportunity to affect the content of the obligation to which the remedy relates, and that opportunity was something that the party in question had general reason to value.

Compared to requirements (1)–(6), the last requirement of EFS is considerably more open. Requirements (1)–(6) specify actions, intentions and states of mind on the part of A and B. By contrast, requirement (7) speaks about opportunities that each of those parties has reason to value. This makes the demands of EFS in specific cases harder to determine in advance. This, however, is a feature of EFS, not a bug. Recall that it was the absence of something like (7) that left EF exposed to the objection that that principle holds only in situations where the four opportunities are valuable for both A and B. If that criticism of EF makes sense, we should expect any plausible alternative to that principle to make explicit reference to what EF missed. Also note that EFS does not make special mention of the cause, structural or not, for which those opportunities might be less valuable for either party. All that it asks (by implication) is that this cause be such that it would deprive a party of opportunities that he or she had general reason to value. Due to their ubiquitous character, structural causes will be the main candidates here, but there is no reason why the application of EFS should be limited to them.

I believe that EFS does better than EF in practice. It explains not only why Worker may refuse to accept the agreed wage, but also why Boss cannot refuse to keep Worker on the job while paying the minimum wage rather than the lower agreed one. That is so because the enforcement of the minimum wage against Boss is now based on the fact that Boss had the four opportunities:

---

[20] My first instinct was to name the revised principle 'EFL' for 'EF for Lefties', but I obviously have an eye to posterity here, and some jokes do not age well.

the opportunity to select a different employee; to negotiate the terms of their agreement; to weigh the available options; and to say yes. Of course, EFS *does* place a limit on Boss's ability to negotiate wages below a certain level. However, the test for whether EFS is justified towards Boss is not whether EFS limits what Boss can do; any moral principle is bound to do that. The test is whether a principle that includes those limitations still affords Boss the four opportunities, and that those opportunities remain valuable for a person in Boss's position. By that token, EFS also explains why the state can be justified in using its coercive power to make Boss live up to the modified terms of the undertaking when the requirements of the principle are met.

Note, moreover, that EFS supplies this justification without relying on the idea that the state would otherwise be allowing Boss to *exploit* Worker. I think that this is an advantage of EFS, even if the charge of exploitation could be reasonably laid on Boss's door. Any account that grounds Worker's complaint on exploitation faces two problems. One is to determine what counts as exploitation. The other, and more difficult one, is to explain why exploitation is the right benchmark for Worker to be able to object to a principle that imposed burdens on Worker on account of Worker's agreement with Boss.

The first problem arises because people can take advantage of another's poor position to secure some gain for themselves in a number of ways. They may take some action that makes the other person's position worse (call this 'active' advantage-taking). Or they may take advantage of the fact that the other person is in a poor position already, or that they are in a much better position than the other person (call this 'passive' advantage-taking).[21] Determining which kind of advantage-taking deserves to be called 'exploitative' is not straightforward, because we can easily think of situations where either kind of advantage-taking is morally OK. I know that you want to buy a certain property, but you are having some difficulty securing the finance for it. I have cash in hand, so I get the owner to sell to me. I then offer to sell the property to you at a mark-up. Here I am taking advantage of the fact that I know your preferences, and my action has put you in a worse position because now buying the property is going to cost you more. But it would be odd if the state were able to stop me from doing this (a lot of commerce works just in that way). Situations in which passive advantage-taking is alright are, of course, even easier to come by. Medical professionals in the private sector take advantage of the fact that the people who come to them want or need their medical care. The former are allowed to use that feature of the situation to make the latter undertake to pay their bills. That counts as advantage-taking, but it too is morally OK.

---

[21] Zimmerman contrasts instead 'exploitative' and 'coercive' advantage-taking through wage offers, above n 19. Mindy Chen-Wishart contrasts 'active' and 'passive' victimisation, *Contract Law*, 3rd edn (Oxford, Oxford University Press, 2010) 396–7.

One is therefore inclined to say: some advantage-taking, active or passive, is legitimate and some is not, and only the latter is 'exploitative'. To draw that distinction, one may argue that advantage-taking is exploitative when it violates a person's moral rights or their autonomy.[22] That sounds good, but here the second problem for the appeal to exploitation kicks in. The other side of making the case for state intervention contingent on the protection of moral rights and autonomy is the implication that the state would not be *pro tanto* justified in intervening, and that advantage-taking would be OK, when such advantage-taking does not involve the violation of a person's moral rights or their autonomy. This claim looks to me much too strong.[23] For a start, note that the practical effect of that claim is to *limit* the kinds of complaint the party taken advantage of is allowed to put forward. The claim entails that, unless that party can argue that their rights or autonomy have been violated, they may not object to a principle for the enforceability of an undertaking that they have voluntarily entered into. The EFS principle does not impose such a limit, as it does not tie the extent of a person's responsibilities to whether that person has been the victim of a wrong or a violation of autonomy, but to whether a principle that sets out those responsibilities is sensitive to the value for that person of the four opportunities. This means that the ground on which a structurally weaker party may object to bearing certain burdens under a transaction with a structurally stronger party is derived from the fact that the social structure has put the weaker party in a position that limits the value of certain opportunities for them.[24] And that party has that objection even if the structurally strong party has been in a thoroughly kind and magnanimous vein. That is, EFS allows persons in Worker's position to object to a principle that enforces

---

[22] For such accounts, see S Shiffrin, 'Paternalism, Unconscionability Doctrine, and Accommodation' (2000) 29 *Philosophy & Public Affairs* 205; D Markovits, 'Contract and Collaboration' (2004) 113 *Yale LJ* 1417; J Kraus, 'The Correspondence of Contract and Promise' (2009) 109 *Columbia LR* 1603; D Kimel, *From Promise to Contract: Towards a Liberal Theory of Contract* (Oxford, Hart Publishing, 2003) at 72ff; R Bigwood, *Exploitative Contracts* (Oxford, Oxford University Press, 2003); C Bridgeman, 'Reconciling Strict Liability with Corrective Justice in Contract Law' (2007) 75 *Fordham LR* 3013; S Waddams, 'Breach of Contract and the Concept of Wrong-Doing' (2000) 12 *Supreme Court LR* 1. For a criticism of wrong-based accounts of unconscionability, see Smith, above n 5, 360–2.

[23] One further difficulty for autonomy-based accounts is that they must make some rather fine-grained distinctions to explain why the autonomy of the structurally stronger party is less worthy of the state's protection. On this point, Shiffrin, ibid, at 249 says that exploiters cannot invoke their autonomy as an objection to the state's refusal to assist their effort, to the extent that market transactions do not tend to impinge on the core of their autonomy rights, as would 'activities that involve intimate uses of the body, the exercise of conscience, or other behaviors that are central to one's sense of self'. I am not so sure. Perhaps Boss considers his business an absolutely central part of his sense of self. Many businesspersons do.

[24] See ch 3(II) on why the value-of-choice account makes responsibility contingent on the choice one *had*, rather than the choice one *made*.

the agreed wage as long as the social structure puts those persons in a position where the opportunity to negotiate has no real value for them. Whether those persons were, in fact, exploited only bears on whether they will seek the help of the state in finding a remedy. But the remedy in question will be a remedy for the 'opportunity deficit' that the structure exposes those persons to, not a remedy for their exploitation in the hands of the structurally stronger party.

III. THREE OBJECTIONS

One could say that EFS demands too much of parties in a structurally stronger position. Or that it fails to improve the position of weaker parties as much as garden-variety redistribution through the tax system would. Or that, even if EFS is justified, some basic features of contract law make it poorly placed to respond to what EFS requires.

A. Transaction Costs and Partiality

Maybe EFS asks too much of parties in a stronger structural position. John Rawls was drawn to this thought. He suggested that trying to do things for parties in a weaker structural position through adjustments to principles for the enforceability of voluntary undertakings would be unreasonably burdensome for other parties, insofar as it would entail that, in order to ensure that an agreement will be enforceable, those parties would need to attend to the structural position of their potential contract partners. This suggestion draws on two ideas. One is that any such requirement would increase *transaction costs* for both parties.[25] Individual agents (persons or businesses) will typically lack information about the structural position of their prospective customers or consumers or employees, or will have to incur prohibitive costs in estimating it. Given the complexity of our societies and the sheer volume of transactions that take place in them, this amount of information would be practically impossible for those agents to process in advance of any single transaction.[26]

---

[25] J Rawls, *Political Liberalism* (New York, Columbia University Press, 1996) 267: 'There are no feasible and practicable rules that it is sensible to impose on individuals that can prevent the erosion of background justice. This is because the rules governing agreements and individual transactions cannot be too complex or require too much information to be correctly applied; nor should they enjoin individuals to engage in bargaining with many widely scattered third parties, since this would impose excessive transaction costs.'

[26] *cf* S Scheffler, 'Distributive Justice, the Basic Structure, and the Place of Private Law' (2015) 35 *OJLS* 213, 220: 'In a complex economy, the determination of how to preserve background justice over time will require massive amounts of information and complex calculations, and only institutions are in a position reliably to gather this information and perform these calculations'.

The second idea is that doing things for weaker parties through adjustments to the enforceability of individual voluntary transactions would fail to make allowance for the degree of *partiality* that stronger parties can reasonably want to exercise with regard to the pursuit of their own transactional aims. We all share a collective responsibility to promote and maintain a just social structure, but we also want to be able to pursue our own chosen projects, both individually and in collaboration with others. A plausible strategy for responding to those two reasons would be to assign the practical responsibility for the former to institutions, leaving ourselves with the responsibility of pursuing our own aims by trying to reach the most advantageous terms of collaboration that we can get for ourselves, given an appropriately regulated social structure.[27]

Rawls thought that these arguments explain why the structural story should not bear on the justification of contract law principles, insofar as those arguments recommend a *division of labour*

> between two kinds of social rules, and the different institutional forms in which these rules are realized. The basic structure comprises first the institutions that define the social background and includes as well those operations that continually adjust and compensate for the inevitable tendencies away from background fairness, for example, such operations as income and inheritance taxation designed to even out the ownership of property. This structure also enforces through the legal system another set of rules that govern the transactions and agreements between individuals and associations (the law of contract, and so on). The rules relating to fraud and duress, and the like, belong to these rules, and satisfy the requirements of simplicity and practicality. They are framed to leave individuals free to act effectively in pursuit of their ends and without excessive constraints.[28]

Let both arguments that Rawls makes in favour of this division of labour be correct. I think that structurally stronger parties could still not appeal to them to object against the particular way that EFS divides that labour. For a start, those parties could not object on the ground that EFS increases their transaction costs. Consider all the familiar statutory regimes for the protection of consumers, employees and insurance policy holders. Instead of asking parties to undertake the cost of working out where their potential contracting partner

---

[27]   *cf* T Nagel, *Equality and Partiality* (New York, Oxford University Press, 1991) 86: 'What we need is an institutional structure which will evoke the requisite partition of motives, allowing everyone to be publicly egalitarian and privately partial'. Note that the partiality reason would apply even in a Coasian world of zero transaction costs; Nagel's point is precisely that partiality matters even when impartiality would be costless.

[28]   Rawls, above n 25, at 268 (emphasis added). On Rawls's conception of this division of labour see S Scheffler, 'The Division of Moral Labour: Egalitarian Liberalism as Moral Pluralism' (2005) 79 *Proceedings of the Aristotelian Society* 229. Scheffler, above n 26, at 217–22 discusses and rejects the view that this commits Rawls to excluding contract law from the basic structure and the demands of justice. I touch on this point in the conclusion to this chapter.

stands in the social structure, such regimes do all that work *themselves*. None of those statutory regimes requires businesses, employers and insurers to make detailed enquiries into the relative structural position and bargaining power of each consumer, employee and insurance holder that happens to knock on their door. And none of them requires those parties, somehow, to plug into the matrix of all voluntary transactions in society and check that their prospective deal with the other party would do its bit in maintaining the justice of the basic structure as a whole. What those statutory regimes do is to identify consumer, employment and insurance agreements as types of agreement, the content of which is generally affected by structural imbalances of bargaining power, which in turn impairs the value of the four opportunities for structurally weaker parties. When the relevant statutes identify the types of transaction and the clauses to which they apply with sufficient clarity, their practical application need not involve unreasonable or excessive transaction costs for anyone. As condition (5) of EFS makes enforceability contingent on the relevant laws being clear and predictable in that sense, parties cannot object to it on transaction-cost grounds.

Moreover, the application of those regimes need not involve any sacrifice of the partiality that people can reasonably want to be able to exercise in the context of their transactions. Those statutes do not ask structurally stronger parties to calibrate their transaction to fit a larger structural or distributive aim. More importantly for the purposes of EFS, those regimes do not deprive those persons of the value of any of the four opportunities. They only place certain limits on the means by which those parties can secure whatever transactional aims they set for themselves. The regulatory regimes that make Rawls uneasy would be too costly or burdensome precisely when they deprive persons of the four opportunities. As the case for EFS depends on those opportunities remaining valuable for structurally stronger parties, that principle has adequate safeguards against this kind of heavy-handedness.

B. Tax-and-Transfer

EFS allows the state to enforce the agreement between a structurally stronger party and a structurally weaker one under terms different than those agreed between those parties, eg with the minimum wage in the place of the agreed one. That injunction is based on the idea that, in some cases, refusing to enforce the transaction would reduce the value of the four opportunities for the weaker party even further, eg because it would condemn Worker to unemployment. One could still argue that this may be an *inefficient* way of trying to improve the situation of persons in Worker's position. As Louis Kaplow and Steven Shavell, amongst others, have suggested, perhaps the best way to do this is to aim for principles of enforceability that increase the total pool of social resources, and then use tax-and-transfer rules to distribute in favour of Worker, and other similarly situated persons.[29] In other words, perhaps contract law can respond better to the concerns of the structural story if it keeps its direct focus on the aim of resource maximisation.[30] If that is correct, then persons in a structurally weaker position may reasonably object against EFS on that ground that this principle makes it harder to implement distributive policies that would improve their position.

This claim seems to me to rely on two ideas. The first and more general idea is that there are several ways in which we could respond to the fact that the social structure puts consumers, employees and insurance holders in a weaker position relative to businesses, employers and insurers, and there is no reason to think that varying the conditions of enforceability for such transactions is the only possible response. We should leave open the possibility that changes elsewhere in the structure could work just as well, or even better. The second and more specific idea is that changes to our tax schedule are a generally better response to our concerns about the value of the four opportunities for parties in a weaker structural position than changes to conditions of enforceability.

The general idea sounds right. Suppose that the economic model of our community allows businesses to use their superior bargaining power to exclude liability to consumers in relation to defective products, and that makes it the case that the opportunity to negotiate has much less value for consumers in the situation. One way to respond to this problem would be to modify our contract law so that any business that uses its superior bargaining power to insert exclusion of liability clauses into its agreements with consumers will be unable to get those clauses enforced. This option would take our basic economic structure (and the disparities of bargaining power that it produces) as given, and attempt to improve the position of structurally weaker parties by taking certain matters off the negotiating table. But this is not the only option we have. Another, more radical, option would be to eliminate the very disparity in bargaining power between businesses and consumers, eg by moving to a socialist economic model, or an economy of very small businesses, where such disparities will be less likely to arise. Now, we may find that, all things considered, we should not model our economy on socialist principles. But the fact that this radical alternative is on the table, and that we could conceivably

---

[29] L Kaplow and S Shavell, 'Why the Legal System is Less Efficient than the Income Tax in Redistributing Income' (1994) 23 *Journal of Legal Studies* 667; A Schwarz and R Scott, 'Contract Theory and the Limits of Contract Law' (2003) 113 *Yale LJ* 541.

[30] Ibid at 677: '[I]t is appropriate for economic analysis of legal rules to focus on efficiency and to ignore the distribution of income in offering normative judgments'. Kaplow and Shavell's distinction between 'tax rules' and 'legal rules' may not be very precise, as tax rules always take the form of laws, but this does not impact on the substance of their thesis.

choose one general economic model over another, shows that whether we have reason to change the conditions of enforceability for certain kinds of voluntary transaction is necessarily contingent on any changes we have reason to make in *other* parts of the social structure within which those transactions take place. This means that laws prohibiting the enforcement of certain clauses in consumer agreements will be necessary to improve the position of structurally weaker parties only insofar as we have reason to model our economic structure in a way that creates or maintains significant disparities of bargaining power between businesses and consumers. Such laws will not be required in case we have reason to model the structure in a way that eliminates those disparities. A socialist economy does not need consumer protection legislation.

The same applies in the example of Boss and Worker. Had the social structure been different, eg were jobs not scarce and unemployment did not have such a dramatic impact on an agent's life prospects, perhaps giving Worker the option of walking out would have been enough. The point is that, again, our reasons for allowing Worker to have the employment contract enforced under terms other than those agreed are sensitive to the shape of the structure as a whole, in the sense that we can only decide whether Worker should be given this option in the light of the way we have reason to model other aspects of the social structure that impact on employment relationships. Structural changes elsewhere may entail that the conditions of enforceability should be appropriately expanded or restricted.

If that is correct, then the debate about the merits of the objection under discussion will turn on the more specific idea that changes to the tax schedule can improve the position of the structurally weaker party more than changes to the conditions of enforceability. Applied to the example of consumer transactions, the claim is that, to mitigate the effect of the structural disparities of bargaining power on the value of the four opportunities for structurally weaker parties, we should focus on redistributing wealth in those parties' favour, rather than changing the conditions for the enforcement of certain clauses that stronger parties manage to insert into transactions due to their superior bargaining power.[31]

This claim is less compelling. Wealth redistribution under a market economic model does not increase consumers' bargaining power, nor does it protect them against the superior bargaining power of businesses. What it does is increase consumers' *purchasing* power, leaving their bargaining position unchanged. The problem with this is that we have no warrant for thinking that consumers have a general reason to favour increases in their purchasing power over increases in their bargaining power (or protection from the exercise by

---

[31] Such redistribution does not need to take the form of taxation. It can occur in the form of lower consumer prices.

the business of its superior bargaining power). Being able to purchase products more cheaply, or to purchase more, is an option that any consumer has reason to value, but it is not always paramount amongst a consumer's reasonable interests.[32] Given a choice between a much cheaper broadband connection fee and a generous statutory right of withdrawal, you may have reason to choose the former, but we can easily think of examples where a considered view of your interests may point in the other direction, eg when the alternative to cheaper broadband is a guarantee that the business will not be able to effect a unilateral change in the terms of the agreement, or to extend unilaterally its original duration, or to terminate without reasonable notice. Besides your interest in getting your broadband cheap, you may also value enjoying a certain degree of security in your broadband connection and the terms under which it is provided, as well as having control over the duration of your service contract. These, however, are interests that you are unlikely to be able to negotiate into any agreement with a broadband provider, no matter how much purchasing power you happen to enjoy. You therefore have reason to value the opportunity to have those interests protected by law, in the form of rules that declare those terms unenforceable, unless you have specifically requested them or had sufficient opportunity to negotiate them. The point is not that the provision of such bargaining protections to consumer is always worth any resulting decrease in purchasing power, but rather that consumers do not have general reason to value increases in purchasing power more than bargaining protections. If that is correct, it follows that the provision of such protections through the restriction or extension of conditions of enforceability cannot be ruled out as an appropriate response to the concerns of the structural story.[33]

C. The Limitations of Contract Law

Let the EFS principle be right that sometimes the proper thing for the state to do is to enforce a transaction between a structurally stronger and a structurally weaker party on terms other than those agreed. One might still object that contract law as we know it is not well placed to carry out that function. A similar objection has been pressed, in various forms and by several theorists,

---

[32] *cf* Kronman, above n 5, at 508–10.

[33] D Lewinsohn-Zamir, 'In Defense of Redistribution through Private Law' (2006–7) 91 *Minnesota LR* 326 arrives at a similar conclusion through a different route. She argues that the economic argument against doing social justice through private law fails if we start, first, from an objective conception of an individual's well-being and, secondly, from an account of consequences that includes information about the impact of the way in which some good is secured on the well-being of the individual who receives it.

against the view that contract law should do social justice. I want to show that, whether or not that objection might succeed against a 'social justice' account of contract law, it does not succeed against the EFS principle. In fact, contract law can do, and has been doing, the job EFS asks of it just fine.

Stephen Smith, James Gordley and Mindy Chen-Wishart have each argued that contract law is not a fit means for doing social justice because modifications to the general conditions for the enforceability of transactions between individuals are unlikely to make any serious or sustained impact on the position of structurally weaker parties. Any such impact, they argue, will be necessarily contingent on three factors: whether agents actually choose to enter into the voluntary transactions in question; whether those transactions involve the particular classes of agents; and whether the volume of the relevant transactions is large and patterned enough to improve the structural position of a class of agents, rather than random individuals within those classes.[34]

Even if contract law is a bad means for pursuing a just distribution of resources, the argument does not make trouble for EFS for two reasons. First, EFS does not require the state to redistribute resources, and puts forward no metric for such redistribution. What EFS asks of the state is to adopt principles of enforcement that impose responsibilities on structurally weaker parties only when those parties have general reason to value the four opportunities. That goes not just for its justification for refusing enforcement to certain undertakings, but also for its justification for enforcing certain transactions under alternative terms. In the latter case too, the justification is protective rather than distributive in nature, in that the alternative of refusing enforcement altogether would reduce the value of those opportunities for the structurally weaker party even further. Secondly, contract law is not just particularly but *characteristically* good at performing that function. The value of the four opportunities for structurally weaker parties turns largely on the prospect of having the exercise of those opportunities backed up by the coercive force of the state. It follows that any principle which bears on general conditions of enforceability is an appropriate means to do the work that EFS requires. Contract principles fit that bill like no others.

---

[34] Smith, above n 5 at 137: '[T]he value of distributive justice ... is a weak basis on which to justify, or even to criticize, contract law generally ... Contract law is a poor tool for altering existing distributions of wealth. Contract law rules can affect the distribution of wealth only insofar as people agree to make contracts'; Chen-Wishart, above n 21, at 28: 'Distributive contract law rules ... can be neutralized by the parties changing other terms of subsequent contracts. Strongly distributive contract rules will make parties more reluctant to contract with the protected group'; J Gordley, 'Contract Law in the Aristotelian Tradition' in Benson, above n 6, at 308: 'if the distribution of wealth is unjust, it should be changed by a social decision, rather than by individuals who go about redistributing wealth on their own, and by a centrally made decision rather than transaction by transaction'.

A natural extension of the point is that EFS shows classical common law doctrines like misrepresentation, mistake, duress, undue influence, unconscionability, and the prohibition on restraint-of-trade clauses as instantiating the same moral principle as statutory regimes about the protection of workers, consumers and insurance holders. The aim of those legal principles, irrespective of their historical provenance, is not to produce certain patterns of distribution, but to protect the value of the four opportunities for weaker parties, eg to ensure that consumers have an extended period of time to say no to purchases of goods made online, or to remove some topics from the negotiating table so that workers do not suffer due to their structural inability to drive a hard bargain, or to allow workers and insurance holders to keep their job or their policy while striking down some offending clauses in the respective agreements. Those principles achieve that aim in either of two general ways, namely by blocking the enforcement of certain transactions or certain agreed clauses, or—when necessary to protect weaker parties against further erosion in the value of those opportunities for them—by allowing the enforcement of those transactions under different terms (or by 'implying' terms into the transaction). The only difference is that classical contract law principles tend to focus on situations where the cause of the weakness in a party's position is the conduct of the parties to the transaction in question (eg the conduct of the party that made the mistake or the misrepresentation, or exercised duress or undue influence, and so on), while statutory regimes are generally focused on situations where that cause is structural.

If that is correct, a discussion of the merits of any of those principles should not be conducted in isolation from the others. Questions about how much we ought to do to protect consumers or workers and questions about what constitutes duress or undue influence or what makes a bargain unconscionable are aspects of the same moral problem. The fact that much contemporary academic discussion of those questions tends to proceed in a rather compartmentalised way, with some questions regarded as falling under contract law and others as falling under consumer or labour law, says more about the state of theorising in those domains than about any inherent differences in their respective subject-matters.

IV. CONTRACT DOCTRINE IN THE LIGHT OF THE EFS PRINCIPLE

In this section I want to explore how the EFS principle might justify and interpret certain familiar contract law principles and doctrines. I propose to focus on the doctrine of unconscionability, the limits and requirements of which are generally taken to be less well settled than those of, say, duress, undue influence, or misrepresentation, and the definition of an 'unfair term' in the Unfair

Terms in Consumer Contracts Regulations 1999.[35] My aim is to illustrate how looking at the relevant doctrines in the light of the EFS principle can help us to identify their requirements with more precision, and to gain a fresh perspective on the debate about whether these doctrines ought to be treated as aspects of a unifying principle of fairness in English contract law.

A. Unconscionability

Compared to the notions of 'duress', 'undue influence' or 'misrepresentation', the notion of 'unconscionability' has proven much harder to unpack in theory and practice. The former notions give us some glimpse of what is wrong with enforcing an undertaking, eg that one party to that undertaking has been put under some sort of illegitimate pressure or has been misled into agreeing. The notion of unconscionability tells us considerably less. All it seems to signify is that it would be 'against conscience' to insist on enforcing a certain undertaking or, from the point of view of our institutions, to actually enforce it. The problem is not just that this description is too generic—after all, it would be against conscience to enforce an agreement procured by duress, undue influence or misrepresentation—but that it does not give us some hint as to which features of the undertaking make its enforcement illegitimate. We might say that whereas notions like duress and undue influence point to certain flaws in the agreement in question, the notion of unconscionability simply states a conclusion that some such flaw exists.

This is not to underestimate the importance of what contract lawyers have achieved so far in elaborating the doctrine of unconscionability, but to highlight how little they had to work with in the first place. The organising distinction between 'procedural' and 'substantive' unconscionability is an important advance in our understanding of the notion: the legitimacy of enforcing an undertaking may be undermined by flaws either in the process that led to its conclusion, or in the balance between the parties' respective entitlements under the agreement, or both.[36] However, the procedural/substantive distinction does not provide us with a criterion that will help us decide in a principled way what counts as a flaw in an undertaking, or how serious the flaw must be for courts to refuse to enforce the undertaking as presented to them (I will call

---

[35] I have discussed some aspects of unconscionability in E Voyiakis, 'Unconscionability and the Value of Choice' in M Kenny, J Devenney and L Fox-O'Mahoney, *Unconscionability in Private Financial Transactions—Protecting the Vulnerable* (Cambridge, Cambridge University Press, 2010) 79.

[36] *cf* A Leff, 'Unconscionability and the Code—The Emperor's New Clause', (1967) 115 *University of Pennsylvania LR* 485, 487 (discussing art 2-302(1) of the US Uniform Commercial Code).

this the normative problem of unconscionability). It simply tells us that such flaws may be found in different aspects of any given undertaking. Perhaps the fact that the undertaking was negotiated between parties of vastly different bargaining power should be enough for courts to treat it with suspicion. Perhaps it is also necessary for the party with the greater bargaining power to have acted in a way that makes it responsible for the other party's weakness in the context of their transaction (eg A may have encouraged B to rely on A's expertise).[37] Or perhaps nothing short of intentional exploitation will suffice.

One aspect of the explanation of why unconscionability is a hazier notion than those of duress, undue influence or misrepresentation seems straightforward. Duress, misrepresentation and (to a large degree) undue influence are typical or 'easy' cases of pathological undertakings, in the sense that any plausible theory of contract law will have to acknowledge that our institutions should hesitate to enforce deals procured by such means. Things get more controversial when we ask whether *less* dramatic flaws (eg that the agreement is exploitative but not coercive; that there was great disparity in the parties' respective bargaining power etc) might justify a similar institutional response. The question then becomes where to draw the line, or how bad things must be for the state to refuse to take an agreement at face value, questions that lie at the heart of all contract theory. To put it differently, the doctrine of unconscionability gives contract lawyers more trouble than those of duress, undue influence or misrepresentation because it requires us to think about the outer reaches of the pathology of agreements, or about the outer limits of the power of our institutions to legitimately refuse to enforce an undertaking as presented to them. Given that these are hard questions, it is only natural that the doctrines we use to tag them will themselves be rather hazy.

Closely related is a problem of taxonomy or range. What sorts of situation should a theory of unconscionability aspire to cover? A quick answer would be: situations like those featuring in common-law cases that invoke that concept. However, that answer would beg two questions. First, it may happen that although courts do not use the language of unconscionability in certain situations, the considerations that they take into account in deciding them are substantially similar to those arising in typical cases of unconscionability (restraint-of-trade clauses are an obvious example). By the same token, terminology aside, the various statutory regimes for the protection of weaker parties to contracts (consumers, employees, insurance holders etc) appear to raise pretty much the same substantive issues as the typical case of common-law

---

[37] This is the view taken in *Chesterfield v Janssen* 28 Eng Rep 82 (1751), 101, where unconscionability was held to arise 'from the circumstances or conditions of the parties contracting—weakness on the one side, usury on the other, or extortion or advantage taken of that weakness'.

unconscionability. After all, statutes like the Unfair Contract Terms Act 1977 or the Unfair Terms in Consumer Contracts Regulations 1999 (to which I turn in the next heading) were adopted against the background of the common law. Had the common law been different, perhaps there would have been less need for them. The point is not that the typical case of common-law unconscionability is identical with the typical case of restraint-of-trade clauses and the typical case of an unfair or unreasonable term in a consumer contract, but that the taxonomic distinctions between them cannot be taken at face value. Perhaps the received taxonomy reflects some substantive differences in the way the law should treat each class of cases. Perhaps it obscures rather than illuminates the structure of the problems it describes.[38] To resolve that issue, we need to ask first whether the pathology of the agreements addressed by common and statutory law is similar or different. The answer to that will depend on the way we identify the flaws of those agreements. So the taxonomic problem folds back into the normative one.[39]

Against that background, consider one of the more authoritative statements of English law on unconscionability, provided by the decision of the Privy Council in *Boustany v Piggott*.[40] Miss Piggott had agreed to extend an existing lease to Mrs Boustany and her husband by a further ten years at a rate that was over five times lower than the market rate for the area. Miss Piggott had made that decision on her own, despite having earlier assigned the management of the property to her cousin George. In laying out the principles of law to be applied, Lord Templeman said:

> It is not sufficient to attract the jurisdiction of equity to prove that a bargain is hard, unreasonable or foolish; it must be proved to be unconscionable in the sense that 'one of the parties to it has imposed the objectionable terms in a morally reprehensible manner, that is to say, in a way that affects his conscience ... Unequal bargaining power or objectively unreasonable terms provide no basis for equitable interference in the absence of unconscientious or extortionate abuse of power.'[41]

On the facts of *Boustany*, the Privy Council found that there had been such 'unconscientious and extortionate' abuse of power, on the ground that Mrs Boustany and her husband had exercised a considerable degree of influence over Miss Piggott. The court reached that conclusion despite having accepted

---

[38] *cf* Chen-Wishart, above n 21, at 381: 'one general principle can be more straightforward: for example facts involving lawful pressures may trigger duress and undue influence as much as unconscionable conduct'; S Waddams, 'Unconscionable Contracts: Competing Perspectives' (1999) 62 *Saskatchewan LR* 1, 10.

[39] *cf* Smith, above n 5, 341–2.

[40] *Boustany v Piggott* [1993] UKPC 17.

[41] Ibid at 23. Lord Templeman's opinion cites *Multiservice Bookbinding v Marden* [1979] Ch 84 at 110 and *Alec Lobb (Garages) Ltd v Total Oil (Great Britain) Ltd* [1983] 1 WLR 87 at 94 in support.

that the parties had no known attachment, and that Miss Piggott had received, and proceeded to ignore, independent legal advice that she should have insisted on a higher rent. The court's basis for reaching its conclusion on the facts was, first, that Miss Piggott had decided to hand over management of the properties because she had become 'quite slow' with age and, secondly, that Mrs Boustany and her husband appeared to have had direct communication with Miss Piggott on the matter. In the opinion of the court, they

> had prevailed upon Miss Piggott to agree to grant a lease on terms which they knew they could not extract from Mr George Piggott or anyone else. When they were summoned by [Miss Piggot's solicitor] the unfairness of the lease was pointed out to them, they did not release Miss Piggott from the bargain which they had unfairly pressed on her. In short, Mrs Boustany must have taken advantage of Miss Piggott before, during and after the interview with [the solicitor] and with full knowledge before the 1980 lease was settled that her conduct was unconscionable.[42]

Before considering how one might decide the case under the EFS principle, note that the claim of unconscionability in *Boustany* would not have been allowed under the different principle of 'inequality of bargaining power' proposed by Lord Denning in *Lloyd's Bank v Bundy*:

> English law gives relief to one who, without independent advice, enters into a contract upon terms which are very unfair or transfers property for a consideration which is grossly inadequate, when his bargaining power is grievously impaired by reason or his own needs or desires, or by his own ignorance or infirmity, coupled with undue influences or pressures brought to bear on him by or for the benefit of the other. When I use the word 'undue' I do not mean to suggest that the principle depends on proof of any wrongdoing.[43]

While the Lord Denning's principle does not require wrongdoing, it requires absence of independent advice. In *Boustany*, it was established that Miss Piggott had received such advice, and decided to ignore it on the strength of the defendant's influence over her.

Suppose that we were deciding *Boustany* under the EFS principle. The obvious issue would be whether, under clause (1) of EFS, Miss Piggott had faced an 'objectionable constraint' when promising to lease the property at a very low rate. As discussed, for that constraint to be objectionable under EFS, it is not necessary for it to have been caused by the wrongful conduct of the other party. It is enough that the person who pleads that constraint found themselves in a situation in which the four opportunities (to say no; to negotiate; to weigh one's options; to say yes) had no general value for them. On the facts

---

[42] Above n 40, at 19.
[43] *Lloyd's Bank plc v Bundy* [1975] QB 326 *per* Lord Denning MR at 339.

of *Boustany*, the question would be whether the effect of Miss Piggott's general condition, of the fact that she had received independent legal advice, and of the contact that she had with Mrs Boustany and her husband, were such that would make it less likely that things would go well for her if she negotiated, weighed her options, and decided for herself. That is, under the EFS principle, the significance of Miss Piggott's condition, the legal advice, and the influence that the defendant might have exercised over her is basically only *inferential*. The same would apply in respect of whether the consideration Miss Piggott received was 'grossly inadequate' or 'unfair' or whether there was a significant inequality of bargaining power between her and the defendant. These considerations too would matter only to the extent that they justify the factual inference that the opportunity to negotiate or to weigh her options had no value for a person in Miss Piggott's position. This suggests that neither *Boustany* nor *Bundy* can be justified as general statements of the conditions under which a person may disclaim responsibility in such transactions. The point is not that wrongdoing or absence of independent advice or inequality of bargaining power or 'gross inadequacy' of consideration are not significant. It is that their significance is contingent on what they tell us about the value for a person of having certain opportunities in the context of the transaction.

The point can be extended to the distinction between 'procedural' and 'substantive' unfairness.[44] If the significance of gross imbalances in the substantive obligations the parties undertake in an agreement lies in what it tells us about the value of for the person most burdened of having certain opportunities, then all instances in which EFS allows that person to refuse the enforcement of that agreement are 'procedural'. They are all concerned with the likelihood that a person's having some options will make things go better for them, rather than with the outcome of them having *exercised* those options in a particular way.[45] Accordingly, the real ground of that person's complaint in the situation is not 'this is too burdensome', but rather 'it was unlikely that giving me the opportunity to avoid incurring that burden would actually allow me to avoid it'. Note here the similarity with Worker's situation. The basis for Worker's complaint too is not 'this deal pays me too little' but 'it was unlikely that giving me the opportunity to negotiate with Boss would actually allow me to get a better deal for myself'.

---

[44] On the difficulty in distinguishing between the two see P Atiyah, 'Contract and Fair Exchange' in *Essays on Contract* (Oxford, Clarendon Press, 1986) 329.

[45] For a view that emphasises substantive unfairness, see Chen-Wishart, above n 21, at 393–4. For the view that either procedural or substantive unfairness might suffice in certain situations, see Smith, above n 5, at 357ff. Smith believes that the justification for this 'mixed' view lies in the fact that the victim of an unconscionable bargain has not given 'real' consent. In ch 3(II) I argued that this packs too much into the idea of consent and voluntariness.

B. Fair Terms in Consumer Contracts

It seems to me that the EFS principle also supplies a good practical standard for assessing the fairness of terms in consumer contracts. According to the Unfair Terms in Consumer Contracts Regulations 1999, a term is unfair, and therefore unenforceable under Regulation 4(1) when, 'contrary to the requirement of good faith [it] causes a significant imbalance in the parties' rights and obligations under the contract to the detriment of the consumer'. That assessment cannot include reference to the adequacy of the price of the goods or services in question—this is excluded under Regulation 3(2)(b), but it may take account of the nature of the goods or services in question, the other terms of the contract, and of all the circumstances attending its conclusion. Schedule 2 to the Regulations provides that, in determining the content of the requirement of good faith, regard shall be had to the strength of the bargaining positions of the parties; whether the consumer had an inducement to agree to the term, or the goods or services were sold or supplied to the special order of the consumer; and the extent to which the seller or supplier has dealt fairly and equitably with the consumer. Schedule 3 then lists several terms which the Regulations consider presumptively unfair, eg terms '(i) irrevocably binding the consumer to terms with which he had no real opportunity of becoming acquainted before the conclusion of the contract'; '(k) enabling the seller or supplier to alter unilaterally without a valid reason any characteristics of the product or service to be provided', and so on.

The obvious difficulty in interpreting the general unfairness clause in Regulation 4 is that the statute gives no clear indication of the position in which the consumer must be placed for a given term to count as unfair. The 'significant imbalance' test could play this role only with the aid of some background account of what a proper 'balance' in the respective rights and obligations of the parties should look like. In particular, given that the performance of a consumer contract by the business and the consumer involves each party doing very different things, and that the content of both performances will be largely dictated by the terms that the business has set out in the contract, the idea of a 'balance' between the parties' respective rights and obligations is really an appeal to intuitions about what it would be *too much* to ask of a consumer in return for what the business is giving them. This, however, requires us to have some working idea of what deal the parties ought to have struck in the circumstances. The Regulation's appeal to good faith may seem to help here, in that it sets a standard for the conduct that the business should take towards the consumer. However, that standard does not tell us how much a business that is acting in good faith ought to do for a consumer, ie what configuration of the parties' respective rights and obligations counts as an abuse of the business's superior bargaining power, and what counts as a legitimate use of that power.

In other words, like the 'significant balance' test, the good faith test does not tell us when the business has done *enough* for a consumer.

The 'how much is enough' issue lay at the heart of *Director General of Fair Trading v First National Bank*.[46] The Bank had sought and obtained judgment against one of its customers who had defaulted on a loan agreement. The law required the Bank to sue in the county court. The county court's judgment would consolidate the original debt and the amount of accrued interest and make an order for its payment by instalments. However, the law at the time did not allow county courts to award claimants (whether or not they were banks) post-judgment interest at the statutory rate on any judgment debt. This meant that the bank was losing out on interest simply because the law required it to sue in a court that did not have the competence to award such interest. The bank had therefore inserted in its standard terms a clause to the effect that borrowers would continue to be charged interest until they had paid off their post-judgment debt in full. Given that the typical payment schedule in judgments for consumer loan defaults would extend to several decades, the amount of post-judgment interest that would accrue was considerable, even if the consumer was paying each instalment on time. The Office of Fair Trading brought action under the UTCCR 1999, alleging that the clause in question was unfair, as it introduced a significant imbalance in the rights and obligations of the parties. The OFT's more particular contention was that consumers could reasonably expect that, in the event of a default on their part, their future liabilities to the bank would be exhaustively reflected in the court's judgment. The post-judgment interest clause was therefore likely to give defaulting borrowers a nasty surprise, as it entailed that making payments in accordance with the court's schedule would not be enough to clear their debt.[47]

Consider how we might approach the question of the fairness of the clause under the EFS principle. Unlike Regulation 4 of the UTCCR 1999, that principle does not ask us to focus on how much each party is undertaking to do for the other, or the balance of their respective rights and obligations. Nor does it ask us to determine whether the stronger party (here, the bank) conducted itself in good faith. Rather, EFS asks us to look into the opportunities that the weaker party had in the context of the transaction, and whether that party had reason to value them. This means that the object of our attention should not be whether the bank ought to be charging defaulting borrowers post-judgment interest, or whether it abused its superior bargaining position in inserting that clause into the loan agreement, but whether borrowers had the opportunity to find out about the relevant clause and its effects, and had reason to value having such advance notice. In turn, it is *that* question which

---

[46] *Director General of Fair Trading v First National Bank plc* [2001] UKHL 52.
[47] Ibid *per* Lord Hope at [44].

dictates the significance of the bank's conduct in the situation. The bank will have done enough for borrowers, in the sense that it will be entitled to ask courts to enforce the clause in question, if it has taken reasonable measures to bring that clause to borrowers' attention, and has not taken actions that would place borrowers under circumstances such that this notice would not be valuable to them.

It seems to me that this corresponds more or less exactly with the approach that the House of Lords took in *First National Bank*. The leading judgment by Lord Bingham focuses expressly on whether the bank did enough to give the borrower the opportunity to find out about the clause, and did so at a time such that this notice would have been valuable to the borrower:

> When the contract is made, default is a foreseeable contingency, not an expected outcome. It is not customary, even in consumer contracts, for notice to be given to the consumer of statutory reliefs open to him if he defaults ... The evidence contains examples of clauses used by over 30 other lenders providing for the payment of interest after judgment, and none alerts the borrower to these potential grounds of relief ... It is readily understandable that a borrower may be disagreeably surprised if he finds that his contractual interest obligation continues to mount despite his duly paying the instalments ordered by the court, but it appears that the bank seeks to prevent that surprise by sending what is described in the evidence as a standard form of letter:
>
> > You need only pay the amount ordered by the Court under the terms of the judgment but you should be aware that under the terms of the agreement interest continues to accrue on your account. It is therefore in your interest to increase the instalment paid as soon as possible otherwise a much greater balance than the judgment debt may quickly build up.[48]

Having found that the bank had done enough on that front, the court rejected the claim that the clause in question introduced a significant imbalance in the rights and obligations of the parties. The EFS principle would seem to me to recommend a similar outcome, with one reservation. In the first part of the quoted passage, Lord Bingham suggests that, when a loan is concluded, the bank ought to provide borrowers with only so much detail about what will happen in the event of a default. This sounds right, but the explanation of why banks need not do more is not, as his Lordship implies, that this is a form of banking custom or typical market practice. Rather, it is that giving borrowers more information about that eventuality *at that early stage* would likely not be very valuable to them, in the sense that one would not expect that having that information would lead a borrower to make different financial decisions. That, however, will cease to be true the closer a borrower comes to

---

[48] Ibid *per* Lord Bingham at [24].

defaulting. When borrowers begin to miss payments, the opportunity to have their attention drawn to the fact that, were they to default and have judgment issued against them, making post-judgment payments will not be enough to extinguish their debt, will acquire clear value for them. It follows that the bank may not insist on enforcing the relevant clause if it draws borrowers' attention to its effect only after judgment has been issued. Under the EFS principle, that clause would count as unfair as long as it is not brought to borrowers' attention *when it would be useful for them to know about it.*

If the EFS principle has the explanatory resources I have claimed for it, it also provides us with reason to give an affirmative response to the question of whether English law features a general principle of fairness. EFS may attribute significance to structural matters, but it is not specific to certain types of voluntary transaction, or to transactions concluded under certain structural conditions, and it has the capacity to justify and guide the interpretation of both common law doctrines and statutory regimes. In that regard, EFS seems to me to survive all the main objections English lawyers have raised against the recognition of a general principle or doctrine of contractual fairness. Ewan McKendrick has summarised them neatly:

> Four principal objections can be raised against the creation of such a doctrine. The first is that courts have difficulty in identifying contracts which are unfair because the adversarial nature of litigation does not make it easy for them to set the transaction which is before them in the context of the market in which the parties are operating ... The second is that such a general doctrine would create an unacceptable degree of uncertainty. The third is that English law as a general aversion to the creation of broad, general principles; the courts in particular prefer to reason incrementally and by analogy to existing categories rather than by reference to a general, overarching principle. The fourth is that it is not the function of contract law to engage in the redistribution of wealth.[49]

EFS survives the first three objections because it makes the task of identifying unfair contracts and contract terms easier for courts, by requiring them to attend not to general ideas such as 'significant imbalance' or 'good faith' but to particular questions about the opportunities that weaker parties had in the situation, and whether a party in that position would have reason to value having those opportunities. And it survives the fourth, because it is not a redistributive principle. The purpose of the EFS principle is not to do social justice, equalise bargaining power, enforce duties of good faith, or transfer resources from stronger to weaker parties. Like the value-of-choice account that drives

---

[49] E McKendrick, *Contract Law*, 8th edn (Basingstoke, Palgrave Macmillan, 2009) 301. For theoretical defences of the claim that no single principle can give a justification of contract law, see M Eisenberg, 'The Theory of Contracts' in Benson, above n 6, 206 at 262–4; Lucy, above n 8, at 382–6.

it, EFS simply aims to ensure that the burdens that people have to bear under their contracts are sensitive to the value for them of the opportunities that the institution of contracting provides them with.

V. 'FAIR TERMS', JUSTICE, AND OPPORTUNITY

Statutes like the UTCCR and the UCTA say that our institutions ought to weed out 'unfair terms' in contracts. John Rawls said that principles of justice ought to specify 'fair terms' of interaction between free and equal persons.[50] The similarity is striking. We want the terms of consumer or employment contracts to be fair. Rawls suggests that we want the same of the basic social structure that governs how we interact with each other. It is no wonder that people have been drawn to the idea that, in order to determine when certain contract terms are fair and should be enforced as agreed, we need to attend to the way Rawls's two principles, the liberty and the difference principle, distribute liberties and basic goods in society.

The problem with that thought is that Rawls's principles may do not exhaust our conception of what is required for the terms of interaction between persons to be fair. As Samuel Scheffler puts it:

> Suppose we want to identify principles of justice to regulate the major social, political and economic institutions of our society and to specify fair terms of cooperation for free and equal citizens. No doubt we will want those principles to articulate regulative standards governing the distribution of personal and political liberties, income and wealth, and opportunities for education and employment. But won't we also want the principles to provide guidance about other issues as well? Won't we want them to articulate standards ... for deciding when agreements entered into by individuals are enforceable and what remedies will be available when agreements are breached, and for establishing when individuals must bear responsibility for damage or injuries that they cause?[51]

Scheffler answers 'yes', and takes this to mean that the principles of justice that Rawls set out are 'not complete, and that additional norms of justice are required to provide guidance on at least some of those issues'.[52] His conclusion is that, when we think about justice, we cannot be thinking only about the distribution of liberties or basic goods. We need to think about non-distributive questions too.

I hope to have shown that Scheffler is right, but only up to a point. The EFS principle gives us a way of telling which voluntary undertakings ought to be

---

[50] Rawls, above n 25 at 54.
[51] Scheffler, above n 26, at 233.
[52] Ibid at 234.

enforceable, which not, and which ought to be enforceable under modified terms. As Scheffler anticipated, it is not a distributive principle, because it does not aim to bring about any pattern for the allocation of liberties and basic goods. Rather, it makes enforceability turn on the value for transacting persons of having certain opportunities. The fact that some people have more opportunities, or are better choosers, or have more bargaining power, are all morally OK under the EFS principle, as long as the person on whom the principle imposes burdens has reason to value the opportunity to undertake them. At the same time, the EFS principle explains why the enforceability of voluntary undertakings ought to be sensitive to the shape of the basic structure of society. That structure does not just affect how much people have in their pocket, what education they get, and what jobs they can do. It also affects the position from which they transact with others. It follows that the value of the opportunities that contracting provides may differ for persons that occupy different structural positions. The value-of-choice account tells us that principles of enforceability should show sensitivity to that difference. Scanlon's EF principle does not do this. Its revision in the EFS principle does. And it tells us that Scheffler is right to encourage us to think about principles for the enforcement of voluntary undertakings in 'non-distributive' terms, but only as long as we do not understand 'non-distributive' to mean 'structure-insensitive'.

7

Vicarious Liability

SOMETIMES WE MAY justifiably require a person to make repair for someone else's mistakes. The principles of vicarious liability in tort describe a range of such situations. Those principles say, roughly, that when A and B stand a relationship of a certain sort, B's conduct amounts to a tort, and that tort occurred in the course or context of that relationship, A becomes responsible to make repair for it. The Latin maxims *respondeat superior* ('let the master answer') and *qui facit per alium facit per se* ('one who acts though another acts through oneself') draw attention to different aspects of that story. *Respondeat superior* indicates that the relationship in question must be, in an appropriate sense, hierarchical, with A being at the top of the hierarchy. *Qui facit per alium facit per se* suggests that the hierarchy in question should take the form of A acting 'through' B, by directing B's conduct. Employment relationships are the typical example.

This basic story already raises two issues. One is that sometimes A may direct B's conduct and still not be responsible to make repair for B's mistakes. Suppose that you are going out for a smoke, and that I ask you if you could get me a can of soda from the shop downstairs on your way back. When you finish your smoke and go to get the soda, you carelessly injure the shopkeeper. To say that it should be my responsibility to compensate the victim of your carelessness would seem to demand too much of me. Or suppose that I am your driving instructor and that, despite the fact that I have been careful in instructing you, you happen to make a bad mistake during a driving lesson, crashing the car and causing injury to third parties. To hold me responsible for making repair for the harm you caused simply because I was directing your action would seem to demand too much of me.

The basic story also leaves open whether action-direction extends responsibility from B to A, or transfers it altogether to A. The typical understanding of vicarious liability sees it as having the former effect, in the sense that it allows claimants to turn against either or both of A and B. This view requires some justification. Under standard conceptions of agency, the agent does not become personally bound by the agreements that the agent has entered into in the name of the principal. The principal directs the agent's action, but it is the principal alone that bears responsibility in the case of non-performance.

If things should be different when B commits a tort, we need some argument to support the differentiation. Moreover, even if such an argument can be made, we have some reason to doubt whether A and B ought to be jointly and severally liable in all tort contexts. Maybe this makes better sense in the context of the tort of conspiracy than in typical workplace settings. For example, if the protection principle I proposed in Chapter 4 is correct, employees may reasonably require their employer to protect them against the burden of repair for workplace mistakes. That, in turn, would entail that, unlike the responsibility of co-conspirators, the responsibility of employers will not be additional to that of employees, but exclusive.

Broadly speaking, these examples suggest that whether action-direction entails responsibility for A, B or both depends not only on the degree of direction that A exercises over B's conduct, but also on the context or the purpose for which that direction is exercised. In this chapter I try to give more depth and texture to that assessment by drawing attention to two ideas that seem to me to play a central role in many different accounts of vicarious liability in tort law. One idea says that A is vicariously liable for B's conduct because A *participated*, in some appropriate sense, in that conduct. According to this idea, accounts of vicarious liability should specify the degree of action-direction necessary for A to count as a participant in B's conduct. The other idea finds the basis of vicarious liability in the fact that A is favourably *placed*, under some appropriate standard, to deal with the consequences of B's conduct. This suggests that accounts of vicarious liability should provide a more refined account of what counts as favourable placement.

I will suggest that both ideas matter in determining A's and B's respective substantive responsibilities, but that received accounts of vicarious liability have not been able to explain their significance adequately. Part of the reason I think, is that those accounts focus their attention either on A—as the person who principles of vicarious liability require to make repair for someone else's mistakes—or on the claimant who can reasonably want to be compensated for the harm that he or she has suffered. While neither focus is misplaced, I hope to show that we can get a much more reliable grip on the position of both A and the claimant if we think about the position of B first. In particular, I will argue that we should understand vicarious liability neither as a way of holding A responsible for entrepreneurial extensions of A's agency, nor as a way of securing compensation for claimants, but as a way of protecting B against the consequences of B's own mistakes, ie as a way for the law to meet the demands of the 'protection principle' I proposed in Chapter 4. Applied to situations of action-direction, that principle says that A ought to protect B against the burden of repair insofar as, absent that protection, B would not have reason to value the opportunity to engage in an activity under A's direction.

Seeing vicarious liability as an instance of protection for B suggests a particular way of thinking about the responsibilities of A. It tells us that we should pay attention not to whether A (or others) participated in the making of the mistake, but to whether A's action-direction affects the value for B of the opportunity to engage in the directed activity (eg whether the fact that B's activity is directed makes it more likely that B will be exposed to situations where B might make a mistake, or aggravates the stakes for B of making such a mistake). Similarly, the principle tells us to focus not on whether A or others are well-placed to deal with the consequences of B's mistake, but whether A or others have reason to value the opportunity to deal with those consequences. This explains, for example, why you may not require me to bear the burden of repair for the harm you cause when you go to buy me a can of soda. While you were acting under my direction and for my benefit, I do not have reason to value the opportunity to pick up the tab for your mistakes in the course of that activity. The reason why the opportunity to do little things in the day for friends or colleagues is valuable for both of us is partly dependent on neither of us having to provide each other with extra protections against liability.

Moreover, seeing vicarious liability as an instance of A protecting B against the burden of repair helps clarify who the victim of B's mistake should be able to claim a remedy from. In particular, it casts doubt on the assumption that the principles of vicarious liability extend the range of persons that the claimant may require to make repair. When the conditions under which B may require A to protect B against the burden of repair are satisfied, principles of vicarious liability ought to block the allocation of that burden on B altogether. Accordingly, when B ought to be so protected, the law ought to not allow the claimant to sue B, or A and A's insurers to claim an indemnity from B, and that where the law still allows such claims or indemnities, it ought to abolish them. The same idea shows the flaw in the—often unstated—assumption that the reason why B is hardly ever sued, or why employers' indemnities are hardly ever exercised, is that B is unlikely to have deep pockets. If the protection principle is right, and to the extent that it applies to B's benefit, allowing B to be sued would be unjustified in the first place. This conclusion is not novel. Several commentators have noted that allowing indemnities for workplace accidents would not help industrial relations.[1] My account shows why that claim ought to be framed in a way that avoids creating the impression that unions are 'bailing careless employees out' of their responsibilities by sheer force of bargaining power. In fact, the opposite is the case. Unions are justified in resisting indemnities precisely because allowing such indemnities in the range

---

[1] See, eg, R Hasson, 'Subrogation in Insurance Law—A Critical Evaluation' (1985) 5 *QJLS* 416, 434–6; R Parsons, 'Individual Responsibility versus Enterprise Liability' (1959) 29 *Australian Law Journal* 714, both criticising *Lister v Romford Ice and Cold Storage Co Ltd* [1957] AC 555.

of situations covered by the protection principle would saddle employees with responsibilities that are not properly theirs.

Aside from helping us get a better grip on the positions of B, A and the claimant, a further advantage of seeing vicarious liability in the light of the protection principle is that this provides a good account of English case-law on vicarious liability, especially cases concerned with the nature of the relationship that must exist between A and B in order for A to be vicariously liable for B's conduct (to illustrate this, I will look both at familiar workplace settings, as well as some more special regimes, like the vicarious liability of car owners). Furthermore, it allows us to distinguish cases in which A ought to carry the burden of repair because B ought to be protected against that burden from cases in which A ought to carry the burden of repair because A has exposed the claimant to the risk of suffering injury in the hands of B, by giving B certain powers over the claimant (eg by giving B the authority of a school principal or a class teacher). Tort theorists have long suspected that the two sets of cases are normatively different and should be dealt with under separate doctrines. The protection principle can explain why that suspicion is by and large correct.

I. PARTICIPATION AND PLACEMENT

Suppose we say that A ought to bear the responsibility to make repair for the consequences of B's mistake. We might be thinking along either or both of the following lines. We could be thinking that A is responsible because it is A, acting through B, who made the mistake. Or we could be thinking that A is responsible because A is appropriately positioned to deal with the prospect or with the consequences of that mistake. The first idea grounds A's responsibility on A's *participation* in the bringing-about of those consequences. The second grounds A's responsibility on A's *placement* in relation to those consequences. The two ideas are distinct because one may endorse one and reject the other. One can say that A may have participated in the making of the mistake, but that some other more appropriately placed person should bear its cost. Or one can say that A was best placed to prevent B's mistake or to deal with its cost, but that liability should rest solely with B, as the mistake is only B's own, and so on. Picking sides here matters, because each idea allows A different ways of avoiding responsibility. If the proper ground for holding A responsible is that A participated in the making of the mistake, A may avoid that responsibility only if A was not, in fact, a participant in the relevant sense. If the proper ground for holding A responsible is that A was well placed to prevent B's mistake or to deal with its consequences, A may avoid that responsibility only if A was not so placed, and so on.

The distinction between participation and placement as grounds of A's responsibility does not map exactly onto the divide between models of wrongs and models of costs in private law, but one can easily see how the two pairs relate. Participation takes as its premise that the separateness of A and B has inherent moral significance and that we need some special argument to justify why and when B's conduct may be attributed to A too.[2] That idea finds a natural home in models of wrongs and their emphasis on singling out the agents who stand in the special normative relationship between a wrongdoer and a victim of a wrong.[3] It is less obviously consistent the consequentialist outlook of models of costs, which judge the merits of tort principles on the basis of their ability to contain aggregate social cost, rather than their sensitivity to the separateness of persons and the special nature of certain normative relationships. Similarly, the idea of placement relies significantly on considerations about a person's ability to manage and contain the costs of an accident (typically, in the case of enterprises, by having access to more affordable insurance and spreading the cost of that insurance through market mechanisms). This finds a natural ally in anyone who thinks that the aim of tort law should be to reduce the social cost of accidents, but it is less obviously in line with the claim the aim of tort law should be to address wrongdoing, rather than all accidental loss. That said, the alignment of the idea of participation with models of wrongs and the idea of placement with models of costs is more a matter of broad affinity than normative commitment. One may emphasise normative relationships and accept that A's placement may itself create such a relationship between A, B and the claimant, just as one may care about minimising social cost and accept that the best way of achieving this might be to impose the cost of making repair for some harm on those who participated in its production.[4]

When we turn to the proposed justifications of vicarious liability,[5] including the view that vicarious liability is not justified at all, the picture is even more mixed, in the sense that the ideas of participation and placement do not map onto the divide between those justifications, as much as they cut across them.

---

[2] OW Holmes, 'Agency' (1891–2) 5 *Harvard LR* 1, 14: 'I assume that common-sense is opposed to making one man pay for another man's wrong, unless he actually has brought the wrong to pass according to the ordinary canons of legal responsibility'.

[3] See, eg, E Weinrib, *The Idea of Private Law*, Rev edn (Oxford, Oxford University Press, 2012) 186: 'Since corrective justice is the normative relationship of sufferer and doer, *respondeat superior* fits into corrective justice only if the employer can, in some sense, be regarded as a doer of the harm'.

[4] It is, however, a matter of note that corrective justice theorists have been generally opposed to seeing vicarious liability as turning on placement (eg see the above quote from Weinrib), while costs theorists have regarded participation as more of a side constraint on the best account of cost reduction (see the quote from Calabresi, infra n 16).

[5] For a critical summary, see J Neyers, 'A Theory of Vicarious Liability' (2005) 43 *Alberta LR* 1, 5–15.

Some justifications, like *deep pockets* and *loss spreading*, are straight appeals to A's better placement: one says that A is better placed because A can afford to cover the cost of the harm, the other says the same because A is able to spread the cost to the community. Similarly, the claim that vicarious liability is not justified at all, ie that responsibility for the harm should lie only with B, makes a clear appeal to A's lack of participation in the production of that harm. However, it may be no coincidence that these justifications are generally regarded as the weakest of the bunch. In fact, all of the more promising justifications of vicarious liability have tended to hedge their bets between participation and placement. Consider the widely endorsed view that A may be vicariously responsible for B's mistakes insofar as A has a measure of *control* over B's conduct. The fact that A has control over B's conduct may matter because it shows A to be a participant in the production of the harm, but also because it places A in a position to take measures to contain the danger of B causing the harm in question (eg by changing B's activity or incentives). Similarly, the fact that imposing responsibility on A could *deter* a harmful activity may matter because it makes A less likely to participate in that activity through B, but also because it indicates that A is well placed to ensure that B does not engage in it. The same applies with regard to the view that vicarious liability is justified as an instance of *enterprise liability*. One might say that A's enterprise should bear responsibility for B's conduct because B's participation in the production of the harm counts as a participation of the enterprise itself,[6] or because the enterprise is best placed to deal with the harmful consequences of that conduct.[7] Sometimes it feels very intuitive to say a bit of both.[8]

Courts and theorists have sometimes looked at this hedging between participation and placement as a sign of weakness, or as evidence that the principles

---

[6] *Ira S Bushey & Sons, Inc v United States* (US Court of Appeals, 2nd Cir, 1968) 398 F 2d 167 at 171: '[R]espondeat superior ... rests not so much on policy grounds ... as in a deeply rooted sentiment that a business enterprise cannot justly disclaim responsibility for accidents that may fairly be said to be characteristic of its activities.'

[7] *Bazley v Curry* (Supreme Court of Canada) [1999] 2 SCR 534 at [33]: 'Beyond the narrow band of employer conduct that attracts direct liability in negligence lies a vast area where imaginative and efficient administration and supervision can reduce the risk that the employer has introduced into the community. Holding the employer vicariously liable for the wrongs of its employee may encourage the employer to take such steps, and hence, reduce the risk of future harm.'

[8] See, eg, *Hinman v Westinghouse Electricity Co* (Supreme Court of California) 2 Cal.3d 956 at 959–60: 'The losses caused by the torts of employees ... are placed upon the employer because, having engaged in an enterprise which will, on the basis of all past experience, involve harm to others through the tort of employees, and sought to profit by it, it is just that he, rather than the innocent injured plaintiff, should bear them; and because he is better able to absorb them, and to distribute them, through prices, rates or liability insurance, to the public, and so to shift them to society, to the community at large. Added to this is the makeweight argument that an employer who is held strictly liable is under the greatest incentive to the careful in the selection, instruction and supervision or his servants, and to take every precaution to see that the enterprise is conducted safely.' See also D Brodie, *Enterprise Liability and the Common Law* (Cambridge, Cambridge University Press, 2010) ch 3.

of vicarious liability have no unifying or coherent justification.[9] This assessment seems to me to encourage the impression that the ideas of participation and placement cannot be accommodated under a single scheme of responsibility. I will argue that this impression is mistaken and that, once we see the principles of vicarious liability as protecting B against the burden of repair for B's mistakes, we can get a better grip on the precise role of each element in justifying those principles.

The next two sections set the background for this claim by looking at placement and participation, respectively. They argue that, considered alone, neither can justify imposing on A the responsibility of making repair for B's mistake. On the one hand, we cannot determine whether A's good or bad placement is significant for the purposes of A's responsibility without considering how A might be involved in the production of B's mistake. On the other hand, deciding whether it is appropriate to treat B's mistake as A's own requires us to consider not only the intensity of A's direction, but also whether A's placement was such that B could have required A to protect B against the burden of repair for that mistake.

II. THE SIGNIFICANCE OF PLACEMENT

The idea that a person's placement makes a difference to that person's responsibilities features in more than one of the proposed justifications of vicarious liability. Advocates of enterprise liability appeal to it when they note that A's enterprise *stands* to benefit from B's activities, or that it will typically *be able* to pass on the cost of insuring against liability to the market.[10] Advocates of control and deterrence theories appeal to placement when they note that A may be in a *position* to affect how B behaves, or that A may *be able* to take measures to avoid B causing an accident or to minimise its costs. The justifications of loss-spreading and 'deep pockets' are appeals to pure placement so understood.

The reason why placement seems to matter in determining one's responsibilities is not hard to see. How one is positioned in relation to some problem

---

[9] See, eg, *ICI v Shatwell* [1965] AC 656 at 685 *per* Lord Pearce: 'The doctrine of vicarious liability has not grown from any very clear, logical or legal principle but from social convenience and rough justice'; G Williams, 'Vicarious Liability and the Master's Indemnity' (1957) 20 *MLR* 220 at 231: 'Vicarious liability is the creation of many judges who have different ideas of its justification or social policy, or no idea at all.'

[10] R Rabin, 'Some Thoughts on the Ideology of Enterprise Liability' (1996) 55 *Maryland LR* 1990 summarises the justification as follows: 'an enterprise should bear the risks of accidents it produces because (1) an enterprise has superior risk-spreading capacity compared to victims who would otherwise bear the costs of accidents, and (2) an enterprise is generally better placed to respond to the safety incentives created by liability rules than is the party suffering harm'. For a key statement of that idea, see G Priest, 'The Invention of Enterprise Liability: A Critical History of the Intellectual Foundations of Modern Tort Law' (1985) 14 *Journal of Legal Studies* 461.

can make a difference to one's ability to address it. To occupy some position is, basically, to have a certain range of options and certain conditions of choice. We say that one is 'well placed' to deal with a problem and mean that one has a range of options that allow one to address that problem, and enjoys favourable conditions for choosing amongst those options. This clearly has some significance when we think about the possibility of *disclaiming* responsibility for some burden. 'I should not bear this burden because I am poorly placed to discharge it' is a very familiar complaint not just in tort contexts (eg situations where the law requires a person to act on knowledge that this person may have a hard time obtaining, or situations where imposing a duty on that person would be financially straining), but also in contexts involving taxation, military service and all sorts of practical burdens that a person may be asked to bear.

But while poor placement may sometimes allow a person to object to being required to bear a burden, good placement does not seem to be enough of a reason for *imposing* a responsibility on a person. The mere fact that I could deal easily or effectively with your problem does not make it mine. To make it mine, you would also need to show that I was in some appropriate sense involved in its coming about. If for present purposes we define involvement in the coming-about of a problem as 'participation', participation seems to set something of a threshold requirement for discussing whether my good or bad placement might make it my responsibility to deal with that problem. In other words, whereas it is clear that participants may sometimes be able to disclaim responsibility on account of their poor placement, it is not at all clear how well-placed persons could be made to bear responsibility for a problem in the creation of which they were not, in an appropriate sense, participants.

Of course, the qualification 'in an appropriate sense' is important, because determining who is a participant in the coming about of a problem depends on how one describes the problem at hand. We can think of that 'problem' as the occurrence of a harmful mistake in a discrete situation (as in 'B lost control of the machinery and injured C's leg'). But we could take a broader perspective, and say that the problem is the occurrence of a certain *type* of harmful mistake in a certain *type* of context (as in 'B caused and C was the victim of an industrial accident', or more broadly, 'B caused and C suffered an accident in the process of mass market production'). An even broader perspective would suggest that, life in present-day communities being what it is, the real problem is that we need to forge a collective response to the occurrence of certain common types of harmful mistakes. Choosing a perspective matters because the more broadly we describe the problem, the more natural it becomes to take a similarly broader view of who might be involved in its coming about. A may not have participated in the physical conduct that constituted B's harmful mistake, but maybe it is *enough* participation that A put in place the system of work in which B made the mistake in question. Or it may be enough participation that someone belongs in a class of agents that have an interest in and stand to benefit from industrial production, eg that person is a market consumer of the goods or services that A's enterprise produces. Or maybe one ought to be counted as a participant in the situation in virtue of being a citizen in a community whose life is such that certain types of accidents are bound to occur. Any one of those perspectives can pass a basic test of causation: without A having set up the enterprise, B's mistake wouldn't have occurred; without consumers, there would be no industrial production and so on. The question is which of those perspectives should matter when we determine whether A counts as a participant for the purposes of allocating responsibility for B's mistake. But we cannot hope to answer that question by appealing to the notion of participation itself.

This, I think, gives us a first indication as to why most justifications of vicarious liability have tended to hedge their bets between participation and placement. The first idea allows those accounts to register how A, B and any other agents *responded* in the situation. The second allows them to describe the *situation* itself. Given that an account of the burdens that one ought to bear in a situation should be sensitive to both parameters, it is no surprise to find that most accounts of vicarious liability will need to appeal to both. Moreover, the fact that we may understand the ideas of participation and placement in different ways should lead us to expect a similar diversity in the content of the justification for requiring A or any other third parties to bear the burden of repair for B's mistakes. Under the value-of-choice account that I have proposed, if A counts as a participant, we will need to consider whether holding A responsible would be sensitive to opportunities that A has reason to value in the situation. If consumers of the goods or services that A's enterprise produces count as participants too, we should tailor the justification for requiring them to bear a fraction of the burden of repair to the opportunities that they would value having, and so on.[11] I will develop an account of vicarious liability along those lines in section V, but I want to preface that discussion by looking at a way of thinking about vicarious liability which purports to rely on the idea of participation alone.

---

[11] One could accept that it may sometimes be appropriate to take a broader perspective of what counts as participation, but still insist that there is moral significance in the fact that some persons may be participants in an accident from more than one perspective. For example, when B injures C's leg, B may count as a participant in the accident all the way from the narrowest to the broadest of those perspectives (ie as the physical actor, as someone engaged in industrial production, as a consumer of the goods or services produced, as a fellow citizen). By contrast, consumers of the products made in the factory where B caused the accident may count as participants only from one of the broader perspectives. This may give us some reason to require that the distribution of the burdens be sensitive to the difference between the position consumers and B. That is, perhaps the fact that B is 'plugged into' the accident in more ways than consumers should mean that B should bear a higher proportion of the cost of dealing with C's harm. It seems to me that this is not the case. The fact that B is more deeply 'plugged into' the accident may entitle us to treat B differently, but it need not entail that this treatment should take the form of having B bear a higher proportion of the burden for repairing C's harm. Perhaps B is getting enough of a different treatment in that B's mistake puts not just B's bank balance but also their employment status on the line.

III. PARTICIPATION AND ATTRIBUTION

The fact that you broke something clearly matters in the assessment of whether you should have to pay for it. Accordingly, one might try to justify holding A vicariously liable for the harm that B caused on the basis that, by directing B's conduct, A participated in the production of the harm. Given that the harm will not have come about from A in the most direct, corporeal sense, treating A as a participant for the purposes of vicarious liability involves thinking about vicarious liability 'as a species of the more general rules concerning the attribution of words and acts of one person to another'.[12] The attribution may involve a fiction in a corporeal sense, but that fiction is no stranger than that involved in the attribution of conduct, both in law and morality, to corporate bodies and other associations, eg to companies or sports teams.[13] What matters is whether the attribution in question is appropriately justified and how its incidence places A in a certain normative relationship with the victim of B's conduct. As Ernest Weinrib puts it in the context of the vicarious liability of an employer for the torts of an employee: '[t]he question here is not whether the employer-acting-through-the-employee is a fiction, but whether it brings out the immanent connection between the doctrinal structure of *respondeat superior* and the normative structure of doing and suffering'.[14]

Weinrib's formulation already suggests that the view of vicarious liability as liability for participation is consistent with a wide variety of justifications. Most obviously, that view fits with the justification of vicarious liability on the basis of A's control over B's conduct. Some versions of the idea of enterprise liability too seem to appeal to that idea, especially when they try to determine what conduct 'belongs' to the enterprise, in the sense of being characteristic of its activities.[15] The same goes for deterrence theories. For example, Guido Calabresi agrees that the goal of primary accident cost deterrence gives us some reason to impose accidental costs 'on those activities that are thought to engender them'.[16] An activity needs an actor, so attribution of a cost to an activity will entail attribution to an actor too.

The question, then, is when B's behaviour may be appropriately attributed to A, making A a participant in the production of the mistake and the ensuing harm. It seems to me that the justification of such attribution raises three issues. One concerns the *purpose* of the attribution, or the particular sense in which we might say that A is or is not a participant in events. Another issue concerns the *object* of attribution, or the identification of the aspect of B's

---

[12] R Stevens, *Torts and Rights* (Oxford, Oxford University Press, 2007) 259.
[13] Ibid at 261.
[14] Weinrib, above n 3, at 187.
[15] See *Ira S Bushey & Sons, Inc v United States*, above n 6.
[16] G Calabresi, *The Costs of Accidents: A Legal and Economic Analysis* (New Haven, Yale University Press, 1970) 54.

behaviour that is being attributed to A for the purpose that we have in mind. A third concerns the appropriate *test* for making that attribution. I consider each issue in turn and conclude that, in each case, we cannot explain why A ought to bear the burden of repair for B's mistake in the context of the directed activity without appealing to the value for each of those persons of the opportunity to engage in that activity.

A. The Purpose of Attribution

The first question arises because, as we have noted at several junctures, there is more than one sense in which we can say that some conduct is mine, yours or A's.[17] I may regard some conduct as (wholly or partly) mine in the context of my own ethical narrative, eg when I think about what I regard as my achievements, failures and other significant moments in my life. I may regard it as mine in the sense that I might deserve praise or blame for it from others. Or I may regard the conduct as mine in the sense that others may require me to bear the practical burden of dealing with its consequences. Although these senses may be related in some ways, the conditions under which the attribution of the conduct to me is justified will depend on the particular sense we have in mind.[18] I may be able to disclaim responsibility in one sense, but not in another. Suppose that I have commissioned your company to construct a new type of vehicle for me and that in testing the new vehicle one of your employees is fatally injured. If I am even minimally self-reflective, this tragedy will obviously figure in my narrative of my own life and my conception of myself and it may even lead me to blame myself for your employee's death. However, it may not *also* make me responsible for dealing with the harmful consequences of the accident.[19] Conversely, I may be responsible for dealing with the harmful consequences of an accident, even though my conduct is not

---

[17]   See ch 2(I).

[18]   This distinction seems to me to cut across Dan Meir-Cohen's distinction between A being 'subject-responsible' (ie responsible as a subject of some conduct) and 'object-responsible' (ie responsible for the production of a certain object through one's conduct), see D Meir-Cohen, 'Responsibility and the Boundaries of the Self' (1992) 105 *Harvard LR* 959, 962–3. One may be subject-responsible for some conduct in a self-narrative sense, but not in the sense of substantive moral responsibility, just as one may be object-responsible for some outcome in the sense of deserving praise or blame for it, but not in the sense of having to bear the burden of dealing with its consequences.

[19]   *cf* J Ronson, 'Jon Ronson is ready for blast-off. Is Richard Branson?', *The Guardian*, 21 February 2014 '[O]n a boiling hot afternoon—26 July 2007—Rutan's team was testing rocket propellant for Virgin Galactic when a tank of nitrous oxide exploded. There had been 17 people watching the test out here in the desert, this place for maverick engineers to push the boundaries. Shards of carbon fibre shot into them. Three of Rutan's engineers were killed, and three others seriously injured. Rutan's company was found liable and fined $25,870 ... When I asked Branson how personally connected he felt to the three deaths, he said, "Well ..."

blameworthy, or a significant aspect of my self-conception.[20] Given that tort principles are concerned with determining who bears the substantive responsibility for dealing with accidents and other harm-causing events, I will assume that when we discuss whether B's conduct may be justifiably attributed to A for the purposes of vicarious liability we are concerned with allocating the burden of dealing with the consequences of B's mistake.[21]

B. The Object of Attribution

The second question concerns the object of attribution, or the identification of the aspect of B's behaviour that is being attributed to A. The question arises because there are at least three different aspects of B's behaviour that we could consider attributing to A for the purpose of determining A's responsibilities: we can attribute the *wrong*, if any, that B committed; we can attribute the *outcome* of B's conduct; or we can attribute the *conduct* itself.

The first option involves saying that, when B has committed a wrong, A has committed that wrong too and, conversely, that when B has not committed a wrong, A has not committed a wrong either. That is often the case. For example, when the claimant's physical injury was not the result of any wrongdoing by B, A may not be held responsible for the cost of that injury either. However, we can think of situations where this view leads to counter-intuitive results. Robert Stevens has pointed to examples in which B's directed conduct amounts to a breach of a contract between B and the claimant. Unless A intended to bring about that result, it seems obvious that the wrong committed by B should not be attributed to A as the directing agent.[22] Similarly, we might contrast a scenario in which A directs B to assault the claimant with a scenario in which A directs B to undertake some conduct that, unknown to B and unforeseeably from B's point of view, A knows will cause physical harm to the claimant. It seems obvious that in the first situation, B's wrong of assault may be attributed to A, while in the second situation A is the only wrongdoer. These examples suggest that whether we can attribute any wrong that B committed against the claimant to A may depend on the

Then he stopped. "If they were working directly for me, I would feel very responsible. Obviously, if we hadn't decided to do the programme in the first place, they would be alive today. So you realise that …'"

[20] The familiar facts of *Vincent v Lake Erie* 124 NW 221 (1910), in which the owners of a steamship whose captain had wisely tied it to a private dock to protect it from a raging storm were held responsible for the damage to that dock, seem to me an example in point.

[21] *cf Launchbury v Morgans* [1973] AC 127 (HL) per Lord Wilberforce at 135: 'I accept entirely that "agency" in contexts such as these is merely a concept, the meaning and purpose of which is to say "is vicariously liable", and that either expression reflects a judgment of value—*respondeat superior* is the law saying that the owner ought to pay'.

[22] Stevens, above n 12 at 263–4.

particular features of the parties' respective situations. One such feature is what A and B know or could reasonably foresee. Another, suggested in Stevens's breach of contract example, is what persons in A's position can reasonably regard as falling outside the domain of their responsibilities (in this example, B's contractual undertaking with the claimant). The point is that even if A *knew* that B would be in breach of contract if B did as directed, A could reasonably disclaim responsibility for the breach on the ground that B's voluntary undertakings with third parties are not A's business. This suggests that while wrongdoing can be the proper object of attribution, the extent to which we may attribute B's wrong to A will depend on certain prior conclusions about A and B's respective substantive responsibilities.

This becomes even clearer if we take the object of attribution to be not the wrong that B committed, but the outcome of B's conduct. It is often natural to say that when B acts under A's direction and B's conduct has brought about a certain outcome, that outcome can be properly attributed to A too and, conversely, that if B's conduct did not bring about a certain outcome, that outcome may not be attributed to A either. Stevens illustrates the idea with the example of a footballer scoring a goal for their team. The fact that the footballer is a member of the team justifies attributing the positive outcome to both.[23] If someone asks who scored the goal in the Barcelona–Real Madrid football match, 'Lionel Messi' and 'Barcelona' are both perfectly good answers.

At the same time, Stevens seems to me to underestimate the complexity of his example. Whether a dual attribution of the outcome is appropriate will often depend on the precise outcome that we are thinking about. Suppose that Lionel Messi's strike brings about two distinct outcomes: a goal and a win. While it makes sense to attribute the goal both to Messi and to his team, a dual attribution seems much less plausible in respect of the win. When someone asks 'who won?', 'Lionel Messi' is not an appropriate answer, except perhaps in jest. The reason is that goal-scoring is an outcome which we take to reflect both a collective achievement of the team and a personal achievement of the goal-scorer (that explains why there is a special prize for the top goal-scorers), while a football victory is an outcome that we take to reflect a collective achievement alone.

To see the significance of this, consider a more complex example, involving penalties for breaches of the rules of football. A bad tackle that results in a red card is attributable both to the offending player as regards the player's further participation in the match in progress, and to the team as regards the total number of players it is allowed to field in that match. However, when it comes to forthcoming fixtures, the red card becomes attributable to the player alone, who may be excluded from one or more such fixtures as a penalty. The card

---

[23] Ibid at 261. Stevens uses the example of Geoff Hurst scoring for England. I have opted for a more updated version of the example in the text.

has no effect on the total number of players that the team is allowed to field in subsequent matches. The way we attribute outcomes and penalties here seems to me to be sensitive to the various opportunities that the offending player and the team have in the situation. Playing football well requires that teams and players refrain from resorting to certain unsporting forms of conduct, which pose risks for players and put the team to which the offending player belongs in an unfairly advantageous position in the field. Players are easily able to avoid engaging in such conduct by keeping to certain basic rules of play. The team is also well placed to avoid and deter breaches of those rules, both by adopting a playing style that discourages them, and by fielding players that are not known to be keen on such breaches. Moreover, the nature of football allows a team to continue playing competitively in a match even if one or more of its players are sent off, so the team has reason to value being able to continue playing despite that setback. That value would, however, be significantly reduced if the rules extended the effects of the red card into the next match, by barring the team from fielding another player in the place of the offender, and so on.

I believe that we are bound to reach similar conclusions if we take the object of attribution to be B's conduct, rather than any outcome that conduct may have had or any wrong that it might constitute. The idea of attributing B's conduct to A encourages the assumption that the description of that conduct will be the same for both A and B. That will be the case in very many typical cases. When A directs B to assault the claimant, it is natural to say that A too is assaulting the claimant. But sometimes the proper description of a person's conduct will depend on the circumstances of that person's situation, and the knowledge and opportunities that this person had in it. Suppose A has a duty to rescue the claimant from some external danger to the claimant's life and that A instructs B, who is best placed to offer help to the claimant but who knows nothing of the situation, to attend to some other task in the opposite direction. Also suppose that the danger materialises and the claimant dies. When we consider who might bear the burden of the claimant's harm, it seems to me that the proper description of B's conduct in the situation does not match that of A's conduct. B simply walks away. A fails to save the claimant. We could, of course, call the behaviour in question 'walking away' as far as B is concerned, and 'failing to save' or even 'killing' as far as A is concerned, but this is the same as saying that the difference between those descriptions is the difference in the positions that A and B occupied, and the opportunities that each had to avert the terrible outcome.

C. The Test for Attribution

The third, and most familiar, question about attribution concerns the test that determines whether B's conduct is an 'extension' of A's conduct, so that A must be counted as a participant in the production of the harm. Obviously, other people can function as my 'extension' in a crudely corporeal sense when I am simply using their bodies for my aims, eg when I suddenly push you onto another person in order to injure that person. The more interesting and complex issues arise when B's conduct is reason-responsive, ie when B acts for what B takes to be good reasons for action, so that A's direction and the impact of B's conduct on the claimant are mediated by B's rational agency.

One particular problem here is that A's direction may be a necessary cause of B's reason-responsive conduct and the claimant's harm, but still not suffice to justify holding A responsible for dealing with that harm. This is a familiar theme in discussions about the exercise of constitutional freedoms. When I address my audience at a political rally and proclaim, with a knowing grimace, that 'somebody ought to do something about those baby-killing doctors', my speech may be causally connected to the damage that my followers go on to cause to your health clinic, but that fact alone does not suffice to make my speech fit for government regulation. The buck of responsibility stops with the persons whose agency is, in Susan Hurley's term, 'proximal' to the actual damage (in this case, the persons who cause damage to your clinic).[24] Why should things be any different when we consider whether I may be vicariously responsible for that conduct in tort?

It seems to me that our intuitions here are sensitive to two issues. The first concerns the nature of the burden involved. Perhaps a 'principle of proximal agency' holds more appeal where the issue at stake is the extent of government's power to limit speech, and less when the issue is the allocation of responsibility for the cost of some harm that the speech is causally connected to. For example, it seems quite intuitive that, had I instructed my devoted followers or members of my gang to go and destroy your clinic, I would have been at least partly responsible for dealing with any damage that my followers go on to cause to you. The fact my *speech* may be protected against government interference, ie that the government may not stop me addressing the rally, may not always allow me to disclaim the burden of responsibility for the consequences of the conduct of those that my speech directs. The second point is that sometimes we have reason to avoid holding the directing agent

---

[24] S Hurley, 'The Public Ecology of Responsibility' in C Knight and Z Stemplowska, *Responsibility and Distributive Justice* (Oxford, Oxford University Press, 2011) 187, 188 states that principle as follows: 'government should where possible avoid regulating actions that harm third parties only indirectly, via their influence on the actions of second parties. Rather, it should regulate the proximal harmful act by the second party directly. If selling alcohol enables someone to drink and then drive, leading to harm to third parties, government should regulate driving after drinking directly, not selling alcohol. If playing a violent computer game influences someone to commit similar violence, government should regulate the aggression directly, not the production or selling of the game.'

responsible for the consequences of the conduct of the directed agents, if that would threaten to stifle an activity that the directing agent can reasonably want to be free to undertake without such constraints. The difference between provocative speech about the tactics that opponents of abortion might undertake and a directive to one's followers to destroy a clinic seems to me to lie precisely in the fact that only the first is something that a citizen can reasonably want to have the opportunity to undertake without fear of anything but moral or political criticism.

These considerations can be helpful in determining whether the buck of responsibility stops with the directed person even when no constitutional freedoms are directly at stake. Consider again the example in which I ask you to buy me a can of soda from the shop while you go out for a smoke. My request that you buy me the soda is both an instance of me directing your action and a probabilistically necessary cause of the harm that you inflict on the shopkeeper, since the shopkeeper would likely have suffered no harm if I had not made that request. However, the idea that I should bear responsibility for dealing with the shopkeeper's harm still seems counter-intuitive, and one way of accounting for this intuition is to say that people value the opportunity to be able to help each other out in little daily projects without assuming responsibility for the consequences of each other's conduct. By the same token, we may think differently when the project in which such help is provided happens to be bigger and more extended in time, when the practical stakes are higher, when the chore involves considerably more direction than one could reasonably give to another in the context of a friendly favour, and so on.

I believe that this puts us on track to see why some widely endorsed tests of attribution for the purposes of attaching liability to A as a participant may not be fit for purpose. Robert Stevens argues that, aside from action-direction, attribution requires the additional elements of *control* and *benefit* to the directing agent. He writes: 'Whenever one party carries out a task for the benefit of another and the beneficiary exercises control over the identity and conduct of the person carrying out the task, the conduct of the task is attributed to the beneficiary'.[25] For Ernest Weinrib, who addresses the issue in the context of employment, the necessary additional element seems to be a high degree of *integration* of B's conduct into A's activity: 'Where the faulty actor is sufficiently integrated into the enterprise and where the faulty act is sufficiently

---

[25] Stevens, above n 12, at 269. Stevens sometimes puts the case in favour of the control test in terms of its 'fit' with the cases: 'One advantage of seeing the relevant test as one of control is that it can be seen as a common factor in all cases where the necessary relationship for the purpose of attribution may be established, even where there is no contract of employment, or indeed any contract at all …. Under this formulation, a contract of employment or the ownership of the chattel used are merely methods of demonstrating the requisite control.' I turn to the cases involving chattels below.

close to the assigned task, the law constructs a more inclusive legal persona, the-employer-acting-through-the-employee, to whom responsibility can be ascribed'.[26]

The view that control and benefit or integration are the proper tests for attribution obviously draws good support from examples involving employment relationships. Employees undertake dependent labour within a system of work designed and maintained by employers, or those who manage the enterprise in the employers' name. While the designation of a relationship as one of 'employment' may differ depending on the purpose for which the designation is made (healthy and safety legislation, tax laws etc), there is little doubt that relationships of dependent labour will typically satisfy both the 'control/benefit' and the 'integration' tests for the purposes of vicarious liability in tort.[27]

However, if the argument I have been pressing is right, both tests are exposed to the same difficulty. Neither test seems to be sufficiently sensitive to the fact that both the directing and the directed agent will sometimes place value in allowing the former to direct the conduct of the latter without assuming responsibility for its consequences. There may be cases in which A exercises control over B's conduct and derives a benefit from B's activity, or cases in which B's conduct is very much integrated in A's project, but we will still have good reason not to hold A responsible for the consequences of B's conduct.

Consider the familiar case of *Nettleship v Weston*.[28] The defendant was a learner driver who caused an accident in the course of a driving lesson, injuring the friend who was instructing her how to drive (to keep both the friendship and the instruction elements in focus for the moment, I will refer to the parties as friend-instructor and friend-learner). Would the friend-instructor be vicariously liable for the tort committed by his friend-learner? It seems clear that the friend-instructor was directing the friend-learner's conduct and that he had considerably greater control over the friend-learner's driving than many employers have over their employees. It is less clear whether the friend-instructor stood to reap a benefit from the learner's activity, but an affirmative answer is certainly plausible. Perhaps it ought to be enough for the purposes of attribution that the friend-instructor stood to reap the moral and ethical

---

[26] Weinrib, above n 3, at 187.

[27] For a critique of the 'control' test as based on outdated assumptions about the ability of an employer 'to direct and instruct the labourer as to the technical methods he should use in performing his work', see O Kahn-Freund, 'Servants and Independent Contractors' (1951) 14 MLR 504, 505ff. See, however, *Various Claimants v Catholic Child Welfare Society* [2012] UKHL 56 at [36] per Lord Phillips: 'the significance of control today is that the employer can direct *what* the employee does, not *how* he does it' (emphasis added).

[28] *Nettleship v Weston* [1971] 2 QB 691.

benefit that friends receive when they help each other out, namely the gratitude of the friend-learner and the deepening of the friendly bond. At any rate,
we can easily think of variations in which the friend-instructor reaps even more
tangible benefits from the friend-learner's activity, eg if the skill in question is
not driving but, say, gardening and the instruction takes place in the friend-
instructor's garden. Finally, under an 'integration' test, the friend-learner's
conduct seems to be firmly embedded into the friend-instructor's activity of
giving her driving lessons, in the sense that her participation is a necessary
aspect of the action-direction. All this notwithstanding, no account of vicarious liability seems to have entertained the view that the friend-learner's mistake in *Nettleship* could be attributed to the friend-instructor. It is important to
ask why that might be so.

One possibility is that it would not be appropriate to attribute the friend-
learner's conduct to the friend-instructor because, unlike employment relationships, the action-direction involved in *Nettleship* does not extend very much
in time. That difference does not seem dispositive, even if we leave aside that
sometimes people need a really long time to learn how to drive. If control or
integration are the right tests for attribution, what matters should obviously be
the *intensity* of that control or integration, rather than their duration.

A better explanation is that the difference between an employment relationship and the relationship between the parties in *Nettleship* is that the latter is a
teaching relationship. This is important because differences in the purpose of
the direction mark differences in the opportunities that the directing and the
directed agents would value having in the course of that activity.[29] The point
of teaching lies, in large part, in helping a person acquire some knowledge or
skill that will allow that person to be able to undertake some activity, and avoid
gross mistakes in it, without the necessity of constant supervision or control
by someone else. At the same time, it is in the nature of the learning process
that learners engage in it from a position of relative weakness. The fact that
they lack the skill in question makes it likely that they will make mistakes in
that process and, at least in relation to some activities, that those mistakes will
pose a risk to others. This suggests that part of the value for learners of learning how to drive lies in the opportunity to receive protection against both the
possibility that their mistakes will cause harm, and the possibility that they will
have to bear the burden of repair for that harm. That value will be clearer
when it is important for learners to acquire the skills in question; the probability of making a mistake during learning is high; and the threatened harms
are significant. In certain cases, putting a learner in a good position to avoid

[29] See also ch 4(V).

the burden of repair for their mistakes may require, say, giving them access to insurance coverage even from the earliest stages of learning.[30]

For their part, teachers value having the opportunity to provide learners with a measure of instruction and protection while teaching them the relevant skill, and so could not object to a principle that made the imposition on them of part of the burden of repair depend on them having had those opportunities. But that value is not unconditional. The nature of the activity may be such that teachers are not always well-positioned to avert every harmful mistake that a learner might make. More importantly, absolving learners completely from the burden of repair by placing that burden on teachers may actually impede the learning process, by failing to impress on learners the stakes of unsupervised driving and lulling them into a false sense of security about the practical impact of their mistakes. This, it seems to me, is the real difference between teaching and employment contexts.

I will return to whether an account that explains the appropriateness of attributing B's conduct to A by appeal to the value for those persons of certain opportunities in the situation, shows the employment and the teaching contexts to be materially different. For the moment, I want to press the broader point that we cannot reach safe conclusions about attribution for the purposes of vicarious liability by reflecting only on the intensity of the action-direction between A and B, either in terms of the control that A exercises over B, or in terms of the integration of their activities. We also need to consider the value for each of those persons of the opportunity to direct the other's conduct, and to have their conduct directed, as the case may be.

IV. AN ILLUSTRATION: VICARIOUS LIABILITY FOR THE USE OF CARS

This account of *Nettleship* emphasises the fact that the case concerned a teaching activity, rather than the fact that the activity took place between friends. There is a further reason for thinking that this is the right focus. Under English law, the fact that the learner and the teacher are friends does *not* bar attribution for the purposes of vicarious liability regarding the use of cars. In fact, English courts have consistently held that the friend-driver is an agent of the friend-owner, to

---

[30] In *Nettleship*, above n 28, Lord Denning MR suggested obiter that a professional driving instructor should not have been allowed to claim against the learner, on the ground that their contract would have included an 'implied term' relieving the learner from such responsibility insofar as the instructor could get insurance coverage for accidents caused by the learner (at 702). This seems to me insufficient. Learners may reasonably require the benefit of insurance protection, but that does not settle whether it ought to be teachers, rather than themselves, who arrange for such protection. The parties' relative ease of access to an affordable insurance mechanism matters in that regard.

whom the accident may therefore be legitimately attributed.[31] For example, in *Hewitt v Bonvin*, DuParcq LJ said:

> The driver of a car may not be the owner's servant, and the owner will be neverthe-less liable for his negligent driving if it be proved that at the material time he had authority, express or implied, to drive on the owner's behalf. Such liability depends not on ownership, but on the delegation of a task or duty ... The reason is plain. The defendant had delegated to the friend the duty of driving and was personally responsible for his acts as the acts, not of a servant, but of an agent. There could hardly be a better illustration of the maxim *qui facit per alium facit per se.*[32]

Similarly in *Ormrod v Crossville Motor Services Ltd*, Devlin J held that

> there must be something more than the granting of mere permission in order to create liability in the owner of a motor-car for the negligence of the driver to whom it has been lent. But I do not think that it is necessary to show a legal contract of agency. It is in an area between the two that this case is to be found, and it may be described as a case where ... there is a 'social or moral' obligation to drive the owner's car ... He who complies with ... a request [to drive the car] is the agent of the other, since he who makes the request has an interest in its being done.[33]

I am drawing attention to this rule not only to reinforce my claim that the teaching aspect was paramount in *Nettleship*, but also because it is not obvious how the rule in *Hewitt* and *Ormrod* might be justified either as a general test of vicarious liability, or as a special rule about the use of cars and other vehicles. For a start, it would be clearly a mistake to say that, as long as action-direction is involved, the fact that A and B are friends has no impact on whether B's con-duct may or may not be attributed to A for the purposes of vicarious liability. It is very often the case that one directs another's conduct, sometimes in con-siderable detail, and yet the fact that such direction takes place in the context of a gesture of friendship suggests that the buck of responsibility stops with the person directed. To return to the can of soda example, it seems implau-sible that whether your carelessness is attributable to me depends on whether I specified exactly what brand of soda I want, which shop I want it from, or whether I gave you the exact change in advance of you buying it. The fact that you were doing me a friendly favour seems to matter more than the detail of

---

[31] Stevens, above n 12, at 269.

[32] *Hewitt v Bonvin* [1940] 1 KB 188 at 194–5.

[33] *Ormrod v Crossville Motor Services Ltd* [1953] 1 WLR 409 at 410–11. See also *Launchbury v Morgans*, above n 21, at 140–1 per Lord Pearson: 'the principle by virtue of which the owner of a car may be held vicariously liable for the negligent driving of the car by another person is the principle *qui facit per alium, facit per se* ... For the creation of the agency relationship it is not neces-sary that there should be a legally binding contract of agency, but it is necessary that there should be an instruction or request from the owner and an undertaking of the duty or task by the agent. Also the fact that the journey is undertaken partly for purposes of the agent as well as for the purposes of the owner does not negative the creation of the agency relationship.' This last point was applied in *Candler v Thomas (t/a London Leisure Lines)* [1998] RTR 214 at 218 *per* Brooke LJ.

the direction I give you. Of course, some other non-professional contexts can be harder to unpack: for example, there is a substantive debate about whether the torts of a child may be attributed to parents and views have varied across different jurisdictions.[34]

Instead, I think that we do better to understand *Hewitt* and *Ormrod* as suggesting two things. One is that, just like me when I ask you to get a can of soda for me, the owner of a car has reason to value the opportunity to pursue their projects through other persons. The other is that the difference between the two examples is that the stakes of a person making a driving mistake are considerably greater. Given those high stakes, those who drive another person's car at that person's request may reasonably require that person to give them a measure of protection against the burden of repair in case things go wrong.

I think that this explanation is broadly right. One obvious difficulty with it, though, is that it still seems strange to have a special rule about *driving*. After all, driving a car (or other vehicle) is hardly the most dangerous thing in the world. Operating a knife or machine equipment can be just as dangerous, but owners of such chattels are not required by law to protect persons who use them with permission from the burden of repair when those persons prove careless, even when they are acting in furtherance of the owner's projects.[35] If I ask you to help me carve the meat we'll be cooking for dinner and, in turning around to greet my other dinner guests, you carelessly injure one of them with it, it seems implausible that your carelessness might be attributed to me. What might be so special about injuries caused by cars?

Maybe the right answer is 'nothing'. But it seems to me that *Launchbury v Morgans*, in which the issue of attribution for car accidents was extensively discussed, gives us an indication as to a possible difference between cars and other dangerous chattels, and the way in which this might matter for the justification of imposing vicarious liability on the owner of a car. The defendant's car was being driven by her husband, who then proceeded to give the wheel to a third party. The third party carelessly lost control of the car and caused injury to the claimant. In the Court of Appeal, Lord Denning MR held that English law should follow the lead of some American jurisdictions and hold

---

[34] For discussion, see P Giliker, *Vicarious Liability in Tort: A Comparative Perspective* (Cambridge, Cambridge University Press, 2010), ch 7. See also *JGE v Trustees of the Portsmouth Roman Catholic Diocesan Trust* [2012] EWCA Civ 938 at [61] per Ward LJ: 'Parent and child could not be closer yet the parent has never been vicariously liable for the tort of the child simply by reason of being a parent'.

[35] *cf* G Schwartz, 'The Hidden and Fundamental Issue of Employer Vicarious Liability' (1995–6) 69 *Southern California LR* 1739, 1750. The odd case in the bunch is *Thelma (Owners) v University College School* [1953] *Lloyd's Reports* 613, which found the owners of an eight (a type of rowing boat) vicariously liable for harm caused by the negligence of the eight's cox. The judge could see no distinction between cars and boats (at 618). Perhaps the difference is that eights are not inherently dangerous in the way cars are.

the owner of a car vicariously liable for the accident.[36] Under this theory of the 'matrimonial' or' family car',[37] attribution proceeded in two steps. The fact that the husband had allowed the third party to use the car was enough to attribute that party's carelessness to the husband, while the relationship between husband and wife was enough to extend that attribution further to the wife-owner. The House of Lords overturned the decision on the ground that the case in favour of the 'family car' rule turned on difficult questions of insurance policy that the court was not properly placed to consider at the time.[38] Lord Wilberforce said:

> The choice is one of social policy ... Whatever may have been the situation in 1913 in the youth of the motor car, it is very different now, when millions of people of all ages drive for a vast variety of purposes and when there is in existence a complicated legislative structure as to insurance—who must take it out, what risks it must cover, who has the right to sue for the sum assured. Liability and insurance are so intermixed that judicially to alter the basis of liability without adequate knowledge (which we have not the means to obtain) as to the impact this might make on the insurance system would be dangerous and, in my opinion, irresponsible.[39]

What makes driving special, in this view, is not just the degree of danger that this activity poses for people. It is also the degree to which that activity is woven into the fabric of modern life and the pursuit of a vast variety of projects. This fact clearly explains why all drivers may reasonably require the state to protect them against the burden of making repair for driving accidents, in the form of giving them the opportunity to obtain affordable insurance by mandating everyone to insure (I discussed this problem in Chapter 4).[40] *Hewitt, Ormrod* and *Launchbury* are concerned with a problem that lies just downstream of that, namely whether such a mandate should apply to vehicles rather than to drivers. In holding the owner vicariously liable, *Hewitt* and *Ormrod* favoured the former policy. In refusing to accept Lord Denning's proposal to adopt the 'family' or 'matrimonial car' rule, *Launchbury* imposed some limits on how far this policy might be extended. However, what is most striking is the reluctance with which the court approached this question. In my view, that reluctance is a sign that the court was focusing its attention on precisely the right issue. Determining whether insurance should be vehicle-specific or driver-specific

---

[36] *Launchbury v Morgans* [1971] 2 QB 245 (CA) at 254 per Lord Denning MR.

[37] See W Prosser et als (eds), *Prosser & Keeton on the Law of Torts*, 5th edn (St Paul, West Group Publishing, 1984) 524.

[38] *Launchbury v Morgans*, above n 21, at 135ff per Lord Wilberforce, 140–1 per Lord Peason and 151 per Lord Salmon. Lord Wilberforce also noted (at 136) that such a solution had been adopted in some Australian jurisdictions, citing s 3(2) of the Motor Vehicles Insurance Acts 1936–45 (Queensland).

[39] Ibid at 137. For a helpful overview of the substantive policy arguments, see Giliker, above n 34, at 113–6.

[40] See ch 4(V).

is a question that goes to the heart of the design of any insurance mandate. Different designs would create different distributions of the risk of bearing the burden of repair, and different 'bundles' of options for avoiding that burden. As Lord Wilberforce notes, determining the value for drivers of each of those bundles of options required delving into complex economic, empirical and actuarial questions.[41] While the court did not consider itself competent to dispose of that question, it made it very clear that the answer ought to turn on a proper assessment of the opportunities that each bundle would provide to drivers, and the value for drivers of having those opportunities available to them.

V. VICARIOUS LIABILITY AS PROTECTION

The idea that the responsibilities of A, B and any other parties involved in the situation should turn on the opportunities that those persons had, and the value of those opportunities for them is, of course, the essence of the value-of-choice account. In this section, I discuss how we could justify the way principles of vicarious liability distribute the burden of repair under a particular entailment of that account, the 'protection principle' that I proposed in Chapter 4. That principle says:

> *Protection principle*: Others ought to protect you against the burden of repair for the outcomes of your mistakes insofar as they have reason to want you to bear certain burdens in the course of an activity, and, absent such protection, the opportunity to engage in the activity would not be something you have reason to value.

The protection principle takes the 'moment of responsibility' to be the moment in which B is presented with the opportunity to engage in an activity under A's direction, and calls for an ex ante assessment of what, if anything, B could have required of A at that point by way of protection against the burden of repair. As we have seen, that protection can take various forms. It may involve A sharing the burden of repair with B; or B being absolved from that burden completely; or A (or others, most notably the state) giving B access to an insurance mechanism that would otherwise be inaccessible to B, and so on.[42]

Employment contexts were one of the examples I used to make the case for the protection principle in Chapter 4. My concern there was to highlight the common moral thread running through the various ways in which private law requires people to protect persons against the burden of repair, from the common law doctrine of contributory negligence to activity- and hazard-specific compulsory insurance schemes. Here I want to explore in more detail the

---

[41] *cf* the discussion of institutional competence on questions of protection in ch 4(II).
[42] See ch 4(V).

implications of seeing vicarious liability as an instance of the protection principle, and to consider more closely how that principle might be justified to B, A, and any other persons on whom the principle would impose the burden of protection. I begin by recapping my explanation of why B (the directed agent) might reasonably require others to protect B in situations of action-direction, especially employment situations. Then I turn to whether A (the directing agent) and others, especially the consumers of the goods or services that A is producing, would be able to object to being required to provide B with such protection. Finally, I consider the position of claimants.

A. Directed Agent

B will typically have one obvious option to avoid the burden of repair for any mistakes that B makes in the course of the activity. B can take care or otherwise discharge the applicable standard of conduct in relation to that activity (eg to avoid defaming the claimant). However, it is not hard to see why B has reason to want additional opportunities to avoid having to bear the burden of repair. Since *errare humanum est*, no matter how familiar the work and how experienced B might be in it, chances are that one day B will make a mistake. Furthermore, the nature of modern dependent labour, especially industrial work, is such that the stakes of that mistake will often be very high and almost always far in excess of B's capacity to make good the resulting harms.[43] Finally, the economic structure of our societies makes it certain that most people will take up work under another's direction, ie some form of dependent labour, in order to secure their livelihood. A principle that made B bear the burden of repair for workplace mistakes in these circumstances, either directly or by allowing A and A's insurers to claim an indemnity from B, would therefore not be sensitive to certain opportunities of obtaining protection that B can reasonably want to have available. In turn, not having those opportunities would reduce the value for B of the opportunity to take up dependent labour. The protection principle puts these points together and allows B to disclaim liability for the burden of repair if, absent some protection against the burden of repair for workplace mistakes, B would not have reason to value the opportunity to take up labour under A's direction.

To the extent that the protection principle is satisfied, it clears B from the burden of providing repair for the mistake and requires A or others to bear that burden, without being able to sue B or claim an indemnity. However, that benefit is qualified in two ways. First, the principle does not secure 'blanket'

---

[43] I discussed this 'asymmetry' between the value of attaining benefits from an activity and the value of being protected from the burdens that it may generate in ch 3(I).

protection for B. The extent of that protection depends on what it takes for the opportunity to take up dependent labour to remain valuable for B. Secondly, how much B may require A, or others, to do is fixed at the moment when B is presented with that opportunity. B cannot appeal to the protection principle *merely* because the burden of repair proves very heavy. Of course, B could still be entitled to a measure of protection in case B is unable to bear that burden, but that protection would be owed to B under special principles relating to personal insolvency.

In this section, I want to ask whether B should be protected for mistakes that did not occur 'in the course of the employment'; in relation to harms that are not the result of 'mistakes' but of B's intentional conduct; in situations where B is an independent contractor; and in situations where B has the option of obtaining insurance coverage against the burden of repair, or of negotiating an exclusion or limitation of liability clause with A.

Consider the claim that B should only be able to require protection only when B's conduct took place *in the course of the activity* in which A was directing B's action, and then only in relation to *mistakes*, rather than intentional or malicious harms. Could A say that the moral 'deal' between A and B ought to be, roughly, 'if you mess up in the workplace, I got you covered, but if you cause harm maliciously, or out of the workplace, you're on your own'?[44]

I think that the answer is yes, subject to one important qualification. For a start, B cannot reasonably object to not having the benefit of the protection principle when B's mistake is unconnected to A's activity or enterprise. The reason is given by the very reasons for which the opportunity to have such protection is valuable for B. B can reasonably want that protection precisely because the fact that B's activity is being directed can increase the risk that B might make a harmful mistake, or raise the stakes for B of making such a mistake. Of course, there will be cases where it will be difficult to determine whether B's mistake took place within or outside the bounds of A's activity. Suppose that the nature of B's work exposes B to great stress and that, one day, B returns home from work and assaults a member of their family, causing them serious harm. When there is a strong causal link between the stress that B is exposed to due to the system of work and B's responses towards others outside the context of work, the value for B of working under such a system will be contingent on B enjoying a degree of protection against the possibility that the stress of work will cause B to harm third parties.

That reason will be clearer in relation to intentional harms that occur in the course of the activity itself, as long as those harms may be plausibly

---

[44] See also Neyers, above n 5, whose 'implied indemnity' theory shares this perspective, insofar as it focuses attention on finding principles that might be justified to both A and B. The protection principle seems to me to provide the basis for deciding whether an indemnity ought to be implied in specific cases.

attributed to the pressures of that activity. 'Situations of friction' in the workplace leading to incidents like common assault between co-workers are the typical example.[45] In that regard, note that sometimes the very nature of B's work will require B to inflict harm intentionally in the course of a 'good faith performance' of his or her duties, eg when B is A's bodyguard, or has been given the task of recovering property belonging to A.[46] Here too it seems clear that B would value the opportunity to enjoy a degree of protection against the burden of repair, precisely because the nature of the activity makes it more likely that B will incur that burden.[47] Things will be different when B's conduct is not careless, the result of 'workplace friction', or a good faith performance of B's duties, but downright malicious. The reason why B may not object to a principle that required B to bear the burden of repair for harms that B caused maliciously is that this principle would make B's liability contingent on an opportunity that this person has reason to value whether or not their activity is directed, namely the opportunity of being able to exercise a certain level of rational self-governance and to keep their malicious intent in check.

Is B entitled to protection when B could self-protect against the consequences of their mistakes, either by negotiating an exclusion or limitation of liability clause with A, or by taking out insurance? With regard to exclusions or limitations of liability the answer will generally be negative, because B will typically not have those options. The matter has been addressed in the well-known opinion by La Forest J in the Supreme Court of Canada in *London Drugs Ltd v Kuehne & Nagel International Ltd*. Showing great sensitivity to the limited range of bargaining options available to B, either individually or collectively with other persons engaging in the same activity, the Justice said: 'I think it ill advised to place the onus on employees to contract out of their tort liability. Despite suggestions going back as far as the aftermath of the *Lister* case that unions should bargain about this issue[[48]], it is apparent that unions and employers have more pressing concerns. It is hardly necessary to refer to any elaborate theory regarding negotiating agendas to recognise that actual employee liability occurs infrequently enough that it is unlikely to get on the

---

[45] *Bazley v Curry*, above n 7, at [17]. Neyers, above n 5, at 16.

[46] *Dyer v Munday* [1895] 1 QB 742, noted with approval in *New South Wales v Lepore* (High Court of Australia, 2003) 195 ALR 412 at [234].

[47] Neyers, above n 5, suggests that B could reasonably object to being required to bear the burden of repair in respect of intentional torts 'where the tort arose out of a "situation of friction" created by the employer *and* the employee's actions could be classified as a good faith performance of the contract of employment' (at 16). I think that the conjunction is unwarranted: either of the two conditions is sufficient to give B a reasonable objection.

[48] La Forest J here cites the discussion of *Lister v Romford Ice & Cold Storage Ltd* [1956] AC 555 in P Atiyah, *Vicarious Liability in the Law of Torts* (London, Butterworths, 1967) 426, n 3.

collective bargaining agenda. In the interim, serious injustice to individual employees can occur.'[49]

As a general matter, the same will hold true of the opportunity for B to obtain insurance against the burden of dealing with the consequences of workplace mistakes. That opportunity may be generally available, but its value for B will clearly depend on whether such insurance is affordable for a person in B's position. In employment settings, the opportunity for employees to obtain personal insurance coverage will not be very valuable for them for a number of reasons. First, given their social-structural position, employees will be likely to be spending most of their disposable income on goods and services that are central to their well-being (rent or mortgage payments, transport, education, health coverage, food, and so on). Requiring them to obtain insurance coverage would therefore ask for a significant level of sacrifice of them. Secondly, the growing use of fractional and zero-hours contracts would sometimes entail that an employee would pay for coverage that they may not actually need.[50] Thirdly, contrary to employers, employees do not normally have the option of shielding themselves from the risk of personal liability by constituting themselves as corporations.

At the same time, I think that we can imagine situations in which B could not reasonably object to a principle that denied them the benefit of protection by A, and required B to insure instead. Suppose that B is A's paid domestic helper. B lives with A and takes care of the household in accordance with A's instructions. One day a friend comes to visit, and suffers injury when B carelessly spills on them the cup of tea that he was bringing to A. Could B object to a principle that denied B the benefit of A's protection against the burden of repair?

On the account I have been developing, the answer depends on whether the value for B of being able to undertake this line of work is independent of the fact that A happens to be directing their conduct. The point can be easy to miss. Given that B's activity *itself* involves responding to A's directions, it seems natural to suppose that the value for B of the opportunity to undertake that activity is contingent on A providing such directions. But that need not be the case. For a start, B could find value in that opportunity even if A does not issue directions at all, and is simply content to put themselves in B's care. The same can be true even in situations where A does issue B with detailed instructions, as long as part of the value for B of the opportunity to be A's helper lies in

---

[49]   *London Drugs Ltd v Kuehne & Nagel International Ltd* [1992] 3 SCR 299 at 353.

[50]   *cf Cairns v Northern Lighthouse Board* (Outer House, Scottish Court of Session) [2013] CSOH 22 per Lord Drummond Young at [37], noting that a requirement for employees to obtain insurance 'would not cater well for employees on short-term contracts, or who simply choose to spend their income on other things'.

having the ability, occasionally, to *disregard* A's instructions if B judges that this is more likely to make things go well for A.

This conclusion entails that we should take with a pinch of salt the widely endorsed claim that a person who employs domestic workers/helpers is vicariously liable for their torts.[51] Insofar as that claim relies on assumptions about the degree of action-direction in employer/helper relationships, it is exposed to the problem I discussed in section III, namely that the significance of action-direction is not independent of the value for each part of having the opportunity to engage in the relevant activity. That claim *is* generally correct when understood as a claim about the degree of protection that domestic helpers/workers may require of their employers, but it would need to be modified in examples like that of the previous paragraph.

I believe that this also explains why B would not be able to object to a principle that required B to bear the burden of repair, without the benefit of A's protection, when B is an independent contractor rather than A's employee. The reason is that such a principle would make B's liability depend on whether part of the value for B of the opportunity to engage in the activity lies in being able to pass on the cost of that activity to the consumers of the services that B is providing. When B is an independent contractor, this is clearly an opportunity that B has reason to value, as the 'passing on' of costs of production, together with a margin for profit, forms the very basis of B's entrepreneurial efforts.

B. Directing Agent

A is the person on whom the protection principle places a direct burden, so we should ask whether A could reasonably object to the protection principle and, in particular, whether the imposition of the burden of repair on A under that principle is sufficiently sensitive to the opportunities that A had, and to the value for A of having those opportunities.

To find out whether A may reasonably object to the burden that the protection principle places on them, it is important to have a clear view of how heavy or light that burden is likely to be. For example, in the employment context, the fact that A will be an entrepreneur is significant not just because it affects what A can do for B, but also because it changes the weight of the burden that the protection principle would impose on A. An enterprise has the option of 'passing on' the cost of obtaining appropriate insurance coverage for workplace accidents to those that purchase the goods or services that the enterprise is producing. Such 'passing on' will require non-negligible

---

[51] See Williams, above n 9, at 441; Stevens, above n 12, at 258; Neyers, above n 5, at 11 (citing *Jardine v Lang* (1911) 2 SLT 494).

increases in the price of the goods or services in question, or perhaps reductions in the enterprise's rate of return to its owners and investors. While these burdens may still be significant, they are not as heavy as the burden of providing repair to the victims of B's mistake. It follows that when A has this 'passing on' option, the burden that the protection principle places on A is not the burden of providing repair for the claimant's harm, but the lighter burden of functioning as a 'middle-person' who feeds the cost of the claimant's harm into the market.

The question, then, is whether A could reasonably object to a principle that places on A the burden of fulfilling this 'middle-person' function. We have discussed a similar form of this question in relation to situations where B is an independent contractor rather than A's employee. In those situations, B too is a 'middle-person', in the sense that B too has the option of passing on the cost of insurance against the burden of repair to the consumers of the services that B is providing. This suggests that the case for requiring A to bear the burden of fulfilling the 'middle-person' function will be similar. In particular, A cannot object to a principle that requires them to bear that burden insofar as that principle is sensitive to an opportunity that A has reason to value, namely the opportunity to act as an entrepreneur, ie to command means of production and have the chance to make a profit by adding a margin to those costs and passing on the sum to the consumers of the goods or services that A is producing.

In that regard, note that the imposition of that burden on A would not risk making A's products or services less competitive, and thereby diminish the value for A of the opportunity to go into business, inasmuch as *all* entrepreneurs get to bear a similar burden in respect of the goods and services that they produce. Similarly, the fact that A has to pass on to the market the cost of insuring against the burden of repair will involve a marginal increase in the price of A's goods or services, but this will not increase the relative risk that A's enterprise will not meet with commercial success, as that risk will be similar for all competing enterprises and therefore unlikely to put A at a disadvantage. Furthermore, this will typically not saddle A with significant transaction costs: all A will need to do in most situations is to adjust the price of the goods or services, while potential litigation costs will either be covered by the relevant insurance policy or incurred directly by the insurer. The costs of insuring against the burden of dealing with the claimant's harm may, of course, turn out to be unusually high for A's particular enterprise, but the significance of this will depend on whether A has a reasonably adequate range of options for reducing the insurance costs in question. For example, if the higher insurance costs are the result of A's choice of production methods, A may be in a position to choose a safer production method, or to introduce safeguards that lower the associated risks.[52] These too are opportunities that any entrepreneur will have reason to value.

Note that this way of making the case for holding A vicariously liable for B's mistakes does not attribute special significance to two considerations that are often considered to merit it. One is whether A's activity is commercial or charitable. The other is whether that activity creates higher-than-normal risks for B or for other persons.

The intuition that A should be liable for the cost of B's mistakes because A is directing B's action for *profit* is very strong,[53] but I think that we should resist it. Of course, A has clear reason to value the opportunity to engage in charitable projects. The value of that opportunity for A will have a special character, in the sense that acting on it would make things go better for A not by making profit for them, but by promoting an independent (and usually other-regarding) aim that A cares for. The question, however, is whether requiring A to fulfil the 'middle-person' function in relation to charitable activities would make it harder for A to pursue the opportunity to engage in such activities. I think that the answer is generally 'no'. No less than a commercial enterprise, a charity has reason to value being able to pass the costs of production onto the market. The difference between commercial and charitable enterprises lies in the fact that the former mark those costs up with a profit margin, while the latter do not. The cost of insurance against the burden of repair for B's mistakes is a cost of production rather than a profit, precisely because the relevant sum is not at A's free disposal. If charities have no less reason to value being able to pass on those costs to the market, they could not object to a principle that required them to fulfil the 'middle-person' function as long as they have that opportunity. This is consistent with allowing charities to trade on preferential terms compared to commercial enterprises in other respects, eg through appropriate exemptions from tax, or from minimum wage legislation.

I think that similar considerations explain why A's liability should not depend on whether A's enterprise creates special, or higher-than-normal, risks.[54] The risky character of A's activity may increase the likelihood that B will make a mistake in the course of that activity, and may accordingly drive up the cost of insurance against the risk of such mistakes. However, a principle that required

---

[52] If anything, the smaller the availability of alternative production methods or safeguards, the lower the probability that A will be facing unusually high insurance costs compared to the competition.

[53] *cf* P Morgan, 'Distorting Vicarious Liability' (2011) 74 MLR 932, criticising the application of principles of vicarious liability to the relationship between a church and its serving ministers on the ground that 'the duty to evangelise is not a suitable hook on which to hang vicarious liability'.

[54] See my discussion of Keating's view in ch 5(II).

A to fulfil the 'middle-person' function in relation to those higher costs would still be sensitive to the fact that A had the opportunity to pass on those costs, and it would not make it any less the case that this was an opportunity that A had reason to value.

C. Consumers

When A is an enterprise that functions as a 'middle-person', the end-payers of the cost for protecting B from the consequences of his mistake are the consumers of the goods or services that A's enterprise produces. Could those consumers reasonably refuse to bear that burden?

It seems to me that the answer is generally 'no'. It is, of course, true that we would all like consumer products to be cheaper. It may also *look* unfair to have to pay more for a product in order to cover the cost of insurance for repairing mistakes that other people could have avoided. That impression, however, is deceiving. In particular, we have clear reason to think that a principle that imposes a fraction of the cost of the burden of repair on each consumer of A's products or services would be sensitive to opportunities that consumers want to have available to them. The fact that consumers want cheap stuff does not make it any less the case that they want that stuff to be produced. A principle that imposed the cost of repair on B or A alone, or even a principle that required them to internalise part of that cost, would make producing stuff less worthwhile for those persons, and would therefore make it less likely that such stuff would be produced. This would give consumers less of an opportunity to satisfy their consumer needs and preferences. It follows that requiring consumers to bear a fraction each of the cost of repair for mistakes occurring in the course of production is a way of making it easier for consumers to get what they want.

D. Claimants

Vicarious liability is generally good news for claimants, in that it allows them to claim against a defendant that is far more likely than B to have adequate insurance against the burden of repair. At the same time, seeing vicarious liability as an instance of protection for B entails that claimants cannot turn against B independently. Could claimants reasonably object to this restriction of their options?

Claimants who are deprived of the option of suing B may be losing either or both of two opportunities. One is the opportunity to gain a degree of satisfaction of their moral sentiments by obtaining an official pronouncement of B's moral blameworthiness for the mistake and, perhaps, by seeing

B suffer a proportionate amount of harm on that account.[55] Another is the opportunity to sue the very person that they transacted with, insofar as this would make it easier for claimants to satisfy requirements of proof, causation and so on.

I think that the loss of the opportunity to have their moral sentiments satisfied would not allow claimants to object to the restriction of their right to sue B for two reasons. First, shielding B from liability for the burden of repair need not entail that claimants lack a way of having their moral sentiments towards B satisfied. As long as A's liability is contingent on B having made a mistake, any legal proceedings will necessarily pronounce officially on whether B did, in fact, make such a mistake, and claimants will not need to incur any additional expense to obtain such a pronouncement. Secondly, and more importantly, the restriction of the claimants' opportunity to see B suffer is necessary in order for claimants to have another opportunity that they have reason to value, namely to be able to sue a defendant that is far more likely than B to be able to compensate them in full for the harm they have suffered. Given that A's reasons for protecting B depend on B's reasons for wanting such protection, a principle that allowed the claimant to turn against B would not just deprive B of protection. It would *also* entail that A would no longer have reason to protect B by taking on the burden of repair. As the claimant has reason to value having the opportunity to turn against A, the claimant may not object to a principle that restricts their ability to sue B.

Things may be different with regard to questions of proof. Requiring the claimant to sue A can make it harder for the claimant to obtain repair when it is difficult to determine A's identity, or to establish that A and B stand in the right sort of relationship under the protection principle. The first difficulty is more likely to arise in situations where the claimant has only ever interacted with B in the course of previous dealings, or in situations where the claimant had no previous dealings with either A or B (eg when B crashes into the claimant in the street while on duty). The second and more common difficulty is likely to arise when B has multiple employers, or when the relationship between A and B does not fall clearly within one of the kinds of relationship that would typically satisfy the protection principle.

The first difficulty is easy to resolve in principle, though applying that solution in practice would require the law on vicarious liability to take a leaf out of the book of consumer law. In particular, given that B values the opportunity to receive the benefit of protection from A, B could not object to a principle that required B to solve the claimant's problem by disclosing A's identity. This requirement is not extraordinary. It is the same requirement that the law makes of 'mere' suppliers of defective products under section 2(3) of the

---

[55] *cf* my discussion of Hershovitz's defence of that interest in ch 1(III)(E).

Consumer Protection Act 1987. Those suppliers have to disclose the identity of the 'producer' of the defective product, on pain of being liable themselves under the Act. It seems to me that B has no reason to object to being placed in a similar position.

The second difficulty is harder to resolve, because its causes will be various. When the cause is that B has multiple employers, it seems to me that none of those employers could object to a principle that held them jointly and severally liable to protect B (unless they have settled on a different understanding between them), as that principle would be sensitive to an opportunity all of them have reason to value, namely to be able to direct B's action without necessarily being tied to B on an exclusive basis.[56] When the cause is that the relationship between A and B is not typical, the claimant cannot object to being required to show that the relationship is one under which A ought to protect B for two reasons. First, having the opportunity to show that A and B stand in the right type of relationship affords the claimant the benefit of a more secure avenue for obtaining repair through A. Secondly, if the claimant fails to show that the relationship is of the right type, they still have the option of claiming directly against B.

VI. LIABILITY FOR PROTECTION VS DIRECT LIABILITY

Recent discussions of vicarious liability in English law have centred on cases unlike those I have been considering. These cases, of which *Various Claimants v Catholic Child Welfare Society*[57] is now the leading example, involve the commission by B of acts of sexual abuse against persons that A had entrusted in B's care and powers. English courts have examined two questions in that regard. One concerns the character and nature that the relationship between A and B must display in order to be 'fit' for the imposition of vicarious liability. The other concerns the determination of when B's acts fall within the 'scope' of the activity that forms the aim of that relationship.

Several commentators have taken issue with the courts' treatment of those cases under the heading of vicarious liability, and suggested that the proper basis of A's liability in them is that A has breached a 'non-delegable' duty of care towards the harmed claimants.[58] Seeing the principles of vicarious liability as an instance of protection for B can explain why those commentators are right. Cases like *Various Claimants* or *Lister v Hesley Hall* are different from cases of vicarious liability precisely because they concern circumstances

---

[56] This seems to me the logic behind the decision in *Viasystems (Tyneside) Ltd v Thermal Transfer (Northern) Ltd* [2005] EWCA Civ 1151 *per* May LJ at [49] and Rix LJ at [85], which held that vicarious liability can attach to multiple employers.

[57] Above n 27; *Lister v Hesley Hall* [2002] 1 AC 215.

[58] See, eg, Stevens, above n 12, at 273–4; Morgan, above n 53.

in which *B does not deserve the benefit of protection.* More precisely, B could not object to a principle that requires B to bear the burden of repair (or, of course, criminal punishment) in situations where B forms and acts on an intention to commit sexual abuse, as long as B had ample opportunity to avoid that burden, and that opportunity was something that B had reason to value.[59] If B is not entitled to protection in such circumstances, then the basis of A's liability cannot be that A is required to protect B. It follows that, if A is liable to the claimants at all, A's liability will be direct (either care-based or, in respect of certain activities, stricter) rather than vicarious.[60]

The practical upshot of treating those cases as concerned with A's direct liability is that we should approach the way they have stated and applied the requirements of vicarious liability with caution. Two points are particularly significant. One concerns the specification of the range of relationships that are 'fit' for vicarious liability. The leading judgment of Lord Phillips in *Various Claimants* notes that employment is not the only such relationship. While not purporting to laid down a fixed list of criteria, his Lordship points to certain considerations that, in his view, justify treating certain relationships as 'akin to employment' for the purposes of vicarious liability: a common aim between A and B; some hierarchy between them; and action-direction.[61] Seeing vicarious liability as an instance of protection shows why one should not be tempted to generalise from this assessment. Sometimes all three of those considerations will be present in a situation, without making the relationship between A and B 'fit' for vicarious liability. *Nettleship* is a clear illustration of this. The second point concerns the specification of when B's tortious act falls within the 'scope' or the 'course' of the activity in question. In that regard, Lord Phillips elaborated on the idea that there ought to be a 'close connection' between A's activity and B's tortious act as follows:

> Vicarious liability is imposed where a defendant, whose relationship with the abuser put it in a position to use the abuser to carry on its business or to further its own interests, has done so in a manner which has created or significantly enhanced the risk that the victim or victims would suffer the relevant abuse. The essential closeness of connection between the relationship between the defendant and the tortfeasor and the acts of abuse thus involves a strong causative link.[62]

Again, one should not generalise this claim into a condition of vicarious liability, as very many enterprises (eg average clothes shops) do not put their

---

[59] See also section V(A) above.

[60] In ch 5(II) I suggested that an appropriate test for deciding whether liability ought to be stricter, rather than care-based, is whether A has reason to value the opportunity to *set the terms* of an activity on his or her own.

[61] Above n 27 *per* Lord Phillips at [56]ff.

[62] Ibid at [86]. The 'close connection' test was proposed in *Bazley v Curry*, above n 7, and adopted by English courts in *Lister v Hesley Hall*, above n 57.

employees in a position that enhances risks to the consumers of their goods or services. If anything, the emphasis on whether B is placed in a position of power over the claimant diverts attention from the feature of B's tortious act that matters for that purpose, namely that it is an act in respect of the consequences of which B may require A to offer B some protection.

VII. CONCLUSION

The principles of vicarious liability in tort have often been treated as a something of a punch bag. A leading textbook describes vicarious liability as 'something without which hardly any cases would be brought to court, but the existence of which has no rational justification'.[63] Several authors have made the milder claim that vicarious liability may not have a unifying justification, applicable to all contexts in which its principles are thought to apply.[64] I have argued that this impression is largely misguided. The fact that most accounts of vicarious liability appeal to both A's placement and to A's participation in the making of the mistake is not a sign of confusion, but of health. Justifying vicarious liability as an instance of the protection principle allows us to see how those parameters jointly determine the value for A, B and other persons of the opportunity to engage in an activity that involves action-direction. Moreover, it allows us to distinguish between cases in which A's liability is vicarious, because A ought to protect B from the burden of repair for the consequences of B's mistake, and cases where A's liability can only be direct, because B does not deserve the benefit of such protection.

Seeing vicarious liability as an instance of the protection principle does not ascribe responsibility for the burden of repair by asking who has committed a wrong, or which principle of responsibility would reduce the social cost of accidents. Similarly, it does not appeal to independent intuitions about 'deep pockets', or which costs 'belong' to which activity, or to the idea that it is 'fair' that those who engage in an activity for profit should also bear the activity's costs. These ideas and intuitions are neither false nor irrelevant, but they state conclusions rather than provide arguments for allocating responsibility to one or another person.

---

[63] N McBride and R Bagshaw, *Tort Law*, 4th edn (Harlow, Longman, 2012) 890.
[64] See citations in n 9 above.

Conclusion

A COUPLE OF weeks after I finished the manuscript of the book, the UK Supreme Court gave judgment in the case of *Kennedy v Cordia (Services) Ltd*.[1] Miss Kennedy was employed by the responders as a home carer in Glasgow. Her work involved visiting clients in their homes and providing personal care, often in evening hours. One evening in December 2010, she was scheduled to visit Mrs Craig, an elderly lady. There had been severe wintry conditions in central Scotland for several weeks, with lots of snow and ice on the ground. A colleague drove Miss Kennedy to Mrs Craig's house, and parked the car close to a public footpath leading to it. The footpath was on a slope, and was covered with fresh snow and ice. It had not been gritted or salted. Miss Kennedy was wearing flat boots with ridged soles. After taking a few steps, she slipped and fell, injuring her wrist. The judge found the respondents liable for her injury, on the basis that they failed to provide her with appropriate footwear. An Extra Division of the Inner House reversed the decision. It held that it was unreasonable to suggest that Miss Kennedy's employer should have provided her with special footwear designed to reduce the risk of her slipping and falling. The reason was that, in this particular regard, Miss Kennedy had been in the same position as any other member of the public who went out in wintry conditions. The employment had not exposed Miss Kennedy to any special risk, or limited any opportunities she had to protect herself against slipping by wearing appropriate footwear.

Miss Kennedy appealed to the Supreme Court. The Supreme Court allowed the appeal, and held that the respondent ought to have provided Miss Kennedy with appropriate footwear. In particular, the court rejected the argument that Miss Kennedy was in the same position, and had the same opportunities, as any other member of the public who took to the streets in wintry conditions:

> One can understand the Extra Division's concern that the law should not be excessively paternalistic. Miss Kennedy was not, however, in the same position as an ordinary member of the public going about her own affairs. It was her duty, as someone employed by Cordia as a home carer, to visit clients in their homes in different parts of the city on a freezing winter's evening despite the hazardous conditions underfoot. Unlike an ordinary member of the public, she could not choose to stay indoors and avoid the risk of slipping and falling on the snow and ice. Unlike an ordinary member of the public, she could not choose where or when she went.

[1] *Kennedy v Cordia (Services) Ltd* [2016] UKSC 6.

She could not keep to roads and pavements which had been cleared or treated. She could not decide to avoid the untreated footpath leading to Mrs Craig's door. Unlike an ordinary member of the public, she was obliged to act in accordance with the instructions given to her by her employers: employers who were able, and indeed obliged under statute, to consider the risks to her safety while she was at work and the means by which those risks might be reduced. In those circumstances, to base one's view of the common law on the premise that Miss Kennedy was in all relevant respects in the same position as an ordinary member of the public is a mistake.[2]

I think that the Supreme Court got it right. The main idea in the passage is that whether Miss Kennedy's safety against slipping while conducting home visits was her problem alone depended on whether she had the same opportunities to self-protect as any other person who chose to go out in dangerous weather conditions. As the court made clear, she did not. Miss Kennedy's employment required her to forego options, and to expose herself to risks, that other private individuals did not have to contend with. And the court saw that this difference was central to determining what Miss Kennedy and her employer were respectively responsible for.

My purpose in this book has been to explain why the way the court reasoned in *Kennedy* is the way we should think more generally about the responsibilities that private law ascribes to people. I have argued that the responsibilities that private law principles impose on persons must be sensitive to the value for those persons of the opportunities that the relevant principle affords them in a situation. Under this 'value of choice' account, the reason why Miss Kennedy could object to a principle of law that regarded her safety against slipping as her own problem is not that she was out of options for avoiding injury. Some such options were clearly available to her. She could have chosen a different pair of shoes. She could have watched her step a little more. She could have called for assistance. She could have refused to take the risk of walking up the icy slope. The reason why the law ought to not leave it wholly to Miss Kennedy to protect herself is that the limitation in her options for self-protecting was not part of the value for her of being able to work as a home carer. Miss Kennedy did not sign up to be a home carer *in order* to expose herself to risks that other people did not have to undertake, and the limitations in her opportunity to self-protect were not necessary for her to do a good job (in a way that, say, exposing oneself to certain risks of injury is part and parcel of being a good boxer or wrestler). Miss Kennedy could reasonably refuse to sign up to the package of opportunities that her employment as a home carer offered her, unless that package included the benefit of certain protections against certain foreseeable and controllable risks that her job exposed her to.

[2] Ibid at [107–108] per Lords Reed and Hodge.

The court did not find it necessary to explain why the burden of providing Miss Kennedy with a certain level of protection ought to fall on her employers, rather than on anyone else. But the tenor of the court's thoughts in relation to Miss Kennedy's position could be easily extended to account for the position of her employers. The employers could not object to a principle that imposed on them the burden of protecting Miss Kennedy, as long as the imposition of that burden was contingent on employers having opportunities that they had reason to value in the situation. A principle that requires employers to supply their home care workers with protective gear, including appropriate footwear for visits conducted in inclement weather, makes employers' liability depend on them having the opportunity to design and run a business that provides home care for the elderly even when the weather is poor. The imposition of the burden of supplying their staff with appropriate protection against inclement weather does not make that opportunity less valuable for employers, at least as long as the protective gear in question is relatively effective and easy to use, and its cost can be passed onto the users of the service (in this case, the local authority). If anything, a putative principle that, say, *prohibited* the provision of home care every time the weather is poor would deprive employers of an opportunity they have reason to value. In fact, the personal and public need for the provision of social care by means of home visits, and employers' incentive to provide it in that form, is arguably stronger when poor weather makes it difficult to supply such care in other ways.

I am drawing attention to the reasoning in *Kennedy* not because it represents some kind of revolution, but because it is very much a standard feature of the way our judges, practitioners and academic lawyers think about private law. We think that a person's responsibilities depend on the conditions under which that person acted, or was presented with practical alternatives, or was required to form a response in a situation. We distinguish cases depending on the nature and quality of the background conditions of a person's choice. We distinguish situations in which giving people the choice is generally likely to make things go well for them from situations in which it is more likely to lead people to make poor decisions. We regard the fact that a person could have avoided some burden by choosing appropriately as making a difference to their responsibilities. My aim has been to convince you that these ideas matter for the justification of private law principles, and that their normative significance need not be mediated by an appeal to notions like wrongdoing, or corrective justice, or be framed in terms of social cost. If there is a theoretical consensus to the contrary, that consensus is mistaken. Private law is not the domain of rights. It is not the domain of wrongs and corrective justice. Neither is its aim to reduce social cost, or to maximise social benefit. The aim of private law is to make our responsibilities to others depend on the opportunities we have to affect how things will go for us.

Index